To my friends, supporters, and other people of questionable judgement.

THE UNITED STATES vs. ABBOTT, ET AL.

A Love Story

GREG ABBOTT

THE UNITED STATES VS. ABBOTT, ET AL. A LOVE STORY

Copyright © 2022 Greg Abbott.

All rights reserved. No part of this book may be used or reproduced by any means, graphic, electronic, or mechanical, including photocopying, recording, taping or by any information storage retrieval system without the written permission of the author except in the case of brief quotations embodied in critical articles and reviews.

iUniverse books may be ordered through booksellers or by contacting:

iUniverse
1663 Liberty Drive
Bloomington, IN 47403
www.iuniverse.com
844-349-9409

Because of the dynamic nature of the Internet, any web addresses or links contained in this book may have changed since publication and may no longer be valid. The views expressed in this work are solely those of the author and do not necessarily reflect the views of the publisher, and the publisher hereby disclaims any responsibility for them.

Any people depicted in stock imagery provided by Getty Images are models, and such images are being used for illustrative purposes only.
Certain stock imagery © Getty Images.

ISBN: 978-1-6632-3752-1 (sc)
ISBN: 978-1-6632-3753-8 (hc)
ISBN: 978-1-6632-4576-2 (e)

Library of Congress Control Number: 2022917617

Print information available on the last page.

iUniverse rev. date: 04/03/2023

PREFACE

> It takes many good deeds to build a good
> reputation, and only one to lose it.
> —Benjamin Franklin

> Then the man and his wife heard the sound of the Lord God
> as he was walking in the garden in the cool of the day, and
> they hid from the Lord God among the trees in the garden.
> But the Lord God called to the man: "Where are you?"
> He answered, "I heard you in the garden and I
> was afraid because I was naked; so I hid."
> And He said, "Who told you that you were naked? Have you
> eaten from the tree that I commanded you not to eat from?"
> The man said, "The woman you put here with me—
> she gave me some fruit from the tree and I ate it."
> Then the Lord said to the woman, "What is this you have done?"
> The woman said, "The serpent deceived me, and I ate."
> —Genesis 3:8–13

Different time, different place, names have changed, but the morality tale remains essentially unchanged. Yes, we did it. We yielded to temptation and paid $125,000 to Rick Singer's Key Worldwide Foundation to support our daughter's college applications and thus became part of the 2019 Varsity Blues college admissions scandal. We believed it was a compassionate, one-off accommodation for her physical disability and had no inkling that it was part of something larger, just as our daughter had no idea that we were "helping" her with standardized tests.

We did it because she was suffering from a debilitating, severe form of Lyme disease, which robs one of focus, inducing brain fog, memory loss, fatigue, joint pain, hair loss, muscle cramps, and other crippling symptoms that put her squarely behind the eight ball in the realm of standardized tests. We didn't want this otherwise stellar soul stripped naked in the garden as she applied to well over a dozen universities (targeting none in particular, contrary to prosecutorial allegations), confident that she'd be cured within a year or two.

Our actions were not motivated out of any lack of faith. Despite being chronically sick and bedridden, she valiantly managed to attain a 4.3 GPA and sing at the Metropolitan Opera. Nor did we try to shoehorn her into an elite university above her ability to satisfy any malignant parental narcissism; she was a credible candidate of them all, and whatever narcissism I possess is more or less the garden variety sort we all have to some degree. We dropped our moral guard to bite from the rotten apple known as Varsity Blues. We succumbed and have suffered, and our child has suffered all the more. Instead of an ivy-walled Eden, we entered a hell of our own making. But unlike Dante, who as he entered the gates of hell saw the following inscription: "Abandon all hope, ye who enter here," I remain robustly optimistic. While I don't expect to remove all the tarnish, I do hope to emerge as wiser and humbler, if not liberated by my public humiliation. As much as possible, I aspire to transform every vile aspect of this into something enlightening and redemptive, to turn it into a gift—especially for our daughter. I am driven to prove Ben Franklin wrong, to tell him to go fly a kite.

We have taken full ownership of our actions. We expect no forgiveness; we have our daughter's, the sole victim in our case, which is what matters. Our friends have universally stuck by us, and fortunately, we are blessed with many. Long-lost amigos from decades past have reached out to express love and support, providing a silver lining and in the process defining the life I have lived. Having fully paid my debt to society (a month in federal prison, $90,000 in fines, and 250 hours of community service, and that was the least of it), I feel I have the right, if not the obligation, to speak my mind, to tell my truth—from remorse to outrage.

Within these pages are unsettling truths about how lives otherwise blessed and even exemplary at times can become cursed by a single false step, one taken out of love and compassion but a false step nonetheless. Read about how that single false step can incur the government's capacity for brute force where none is needed and become grist for media and internet mills, which require endless grist (truthful or not) for their survival, and our collective insatiable appetites for schadenfreude.

So, why write this book, risking that it might simply provide even more grist for hostile mills? Because in this digital, social media age, information (and misinformation) never dies, and because we and our story are very different from the sensational, smearing narrative you've read in the papers or seen on the internet and TV. Yes, we had so much yet still reached one branch too high for that apple. Though we are privileged, we are still humans caught up in the human condition. This cautionary tale is my effort to humanize our legacy, to wrest it back from lurid headlines, fabricated news reports, financial persecution, prosecutorial lies, and federal prison—of having our lives trashed for a single mistake made out of pure love at an *extremely* vulnerable moment. Bad choices make good stories, and our story, in the mere telling, lays bare how press/prosecutors/politics (a.k.a. the media-governmental complex)—as well as our venal educational institutions—operate in this country and why we as citizens of all political stripes should be concerned. What happened to us could happen to virtually anyone. We are merely one side of this multifaceted infamy, which is why this story *must* be told.

"The more society drifts from the truth," wrote Orwell, "the more it will distance itself from those that speak it." I'm already a pariah, so what do I have to lose?

PART I

CHAPTER 1

> Life is what happens when you're busy making other plans.
> —John Lennon

March 12, 2019. Dawn. New York City. Fifth Avenue. Loud knocking, murmuring voices piercing sleep. Whose sleep? My sleep. The time? No idea. It felt like the middle of the night. Before I could get my bearings, "FBI, FBI!"

It was a dream; it had to be a dream. And it was until I was blinded by a flashlight. Who were these people? Four, five, six—I was too disconcerted to count—had streamed into my bedroom and were now standing around my bed. They had guns on their hips and badges, and they meant business.

"Are you Gregory Abbott?" barked a no-nonsense young woman.

"Y-y-yes," I faltered, half-asleep but waking up quickly. "What are you doing here?"

"We have a warrant for your arrest."

Heart pounding, adrenaline racing, there was no need for my très chic, Eurotrash caffeine jolt at Sant Ambroeus. While I hoped this was one big mistake, I somehow didn't think so. There were too many of them for this to be in error, and they had obtained a warrant, though I had no clue whatsoever as to the reason. It was utterly surreal.

"*Excuse me?* How did you get in here?"

"None of your business. Get dressed, sir. You are under arrest."

"Arrest?" I shrieked, sitting up in bed, protecting myself with the covers. "Why? For what?"

"Conspiracy to commit mail fraud and honest services fraud."

I had no idea what she was talking about, what those alien-sounding phrases even meant, but frantically tried to make sense of it. My thoughts immediately went to the small and vulnerable company I had founded, for which I had been bleeding emotionally and financially for fifteen years. For those fifteen years, my entire working life had been devoted to it and the far-reaching social cause it represented. Jane Goodall—yes, *that* Jane Goodall—had endorsed our game-changing aseptic dispensing device for its humanitarian benefits. I wracked my brain for what wrong I might have committed. Had I inadvertently divulged some kind of inside information to an investor? Had something been improperly stated in our quarterly report? Had extroverted "Gregarious Greg" said too much to someone? The company had been on the cusp of breakout success for too many years—such is the nature of the beast with aseptic packaging innovations—and all it took was one disgruntled investor or even a competitor to make a spurious call and fabricate something.

"Conspiracy to commit *what*?" I asked in disbelief.

"Mail fraud," a male agent said in a snarky tone, as if I knew perfectly well what atrocity I had committed. His contempt was palpable; clearly, he thought this silver-fox Fifth Avenue denizen in the fancy cotton pajamas was a lying sack of shit.

"Mail fraud!" I expelled a nervous laugh that sounded guilty even to me. "I don't understand. There must be some mistake!" Resounding silence. I resisted the urge to ask, *What, did I not put enough postage on a letter?* This was no occasion for sarcasm. "What time is it?"

"Quarter to six," snapped the lead female agent, whose young earnestness reminded me of Clarisse Starling in *Silence of the Lambs*. "Get dressed. We don't have all day!"

My six-foot, three-inch twenty-four-year-old son materialized in the doorway, his handsome face etched with horror. At that moment, all my concerns turned to him.

I climbed out of bed and wobbled toward my son, where I found five or six more agents milling around outside my room in the hallway. Such a show of force! Did they think I was Jackie Chan? Between these goons and the ones in my bedroom, I think I counted ten in all—a veritable SWAT team of armed fed invaders to arrest an almost sixty-nine-year-old man with a torn ACL and a totally clean record, who had not the remotest idea what he had done to merit this. My mind flashed to what my Princeton classmate and friend of fifty years, Judge Andrew Napolitano of Fox News, once told me over dinner: a man commits an average of three felonies a day without knowing it—the libertarian judge's commentary on how many elasticized laws there are on the books and how the government can destroy anyone it chooses. "Show me the man, and I will show you the crime," Stalin's chief of police (and pedophile), Beria, once boasted. But which crime had I committed? What had I done to earn the charge of "conspiracy to commit mail fraud"? I couldn't associate it with any action. This wasn't supposed to happen—not in America!

"Please get dressed, sir," Clarisse said a bit more politely, perhaps out of respect for my son. Saying "please" was hardly enough to make up for this grotesque intrusion. A simple phone call would have sufficed, and in this age of information, they surely knew the physical threat I posed was nonexistent.

"May I at least take a shower?"

"No!" snapped Clarisse, though she didn't object to me brushing my teeth and peeing, as long as one of her armed male colleagues accompanied me to the bathroom and stood over me, just in case I was plotting to jump out of the fourth-floor window.

After my rush-rush bathroom stint, I threw on some clothes and gave my eldest son a long, soulful hug in the hallway. "I love you," I whispered urgently into his ear, kissing his cheek and squeezing him hard, reassured by his squeeze back even while feeling the distress pulsing through his body. For years, he had often (but not always) looked up to me as his hero; his admiration and respect meant the world to me. This was beyond heartbreaking for both or us, a lasting trauma on our psyches. "Please don't worry," I said, trying to reassure him. "I'm sure it's some mistake, something overblown. I love you."

"Did you do something wrong with IDC?" he asked anxiously ("Say it ain't so, Joe"), referring to the dispensing company that I'd been nurturing for well over a decade.

His eyes searched mine, pleading for a definitive answer, but all I could do was shrug uncertainly and clasp his broad shoulders. "I have no idea what this is about. I promise."

The FBI brusquely cuffed my wrists and ankles and led me away from my forlorn, slack-jawed son into the elevator. Once in the lobby, they escorted me past the astonished doorman and one resident who happened to be there at this ungodly hour to witness my humiliation. Out of pride, since, as far as I was concerned, I was innocent until proven otherwise, I made eye contact with each of them. The doorman looked at his shoes. My fellow resident was expressionless, eyes noncommittal, though having lived in the Upper East Side for decades, I knew schadenfreude when I saw it. Due to the ankle cuffs, I had to shuffle along with baby steps, but even then, the iron dug into my skin and bones.

(There was one group that wasn't at all surprised by the appearance of FBI agents in my bedroom at the crack of dawn. The government had notified all media outlets of its nationwide sting twenty-four to forty-eight hours in advance in order to assure maximum coverage, headlines, and glory, to make sure cameras and reporters were situated in all the right places. One teen involved in the case went on suicide watch; had anything tragic like that actually happened, the government and press were ready to point fingers at the "cheating" parents and categorize us as child murderers. Surely in the name of human decency, the feds could have given me, all of us, a few hours to engage a lawyer and surrender voluntarily, but the headlines, photo ops, and potential career enhancements wouldn't have been nearly so impressive.)

I was led to the cramped back seat of a parked car in front of my Fifth Avenue co-op building. As we headed off, the third world condition of New York City streets was never more apparent. Each bump and pothole (the car seemed to hit them all) caused the shackles to pinch my wrists and ankles and my head to bang against the plexiglass divider as they took me all the way downtown to the Daniel Patrick Moynihan Courthouse at 500 Pearl Street. The next thing I knew, I was in the offices, where my cell phone, wallet, and passport were confiscated. I was photographed, fingerprinted, and asked a slew of biographical questions about everything from the schools I had attended to the medications I took. Feeling like Dan Aykroyd (*Trading Places*), agents teeming all around me, imagining Billy Ray Valentine smoking a huge cigar in my Fifth Avenue flat, I sat on a bench in shackled silence and waited ... for what exactly I didn't know. Three hours or so into this nightmare, Clarisse informed me that I was allowed my phone call.

I know a lot of people, and I mean *a lot*, but not the name of a single criminal attorney. Apart from my three theoretical felonies a day and a smattering of speeding tickets decades ago (in a Porsche, full disclosure), I had never had a single issue with the law. I would have ample time to retain a lawyer, so I used my call on my son, to make sure he was OK.

"Hi. It's Dad. You OK?" I asked, trying to projected fatherly strength.

"Mom's been arrested in Colorado," he said somberly, unable to mask his angst. He is a strong, silent type, not one to reveal vulnerability, but he feels things deeply. "It's happening all over the country. Dozens of people are being arrested. Something to do with the SATs?" He intoned the last sentence like a question, which I let wash over me. Finally, I knew what this was about, sort of. But I couldn't comment directly, even to my son. It was all so new, so raw, with so many open questions, and I was in a discombobulated daze.

"How's your sister?" I asked, heart rapidly sinking, imagining how my Lyme disease–ridden daughter felt seeing the mother she worshipped dragged off in handcuffs, left alone in our home seven miles from town with no driver's license. *More trauma in her life*, I lamented. At least she was eighteen; had she been a year younger, the state would have taken her into "protective custody." I remembered Ronald Reagan's classic admonishment about the worst thing a citizen can hear: "I'm from the government, and I'm here to help."

"She's freaking out," said my son, "but I calmed her down. We're in constant touch."

"Good. Stay close to her. Be a good big brother. Tell her I love her and that everything will be OK." As if anything I said could possibly ameliorate or reassure my daughter. For reasons to be covered later, she hadn't spoken to me in weeks, except to tell me that I was no longer her father. I didn't expect that this episode would alter her views in that regard.

They deposited me in a stark, empty jail cell—ankles still shackled but hands free—where I had several hours to reflect amid all the cacophonous hooting and rattling emanating from neighboring cells, like it was feeding time at the zoo. Lonely as I felt, I was grateful not to have a cellmate.

Sitting on an iron bench, I tried to put the pieces together, to recollect past events and imagine what the government had in store for my wife and me. One bedrock reality kept me reasonably composed: this was the United States of America, not a banana republic.

Rick Singer was obviously at the center of this. Surely, you've heard of him. Through something he called the Key Worldwide Foundation, he lured millions and millions of dollars, some of which were used as bribes (or whatever you wish to call it) to grease application skids to various universities. I will get into my family's connection with him soon enough, and how we had no idea that this was part of something larger. For now, suffice it to say that Singer is not a man without gifts. Over the phone, I could almost hear him tear up when discussing all the good works his Key Foundation accomplished for underprivileged kids. My involvement with him consisted of three short phone conversations spaced out over several months, one almost a year before after the plan was hatched without my input, another about nine months before, and the last around seven months before. That was the extent of it. I had never met him, had no idea what he looked like, and barely remembered our conversations. I wondered how many people were being arrested that day. From what my son had said, it was a nationwide sting.

In my cell, I thought about how my marriage had come apart in recent years, unpeeling the onion to blame my wife, Marcia, then myself, and so on. The more I unpeeled (back to 1987 when we were married), the more I realized that it didn't matter who was to blame, that both of us were, that neither of us were, that it was simply due to the vicissitudes of life. Maybe this would reunite us somehow. Awash in compassion, I pictured her in a Colorado hoosegow, hoping she was holding up and not being treated harshly. She was delicate and refined, not built for this. Despite the rancor between us—and God there had been a lot, and still was on a daily basis—it was impossible not to feel love for the mother of my children, the girl I had fallen for and married thirty-two years before. She had dedicated her life to being a mother, the most thankless profession (certainly on this day). I bristled that this loving lioness to her children, who had borne the brunt and complication of raising our sick daughter during our separation, could be arrested in such barbaric fashion. How could our lives—decent, generous, productive—have suddenly come to this?

I want you to meet our daughter and her constant companions during high school, Babesia and Bartonella. These hangers-on have much to do with how we became involved with Singer, so it's important that you know them sooner rather than later.

Babesia and Bartonella are a variety of infectious diseases brought on by bacteria. Ticks carry Babesia, while Bartonella is often referred to as cat scratch disease, implying that sometimes, but not always, its problems follow a bite or scratch by an infected pet. Babesia brings on Lyme disease, and Bartonella can cause its own autoimmune symptoms, ranging from mild to severe. My daughter had both, severely. A doctor's report:

> She had active Lyme Disease, with more co-infections than almost any other patient I've seen ... Lyme Disease and its co-infections—Babesia and Bartonella—affect focus and memory in profound ways, and despite [her] intelligence and determination, she simply cannot sustain attention ... This is a hard-working young woman who has been at the top of her class in high school, and she should not be penalized because she is fighting (and taking many medications for) a disease which robs its victim of normal brain function.

Shortly after our March 12, 2019, arrest, the *New York Post* published an article following our first appearance before the Boston court, misreporting that our daughter "would have gotten a 23 on the ACT, *according to court papers.*" Italics are mine to highlight the phrase that insulated the paper from claims of libel. The court papers rested on a self-serving and false assertion by Rick Singer himself that our daughter would have gotten a 23 rather than the 35 recorded. Singer, hardly a credible source and under pressure by the feds to craft a certain narrative, pulled that number from his nether regions. The lower our daughter's scores, the more culpable, venal, and disgusting her parents were—exactly the narrative the government wanted.

Now for the truth: In his letter to the court, our daughter's ACT/SAT tutor made clear that Singer's assertion was absurd: "I heard [Singer's] claims that she scored a 23 on [the ACT] test. I find that impossible to believe. On her absolute worst day with Lyme she would have scored much better than that." He went on to write of our daughter as "one of my favorite students. Bright. Engaged. Funny. Hardworking." Due to Lyme disease, he said, "maintaining her focus for five hours (the single day extended time accommodation) was extremely difficult for her." When he allowed her "much needed" extra time in practice tests "over multiple days ... to accommodate her disability, she consistently [scored] above 30 across the board." This letter is in the court papers, but I do not believe it was reported in any press account—for reasons I leave to your imaginations.

While many have Lyme disease and most recover following a course of antibiotics, many don't, and the consequences can be dire.

To cite one illustration: the husband of my former assistant, whose Lyme disease went undiagnosed for fifteen years, was rendered a vegetable. That was my chilling introduction to Lyme disease. To cite another: For many years, it was believed that Kris Kristofferson had been suffering from dementia or Alzheimer's disease. It was eventually learned that he had been suffering from undiagnosed and thus untreated Lyme disease.

Witnessing our daughter was like witnessing a young, otherwise capable person suffer from a form of dementia, only with the addition of hair loss and rashes all over her body. On one terrifying occasion in a taxi, she forgot where she lived. Lyme limited her focus to varying degrees, sometimes to just thirty to forty-five minutes at a time. Once brain fog sets in, you're done for the day; she needed not only extra time but *multiple days on each test* (roughly nine to twelve days of testing in total for a single go-round) to reflect her true ability, as her tutor had verified and her physician had recommended. Too much for a girl who, when she wasn't gutting out an opera performance or doing her studies, spent her time in bed.

CHAPTER 2

ET TU, BRUTUS AMERICANUS?

March 12, 2019. The day of the arrest, late afternoon. Prison cell, Daniel Patrick Moynihan Courthouse, 500 Pearl Street, downtown Manhattan. Since my dawn arrest, I had been given no food or water. Mouth parched, stomach achy and hollow, energy faint, the time behind bars seemed interminable. There was only that iron bench and no way to be comfortable. Six hours behind bars brought on an onset of paranoia and claustrophobia ameliorated only somewhat by deep breathing and half-assed meditation. I tried to imagine what a real prison sentence might feel like and questioned whether I could survive prolonged confinement.

My heart kept returning inevitably to my daughter, living in Colorado with her mother, my wife, from whom I was estranged. Though she was all alone in our house seven miles from town, I was confident she would be physically looked after. We had many friends there, having lived there full-time for twelve years and then summers and Christmas holidays since 2002, and everybody loves my daughter. She is one of those rare souls who is impossible not to love.

I prayed for her tender psyche, wondering what was going through her mind and how she was processing whatever it was she actually knew. She had known nothing of our attempts to help her. We had taught her right from wrong, and on that score (and others), she was a parents' dream. Yet now, wracked with guilt, I imagined that her college dreams were toast—through no fault of hers, solely that of her parents. What had we done to her!

In return for my family foundation's two donations to Singer's foundation—the take-it-or-leave deal Singer had wrung out of my wife, with my eventual consent, after serving as a college counselor long enough to appear credible—I knew my daughter had gotten some sort of ACT and SAT test help that was outside the rules. I didn't exactly know the details and didn't want to know. The fact that she was seriously disabled with Lyme disease and estranged from me had trumped all other considerations. Not all of the $125,000 could *possibly* have been spent in altering tests—maybe ten grand at most. I had no reason to believe that the rest hadn't gone to a noble cause. It was clearly a devil's bargain, something we'd succumbed to, but had we actually committed a *crime against our country*? "Conspiracy to commit mail fraud" for donating to a bona fide 501c3 charity and in the process lending a hand to our sick daughter who, in the realm of standardized testing, had the deck stacked against her? It was wrong, reprehensible one could argue, but what did any of it have to do with mail fraud? Wasn't the word *conspiracy* a tad dramatic? Was this bombastic arrest proportional?

It was late afternoon when a couple of men in blue arrived to fetch me. They snapped handcuffs back on me and led me down several long corridors to a closed doorway, where my public defender awaited. The police finally unlocked my wrist and ankle cuffs, to my relief. I had been in shackles since dawn.

"Just take your cues from me," was all the public defender told me, whereupon she opened the door leading into a packed courtroom. Culture shock. The entire gallery in back was jam-packed, though at the time I was too dazed and addled to realize that they were from the media. I actually assumed they were friends and relatives of other people about to be brought before the judge after I was disposed of.

There were some legal formalities where I answered, "Yes, Your Honor" or "No, Your Honor," to each question on the fly, depending on the cue from my public defender in the corner of my eye.

A young prosecutor, who looked like she was a week out of law school and who obviously knew zilch about me, began addressing the court. She was adamantly telling the judge that I was a flight risk. Why, because I lived on Fifth Avenue? How bigoted and dehumanizing, and what did she know about me or my finances? From raising money from well-healed investors for my dispensing company, I had learned never to assume anything about another's finances, liquidity, or personal issues; for as long as I can remember, I never objectified people just because they were rich. Or poor. Or black or white. Flight risk? Exactly what grounds did she have to suggest that I was so hard-hearted as to abandon my family? Everyone I loved and everything I owned was in the United States! How could they allege such a preposterous thing in a court of law without a smidgeon of evidence? I tried to whisper my outrage to my public defender, who shushed me but still managed to say the right things.

The prosecutor, whose callow, woke-soldier vibe told me she knew squat about squat, recommended to the judge that my release from jail be contingent on bail of $1 million—hard cash I couldn't afford to part with given my current crunch! Would I be going back to jail for the foreseeable future? The notion momentarily filled me with terror.

"I'm very disappointed," the crusty old judge chastised her. Each time the prosecutor tried to mount a counterargument to smear me, the judge cut her off, reiterating his displeasure at her draconian request. This caused tears to well up in me. As I sucked them back with physical exertion and a suppressed snort, my public defender kicked me under the table. In the end, the judge hit me with a $500,000 bail bond, one requiring I obtain a personal guarantor, payable only if I broke the conditions of my release. No cash outlay, at least, but upon whom could I impose to be my guarantor?

Embarrassing as this is to admit, one of the most uncomfortable aspects of the ordeal was spending the day without my cell phone. I am addicted to my device. Who among you isn't? Interesting that only the high-tech and illegal drug industries refer to their customers as *users*. Despite having been on the cutting edge of the internet revolution, before most of you knew what the internet was, I have a love-hate relationship with technology. Apart from the benefits of connecting people and speeding access to information, it kills intimacy, imperils happiness by depersonalizing interactions, increases pressure by eliminating useful excuses, and, worst of all, is the greatest instrument for totalitarianism and spying the world has ever seen. Call me Abbottosaurus, but I was happier in the era of pay phones, back when human instincts and personal connections were valued and algorithms barely existed.

Besides my obvious concerns throughout the day, I was compulsively worried about my little struggling company—where the stock price was trading, what was happening in way of customers and funding. Without my phone, I was helpless, half-sick. What would the impact of my arrest be on my labor of love? Would it be fatal? The company was so intertwined with my life, finances, reputation, identity, and family. Were all of the above being sucked down the great abyss?

Upon my release at around 5:00 p.m., my phone and wallet (but not passport) were returned to me. I grabbed them like a crack addict grabbing his pipe. As soon as I powered on my cell, texts began pouring in, several of them from the media. Two were from my biggest investor, who expressed profound disappointment and demanded that I call him immediately.

My heart sank to my stomach; I had revered this man since 1994 and considered him a mentor but was too disoriented and disconsolate to call him. Had my best friend, George Kriste, been alive, that would have been a different story, but outside of family, that was it. First and foremost, I called my daughter, who answered immediately. "I'm so sorry, I'm so sorry," I remember telling her over and over, but I can recollect little else other than the impression that she was shell-shocked and not all that keen on talking, much to my heartbreak. I tried Marcia, and it went straight to voice mail. She was on mountain time and probably still behind bars.

As I headed for a side exit, a reporter materialized from behind a marble column. He said he was from the *Wall Street Journal* and asked if I wished to comment. Flashing a weary smile but saying nothing, I shook my head and continued toward the exit, craving fresh air and freedom. Immediately upon stepping outside, I was accosted by four or five members of the paparazzi. Camera lenses came within inches of my face, rapid-fire clicks and flashes from all directions capturing me at my worst and robbing me of my soul, or so it felt.

Still not appreciating the gravity of what I was involved in, feeling drained, famished, and well past my boiling point, I waved my arms to shoo away these "hyenas with cameras," as a friend aptly described them. Had you gone through what you have to agree was a pretty difficult day, you might appreciate my eloquence in snapping, "Get the fuck out of my face!" These were my only words to the media throughout the scandal (other than some off-the-record discussions with certain TV news luminaries to be discussed later). For the moment, I wondered whether I had supplied the *New York Post* with its following day's headline.

The hyenas pursued me, pack style, as I headed toward the nearest avenue, then suddenly abandoned their pursuit. I'd supposed they'd gotten all the tortured pictures they needed. I turned back, and my eyes met with one of them at a distance for several curious seconds before he scurried away. It reminded me of the eerie, Ace Ventura–like eye contact I had with an elk through my Colorado bedroom window one early morning over a decade ago. The huge creature, whose head was the size of my torso, and I were three feet apart, separated by a mere pane of glass. There was that one terrifying moment where we forged a connection before the antlered beast thankfully bounded away rather than through the window.

I hailed a cab and headed back to the scene of this morning's raid. *Home sweet home*, until the government decides it isn't. Again, I tried calling my wife, to no avail. I called my daughter again, over and over; with each no answer, I died a small death. My eldest son and I ordered out burgers and ate them on the bed in loving, emotionally drained silence. Only when I switched on the TV did I learn of the term "Operation Varsity Blues." It was the lead story on the national news, the opening joke on the late-night talk shows. Thirty-three parents—including celebrities Felicity Huffman (*Desperate Housewives,* Oscar-nominated actress) and Lori Loughlin (never heard of her or Aunt Becky until now), as well as prominent lawyers, capitalists, and the like—and nineteen coaches had been arrested that day. Cheating on tests wasn't the half of it. Much of the coverage centered on elaborately fraudulent athletic recruiting schemes and of course the topical issue of white privilege. Move over, Robert Mueller.

All this on March 12, 2019—my personal Ides of March, the day my life as I knew it changed forever. *Et tu, Brutus Americanus?*

CHAPTER 3

FROM SYRIA TO SAYRE TO PRINCETON

Your Honor, I grew up to romanticize the American dream, where anyone regardless of background can carve out a good life by virtue of honest, hard work. My parents, children of immigrants, grew up during the Great Depression and couldn't afford college. But they were smart and worked themselves to the bone to make a better life for themselves and their family. I was the first in my family to go to college. My parents taught me the virtues of hard work and sacrifice; honoring a handshake even when it works to your detriment; taking away something positive from both victory and defeat. To treat everyone with respect and humility, whether king or pauper. To strive mightily but never put money and success on a pedestal, as they are hollow without personal integrity. These are the values I have tried to live by and instill in my three children—values which in this tragic instance I failed to uphold.

Just who *is* this disgraced felon and where did he come from?

I was born in what President Trump might refer to as "shithole" Sayre, Pennsylvania, population 5,000 and home of my mother (who bottle-fed her two 1950s boys; breastfeeding "never occurred to me," she declared decades later when my wife was pregnant). A family joke used to be of a fictitious billboard saying, "You Are Now Entering and Leaving Sayre, Pennsylvania."

When I was two and my brother a newborn, we moved to the metropolis of Ithaca, New York, home of Cornell University, Ithaca College, and my father. Mine was a wholesome childhood, playing baseball and other sports, riding my bike to school, and growing up far above Cayuga's waters in a middle-class-plus neighborhood replete with children of all ages, kids named Jimmy, Tommy, Stevie, Eddie, Chuckie, Chet, Skip, and Ruthie (the neighborhood tomboy who could really hit a baseball). We played baseball and football in the backyard of an empty nest couple. Their yard was a perfectly symmetrical, multipurpose sports "stadium," with a short right-field wall of pine trees like Yankee Stadium and an oddly shaped tree branch parallel to the ground that served as a goal post. The neighborhood kids trashed that plot of land so badly that my father took it upon himself to have it reseeded every spring. A generous, take-charge guy, he never allowed anyone to buy him dinner. My parents never once spanked me (maybe the core of the problem, though I didn't give them reason to), and nobody seemed to care a lick about how much money anyone had. The closest I ever came to discussing money was when a couple of friends, sons of a pizza parlor owner and a Cornell professor, told me after school, "You're richer than most of us, but you don't act like it." High praise in late 1950s Ithaca, and it meant a lot to me. Boys that age seldom give each other compliments. Money and status were almost alien concepts where I grew up. We all had middle-class values, where being a decent person was what counted.

We were Ithaca-rich, meaning that our redbrick house was slightly bigger than those of our neighbors. My father, who also was partial to the large Cadillac tail fins of the day (as ostentatious as one ever got in our sleepy college town), had his own cut-and-sew ladies' underwear plant. Ithaca Textiles produced nylon and acetate bloomers (in white, pink, or mint green) that came in packages of three. One hundred percent of these packages carried the label of JCPenney. Like a pit bull on a pantleg, he cultivated JCPenney as his only customer, focusing all his energy and fealty on what was then America's largest soft goods purveyor. Saturday mornings, he would sometimes take me to the plant, where he taught me to make markers, tracing the silhouettes of fronts, backs, and gussets on a long sheet of paper, which was later laid atop a pile of fabric for cutting.

"What's a gusset?" I asked my father each time. "Crotch," he grunted, as I giggled. Obviously, it was paramount that the fronts, backs, and crotches fit like a jigsaw puzzle in order to minimize fabric waste. Whenever I messed up, my father never chided me but simply corrected my mistakes and taught me how to do it better. Amazing patience for a man not known for it, an ambitious Syrian American hell-bent on covering the asses of the masses. He used to joke that he skipped three grades and graduated at sixteen because Ithaca High wanted to get rid of him as quickly as possible. He went straight from high school to work. While he could be volatile, he was hyperalert and seemed to be aware of everything going on around him. He frequently traveled to New York City, as JCPenney was headquartered there, and was the most bighearted, hardworking man I have ever known.

For reasons never explained to me, the International Ladies' Garment Workers Union tried to unionize Ithaca Textiles in 1959. They disrupted production, straining the one-customer relationship and almost ruining my father's company. In school later in life, I was taught that unions were essential to prevent the exploitation of workers. My college history professors romanticized labor unions. My firsthand experience through the eyes of a nine-year-old was quite different. Dead Cayuga Lake carp—oozing blood from the gills—greeted us on our welcome mat each morning as my brother and I left for school. Company trucks were run off the road into ditches. Despite my parents' efforts to maintain a semblance of normalcy, tension engulfed our family. When my father was in New York on business to shore up his crumbling relationship with JCPenney during the strike, my mother received menacing phone calls that left her visibly shaken. She didn't talk about it—nobody, and I mean nobody, kept a secret better than my mother—but try as she might, she couldn't mask her terror, which made me want to be her protector when Dad was away.

Legions of union protesters were bussed up from New York City, joining leftist Cornell students and a smattering of disgruntled workers to lay siege to my father's plant. One day as I, a chubby nine-year-old carrying a BB gun and sporting a Davy Crocket coonskin cap, patrolled the property for imaginary big game, I spotted a stranger rummaging around in our open garage. This character didn't look like he belonged. Warily, I entered the garage. His startled mug told me all I needed to know: He was a trespassing goon from the union. From behind a jutting Caddy tail fin, I aimed my BB gun straight at him. "Get out!" I demanded, brandishing my musket to mask my trembling. "Get out before I shoot you!" To my relief, he took off without a word. Breathlessly, I followed the weasel with my gun as he exited the garage, trailing him at a distance, aiming at his back long after he was out of range of my pellets as he ran to the end of our driveway, where an idling getaway car awaited him. It is the only time in my life where I exerted my Second Amendment rights.

The efforts to unionize Ithaca Textiles failed—my father engendered great loyalty—but it also took its emotional and financial toll, and things in the country were changing. Textile companies throughout New York and New England were making a mass exodus south. My father hired a manager and moved the plant to tax-friendly, union-averse Cairo, Georgia (birthplace of Jackie Robinson, the main reason I grew up a vociferous Dodger fan and remain one to this day, an homage both to my humanity and arrested development; thanks to Dad, I actually saw Jackie play at Ebbets Field, Game Two of the 1956 World Series, the "other" game Don Larsen pitched in that series, where he was chased in the second inning and lost 13–8; Jackie went two for four—but I digress). A cadre of Dad's Ithaca employees stayed on and relocated south. My parents began planning their move to New York City, a bold step at their ages (midfifties), given they knew no one there except the JCPenney people with whom my father interacted, most of whom lived in New Jersey. The *Cornell Daily Sun* published a cartoon of a train heading south from Ithaca, driven by an excellently rendered (I must admit) caricature of my father smoking his trademark cigar, with the derogatory caption "Abbott's Gravy Train." A *Daily Sun* reporter entered the plant unannounced and walked up the stairs to my father's office, expecting to interview him, only to be dragged by his long hair back down the stairs and out of the place by a muscular, cigar-chomping, Patton Third Army vet of Syrian descent with whom you didn't want to mess. It was the 1960s, when the country was as divided as it is today.

Speaking of divided, my father's six siblings (apart from the brother who died of whooping cough) were either card-carrying members of the Communist Party or fellow travelers—the eldest, ironically, my uncle Sam. After earning a Bronze Star fighting Hitler, Uncle Sam was arrested more than thirty times for fighting fascism on his native soil, advocating subversive things like racial and social justice, banning the bomb, and opposing the Vietnam War. Because Mom didn't want her sons exposed to far left radicalism, our families never interacted. My sole memory of Sam was seeing him on TV—a demonstrator being shoved into the back of a police wagon. Later, he was elected mayor of Tacoma Park, Maryland, a beloved corruption fighter and, according to Dad, a local legend for keeping freeways from displacing citizens from their homes. Sam's seventy-nine-year-old son, whom I'd never met, called and introduced himself upon hearing of Varsity Blues. We bonded, Facetimed, and have become chums. What a lovely guy, son of Sam, cuz of Greg! We even see eye to eye on most things political. Back then, however, through my young, Mom-tinted lens, Dad was the sole white sheep in his family.

—

Somewhere in all this, I learned what a prep school was. With my parents planning their move to New York, I suddenly was shown brochures of schools that looked like colleges. I was intrigued but even more intimidated. Exeter, Andover, Deerfield, Hotchkiss, Choate … How my Sayre-born mother even knew about these places was a mystery to me; she obviously had done extensive research and had no bones about shooting for the moon. My parents wanted to rise above their circumstances, and I wanted to do my part. Back in the early 1960s, such upwardly mobile ambition was deemed a virtue, as American as *Ozzie and Harriet*.

My mother also introduced me to the gentleman's game of golf, where you learned the etiquette before you learned how to play. I excelled at both facets of the game, eventually winning the Ithaca Country Club Men's Championship at the age of seventeen, the youngest "man" ever to win the title to this day. The thirty-six-hole final ended in sudden death on the thirty-seventh hole, when I hit a wedge shot within a foot of the hole for a trembling, pubescent tap-in. Somewhere in the subterranean bowels of the clubhouse, I'm told, is my championship plaque. A surprising number of middle-class kids played golf in Ithaca, some of my peers better than I despite my coveted title. It was hardly an elitist sport in our community at that time—the courses were like cow pastures—but both the game and the etiquette that came with it did me no harm when it came to discipline and life preparation.

I took the prep school standardized tests and bombed them. With apologies to Jane Goodall, who would find my comparison to her primates an affront, a chimpanzee would have fared better. For Jane's sake, let's just say I was a deer in headlights. That my parents never shared the results with me says it all (*ooh ooh ooh*). We toured the New England prep schools. Exeter and Andover scared the bejesus out of me; they were so much like real colleges and so out of my league. My mother liked Choate best because the students she met were unctuously polite. Eddie Haskell would have charmed circles around her ("How nice you look, Mrs. Cleaver!"). She loved Choate's in loco parentis philosophy, despite mispronouncing the phrase. During my interview with William St. John, the headmaster's brother, I was asked to spell *lieutenant*. "L … e … u …" I began, thinking I had nailed the trick question, only to learn I was one vowel shy. By some miracle, Choate accepted me. Was admitting a half-Syrian from Ithaca an early form of affirmative action? I suspect I got in because of my interview. Thanks to my mother and golf, I was extremely well mannered and no Eddie Haskell. I was sincere and didn't know how to be any other way. Thanks to my Episcopalian mother's genes—high cheekbones, blue eyes—I projected few disqualifying traces of ethnicity and could, outwardly at least, pass for Choate material. "I like him," St. John told my parents, back in the era when good manners, gut feelings, and blue eyes mattered.

My parents never revealed to me the verdicts of the other schools, I assume because I was rejected by them all. William St. John's gut feeling was all that stood between me and a total wipeout, proof of how life can be a game of inches. I was an inordinately naïve hick with an upstate twang and twenty percentile test scores (at best). However, once I learned from Mom that President Kennedy had gone to Choate, I quietly basked in the JFK cachet, which had grown to epic proportions after his recent assassination. None of the kids I knew in Ithaca went away to prep school. Ithaca High, with two local colleges, was considered a better than average public school with excellent college placement, thanks in large part to Cornell. My matriculation to the school President Kennedy had attended caused some distance and envy among certain friends. "Choke?" one kid errantly said of my future school. "Choke my dick!" Suddenly I was different from them, which bothered me. I hated elitism back then and always have.

Once there, it didn't take long for the JFK patina to wear off of Choate and for monumental alienation to set in. Perhaps the greatest miracle of the Varsity Blues scandal is that two Choaties actually wrote me strong character letters, since during those four years I made no friends; was teased unmercifully; was unjustifiably cut by the basketball coach; was passed over as golf captain; and was voted "Most Out to Lunch" by my senior class. I don't think the OTL award existed previously but was inspired by me and retired after my graduation, like Jackie Robinson's number forty-two. Like AOC, I attained acronym status. It wasn't that I was disliked as much as a big, open boondock-y target for snarky preppies from Manhattan,

Greenwich, and Darien. I was too wrapped up in my own ostracism to consider how the one black kid in our class or the one American Indian kid in the class behind me (Russell Red Elk, of the Lakota Red Elks, not the Greenwich Red Elks) might have felt. After rooming with the *Herald Tribune* scion fourth form (sophomore) year, I couldn't get anyone to room with me for the final two years. Even the scholarship kid from Hudson Bay, Canada, considered me a rube. The OTL award caused me to burn my graduation yearbook. Even then, I deplored book burning, which reminded me of what I'd learned in history class about the Nazis. But I couldn't bear the idea of my parents seeing me cast in such an unflattering light. Making them proud was still my biggest motivation in life.

A basketball cocaptain, my nemesis for four years, was one of my Varsity Blues letter writers. He told the judge, "… the last full-fledged fist fight I had was with Greg when we were fifteen over remarks made after a game of one-on-one basketball." Actually, it was the only time I *did* beat him. Elated and endeavoring to be a good sport, I blurted, "Nice game," which caused his fists to fly. Being a Buckley School boy from Manhattan, he couldn't fathom my Ithaca purity. We joke about it now, though he still suspects I gloated. I remember it like yesterday and assure you I was only trying to exhibit good sportsmanship, though I'll concede it may have bordered on OTL behavior. A clinical psychologist and award-winning musician who was voted both "Most Cynical" and "Most Likely to Succeed"—kind of my antithesis—my classmate thoughtfully added, "Greg, to his horror, was voted 'Most Out to Lunch' in our class poll, which meant, in my translation, the person who least understood how to play the requisite cool guy game … There was, and remains, something about Greg that seemed ingenuous and innocent, even when he was trying hard to pretend otherwise. He couldn't fully disguise the terminally uncool element of being blessed (and cursed) with a good heart."

The other Choatie who chimed in on my behalf was in the class ahead of mine and the undisputed golden boy of the school. I only got to know him later in life in New York City. "Deception, cynicism, and conspiracy," he wrote, "are, to put it succinctly, simply not in Greg's DNA. Never have been, never will be. Greg is one of the most open and fair-minded people I've ever met and is incapable of doing a malicious deed."

I consider myself a Choate survivor. I imagine that many of my class of '68 classmates feel the same way, though perhaps for other reasons. It was a tumultuous time to be in school. Our class staged Choate's first on-campus demonstration and still reputedly has the lowest donor participation of any in school history. The mere mention of the name *Choate* caused me PTSD seizures for at least a decade after graduation, yet oddly enough, I never regretted going there—partly because it got me into Princeton and partly because I saw it as part of my and my family's journey.

My SATs were good enough to land me facedown in a Nam rice patty. But mine was a different era, the same era Dubya went to Yale— ah, the good old days! Simply by virtue of being a Choatie, my grades, recommendations, and college interviews were good enough to get me into the Universities of Virginia and North Carolina (considered safeties back then, if you can believe it) as well as Duke and Princeton—but not my first choice, Harvard, which might have taken me were it not for the fact that my college guidance counselor deemed Princeton a better fit. Back then, Rick Singer was about seven years old and of no help or harm to anyone.

The Ithaca kid wanted the Harvard brand for all the wrong reasons: to stick it to all those schoolmates who had teased him, short-sheeted and urinated in his bed, and voted him "Most Out to Lunch"; to the coach who cut him from varsity basketball and banished him to JV, the only Choate senior ever to play JV basketball (I sang the junior varsity blues five decades before I sang the Varsity Blues); to his golf teammates who didn't elect him captain but picked a junior instead. My college counselor did me a favor. Go, Tigers! You've become a better brand than Harvard anyway!

Let it be known that despite rotten standardized test scores, I finished in the top quintile at Choate and graduated cum laude in history from Princeton. I mention this not to boast but to join the mounting criticism of standardized tests, which in our case were the sine qua non of the Rick Singer trap and Varsity Blues scandal. My long-held contempt for such tests may indeed have factored subconsciously into my wrongheaded decision to wire money to Singer's Key Foundation for other considerations. Many colleges are abolishing them, and hopefully the trend accelerates until they are eradicated. They mainly prove one's ability to take a pedantic test under artificial time pressure. They do not measure intangibles like character, drive, creativity, or even reasoning and vocabulary—especially if, like my daughter, you're suffering from the loss of stamina, loss of memory, and brain fog of chronic Lyme disease. We are so much more than lab rats, though I realize it was not my prerogative to play God.

GREG ABBOTT

Princeton gave me a much-craved fresh start. After the *Catcher in the Rye* angst and alienation of Choate, it took one wake-up call semester of Cs and Ds for me to get my arms around my newfound freedom. My parents were so proud that their son was a Princeton man that they didn't give a damn about his grades. In this less regulated atmosphere, where pretty much every student felt good about himself simply by virtue of being there, I effortlessly made friends and joined the same eating club joined by half the varsity basketball team. After that throwaway first semester, I breezed through the school of Einstein. Though I skipped numerous lectures and spent more time in Dillon gym playing basketball with students, townies, and black kids from Trenton than studying, the atmosphere engendered intellectual curiosity and a love of learning. I majored in history because there were no right or wrong answers (unlike the orthodoxy of today) and because history encompasses everything else in life: politics, art, literature, philosophy, religion.

I must confess that I joined a cult in college and have been a member ever since: the cult of Princeton basketball, whose Charles Manson in this case was now Hall of Fame coach Pete Carril. In a short span during my senior year, unranked Princeton beat number two North Carolina, number three Penn, and number six Villanova all by double digits, with inferior talent and relentless backdoor cuts. My sophomore year, the Princeton Tigers came within two seconds of ending UCLA's longest winning streak in college basketball history, on UCLA's home court, Pauley Pavilion. Our defender slipped on some sweat as an unguarded Sydney Wicks made a fifteen-foot buzzer-beater, dashing Tiger dreams of immortality. UCLA beat us by a single point but should have beaten us by twenty-five. Carril once told me that that game was the biggest disappointment of his career. His book title, *The Smart Take from the Strong*, says it all. He's a bona fide genius, smarter than most Princeton professors. Basketball, even more than history, was a critical part of my formative Princeton experience. It was perhaps the only area in life where Princeton was the underdog, at least during March Madness. As one big conference coach pep-talked his team before a March Madness game against the Tigers, "Beat the hell out of these sumbitches, 'cuz someday you'll be working for them."

It is not incongruous to say that I am both privileged and identify with the underdog, with people like my parents and teams like the Brooklyn Dodgers. I've always considered myself an underdog. Princeton basketball taught me that underdogs—even slow white guys playing bigger, stronger black guys in basketball, or me with meager test scores against high school valedictorians with bigger, stronger scores—can win, and when we do, the glory is sweet. Even when we lose (say, by a point to number one Georgetown—"the game that saved March Madness"), we earn honor and even a smidgeon of immortality. I played JV at Princeton, which unlike Choate was no humiliation, not when you're 5'11" and the varsity is beating North Carolina.

Princeton's rite of passage is the senior thesis. Mine, *From the Center of Sorrow*, about Whittaker Chambers and the Alger Hiss case, received a flat A, surprising given my right-of-center conclusion that Hiss, while understandingly concerned about the rise of fascism in the 1930s, was nonetheless guilty of espionage. It also delved into the complex psyche and intellectual journey of his accuser, Whitaker Chambers, and his conversion from communism to conservatism. Considering that the Hiss case spawned the political prominence of Richard Nixon, not exactly beloved in academia, my professor was remarkably tolerant to give me an A. We were decades away from word processors and computers, and my mother (whose vision and drive had made my unlikely education a reality) insisted on taking my chaotic, note-riddled 120 pages and typing the final copy herself. "My Episcopalian Jewish mother," I affectionately dubbed her, which threw her into a mild hissy fit. I dedicated my thesis to her, which made her cry.

I took Mom's original immaculate copy to a local binder on Nassau Street, who constructed a black leather-bound book with "From the Center of Sorrow, by Greg Abbott" gaudily embossed in gold on the cover like an oversized Koran. I found a quiet place in Firestone Library to read my beautifully adorned masterpiece—savoring every word and footnote until I came to page 81, which had been inserted upside down! "Fuck!" I seethed aloud, causing library denizens studying for exams to scowl and self-righteously wag fingers as only Princetonians can do. I quickly turned philosophical. This fateful mishap was a lesson in humility—a sign that I must never take myself too seriously or forget my roots. I am strangely grateful that page 81 is upside down. Wouldn't have it any other way.

Picture my ultra-right-wing parents four years later (1976) at a Manhattan cocktail party hosted by a gay male couple. Once you've absorbed that, picture my mother being introduced to Alger Hiss.

A bell went off in her head. "Oh, oh, oh," she gushed, refreshing her memory on the fly, "my son wrote his Princeton senior thesis about you!"

Alger Hiss perked up. "Really?"

"Yes. He got an A," she said with motherly pride. "I typed it for him."

"What was the gist of his thesis? What did he say?"

My typist had given me a flawless copy, but perhaps she'd focused too much on avoiding typos to fully grasp its content. Nothing else could have explained what she said next: "Oh, it was positive … *very positive* … about Whitaker Chambers."

A dumbfounded Hiss turned gray as a ghost and walked away. His reaction suddenly caused my mother to realize her colossal faux pas. Mortified, she followed Hiss and relentlessly tried to atone. Like Edith Bunker, the more she talked, the worse things got. I wish I could have witnessed their exchange firsthand; I can't even imagine it. Finally, the world's most famous spy since Mata Hari graciously put Mom out of her misery (and surely himself out of his) by handing her his business card. "Have your son call me. I'd love to have lunch with him."

One of my greatest regrets in life was not taking Alger Hiss up on his offer, or at least not storing his card inside a hollowed-out pumpkin for later. Aren't experiences like that what education is all about? I wasn't timid about meeting and mixing it up with him. I simply had moved on from my formal education and was absorbed in business and the rhythm of big-city life. I later promised myself never to make that same mistake again. Squandering such opportunities when they come along in life is a sin.

My Ithaca-rich parents never gave a dime to Choate or Princeton beyond tuition, nor did anyone twist their arm. They had no connections whatsoever to either school. I never had a tutor in my life (apart from a Choate teacher advising me to look up all the words I didn't know in the latest *Time* magazine, from back to front, a technique that boosted my verbal SAT score 120 points, from reptilian to low-level mammalian). I was no legacy but the first in my family to go to college. I was born in "shithole" Sayre and grew up in sleepy, twangy Ithaca. My father almost lost his business in 1959 but persisted, with an assist from nine-year-old Davy Crockett, to save it and his family from financial ruin. Only by a fluke was I was lucky enough to get into even a single prep school, where I spent four socially and athletically traumatic years riddled with low self-esteem and OTL branded on my brow. Finally, I managed to make friends and graduate from Princeton with honors in 1972 despite simian SAT scores. Dismiss it all as la-di-da white privilege if you must, as is your God-given right, but it never felt that way to me.

CHAPTER 4

PARIAHS

March 13, 2019, to March 29, 2019. For the next ten days after my arrest, the hyenas with cameras camped outside my apartment building day and night, much to the annoyance of my fellow co-op residents, not to mention me. It's a relatively small, some would say snooty, building of only thirteen floors, with essentially one apartment per floor and residents who value privacy and detest this sort of notoriety. That's why they have co-op boards, to keep out controversial rabble who attract media attention. Each time I left or entered the building, the hyenas swarmed to snap my picture or ask questions, like I was Madonna (who *never* would have been allowed to reside there). Pressing camera lenses against the window of my taxi, they were persistent buggers, I'll give them that, though occasionally I managed to avoid them with the diversionary help of the doorman.

For my then twenty-two-year-old middle son, their presence represented opportunity. Known to us as Malcolm but to his rap public and social media as "Infamous Billa," he went outside and held court with the hyenas. I was horrified but not entirely displeased by the ensuing *New York Post* article: "Blunt-Smoking Son of Alleged College Admissions Cheats Asked Us to Review his Rap CD." Good for him for defending his parents; good for him for promoting his CD, which the *Post* predictably trashed. Had it been a masterpiece, they would have trashed it anyway to suit their defamatory narrative.

It states the obvious that, thanks to Malcolm, we received more media attention than we would otherwise have. Like all defendants, we were advised by counsel and friends to lay low and speak to no one, especially the media. Infamous Billa got the memo, but he marches to the beat of his own beats. He was Malcolm in the Middle before the advent of the TV show, and like the stereotypical middle child, he had been a handful to raise. Out of the womb, he was wired differently: spacey, tangential, physically awkward, incredibly sweet. The frustration of being different and out of step in the cookie-cutter Upper East Side eventually led to rage, rap music, and drug abuse—all of which became stress points between my wife and me. Despite the difficulties Malcolm presents, he possesses an enormous heart and exceptional talent. It was that heart—and some pot-addled judgment—that inspired him to go outside with blunt in hand (somehow, without parental knowledge, our resourceful son had managed to procure a medical marijuana license) and speak to the *Post* a day or two after the scandal broke. His mission was twofold: defend his parents and, in the process, plug his new rap album.

"I would take a bullet for my parents," he declared to the reporters outside our building, who must have thought Christmas had come early. "Leave them alone, they're great people …. My father always taught me to treat everyone with respect, whether king or pauper … The media is blowing this out of proportion … I believe everyone has the right to a free education, man …" Then the pivot: "Hey, check out my new album, *Cheese and Crackers*," he said, handing out CD demos. This Aspbergery display led to a *Vanity Fair* interview. It even landed him coverage on *Fox and Friends*, an indignity mollified a tad by the sight of conservative pundits squirming like whores in church while saying "blunt," like they'd only learned what a blunt was moments before going on air. The news spread through social media like wildfire.

Thus far, I have resisted all forms of social media—truth told, I don't know my Facebook from my Assbook—but Marcia and our daughter living in Colorado were horrified, as were virtually all our friends. Based on this unanimous disgust and how it reflected on me as a father, I ripped Infamous Billa a new one and told him what a deplorably dumb move it was, especially with a blunt, a horrible optic on so many levels. Privately, I took some solace that he had said positive things and honestly believed, albeit misguidedly, that he was displaying loyalty. He's a work in progress, and I see much goodness and potential in him. My newly retained defense lawyer expressed similar sentiments, noting that Malcolm "really cares about his parents." Still, we would have exchanged a little less caring for a little less media fallout.

USA VS ABBOTT

Thanks to Infamous Billa's unforced error, my wife and I, private people to the core, appeared on the cover of the *New York Post* (not exactly a local paper, with the fourth largest circulation in the USA) with the caption "The Parent Rap." Inside, we took up an entire page. "Wealthy NYC 'Bribe' Couple Face Judge" read the excessively bold, war-sized headline, just above our pictures and a disparaging article, one written in a manner to suggest that Marcia and I were weed heads who had to be restrained by a court order. As one caption read, "Millionaire Manhattan couple faces judge in college admissions scandal, told they must abstain from marijuana as blunt-smoking rapper sells t-shirts online." (Malcolm had expanded his commercial aspirations from CD sales to T-shirts at thirty dollars a pop, imprinted with the words "Free Education" on the front and a photo of him smoking a blunt on the back. An aspiring hip-hop artist with 150,000 followers on Instagram and a blue check signifying influencer status, he values publicity as much as my wife and I value privacy. He also donated the T-shirt profits—approximately $3,000—to the Nyack Center, an organization that brings kids from all backgrounds together through art. A fact the muckrakers failed to report.)

The judge in this instance was Magistrate Paul Kelly, Federal District Court in Boston, where all the cases against the thirty-three parental defendants had been assigned. The purpose of the hearing was to have us hear the charges against us. No, the judge did not admonish the Abbotts about smoking weed but rather informed *all* defendants of the *standard conditions* that we had to meet in order to sustain our release. The ones I remember included: no contact with fellow defendants (my wife and I, though charged separately, were granted special dispensation to speak to each other; when I politely murmured, "Thank you, Your Honor," the gallery sniggered, which the *New York Post* gleefully lampooned); no leaving the country; any travel within the US had to be preapproved; any contact with police had to be reported immediately to your pretrial officer; and no marijuana use, for even though it was legal in Massachusetts, it was illegal federally, and we had been charged with a federal crime. The *Post* did not report all the instructions or the fact that they were routine, for the obvious reason that, in our case, nothing titillated so much as "abstain from marijuana."

Not content to suggest that Marcia and I were dope fiends, diminish our daughter's intellectual capacities, and poke fun at our blunt-boy's promotional activities, the same *New York Post* article, digressing from the case to pump sales by scandalizing us, claimed that I had paid Aspen

GREG ABBOTT

Christmas carolers to go around town and sing my "self-penned holiday ditties." I may be out to lunch, but I'm not a pedantic bozo. Nearly thirty years earlier, I had composed some irreverent Aspen Christmas carols, which I sang and recorded myself, accompanied by my own piano playing, and which the local radio deemed amusing enough to play for a short while—and, no, there was no payola involved. My radio local celebrityhood abruptly ended when some born-agains complained. The *Post* article even butchered my lyrics in order to drain whatever wit they might have had.

Still, I gotta hand it to the *Post*, however begrudgingly. It has a gift for making priceless headlines out of thin air. Milking our woes for all they could, they ran yet another story translating the court's routine hearing to: "Abbotts Told by Judge to Lay off the Weed." I can only imagine what the *Post* might have written about Hitler's death: "Amateur painter, noted vegetarian, and excellent ballroom dancer yesterday took his own life in reaction to continuing professional setbacks"?

A *New York Post* talent, which I used to enjoy until it was used on us, is printing photos to show their prey in the most unflattering of lights. Not even they could make my wife look bad, but in their March 12 photo of me exiting the courthouse, only a ski cap spared me from Nick Nolte comparisons. In another photo, sans ski cap, with my white hair all puffed up like a perm, I resembled Barbara Bush. A blue dress and string of pearls would have made the impersonation complete. Barbara Bush was a great lady, but I'm sure she wouldn't have wanted to look like me either. With all the smearing and slandering to be done, I began to wonder if the *New York Post* had a team of embellishers rather than fact-checkers.

Let me be clear. Both my wife I had always loved the *New York Post*—loved its witty and imaginative headlines; its iconoclastic attacks; its delight in the scandalous. It was for me the paper of record of New York. I have since cancelled our daily subscription.

The venerated *Wall Street Journal* (second largest circulation in the USA) was the most despicable rag of them all. The *WSJ* quoted me several times, although I never, *ever* spoke to them. I told you of my one and only encounter with the *WSJ* in chapter 2, in the courthouse hallway as I was leaving after my day-long arrest. I was asked to comment but didn't utter a single word. That did not prevent the *WSJ* from printing the following, every word an utter fabrication:

"Mr. Abbott said his family had spoken to the FBI about the alleged cheating scandal, and on Tuesday called the situation 'insane.'"

"'Literally, we were involved with this guy for our daughter to help out with college counseling and he gets f*****g arrested,' Mr. Abbott said. 'We didn't know he was doing this s**t.'"

"'A network of New York City mothers uses this guy and they all say he's the best,' Abbott said."

I didn't know a single New York City mother who used Singer, except my wife, who was living in Colorado and introduced to him by a friend from California. It was primarily a California scandal. I would never say such an idiotic thing, nor any of the other idiotic and profane things the *WSJ* alleged I said. At least the *New York Post* had some kernels of truth, albeit woven to be misleading. The *WSJ* simply made everything up, all of it, out of thin air, which is not only deplorable but probably actionable.

Worse than simply skewering someone in the public mind, a false press article can cause real and tangible harm. In this instance, six months later at the sentencing hearing, prosecutor and officer of the court, Eric Rosen, Esq., cited the *WSJ* fictitious quotes to illustrate my "lack of remorse," in an attempt to send me to federal prison for one year!

—

The day following my arrest, I returned the calls of IDC's largest investor (besides me), who had left two urgent messages the day of my arrest. I got more than an earful—an earful I deserved far more, in my opinion, than my eventual one-month prison sentence. This iconic investor had been with me from the beginning. He was a major benefactor to Princeton, including donating a building, and also helped manage its endowment funds. During a casual phone call in February 2019, three weeks before the Varsity Blues sting and five weeks before colleges sent out their decisions, I was telling him that Princeton had invited my daughter to attend a choral concert later that month, obviously because of her opera. I *did not ask him* to put in a good word for her; he graciously volunteered out of friendship. When he asked me for some background info, I impulsively (and regretfully) rattled off the following email:

> Attached are [my daughter's] Princeton essays plus a couple of short (one minute each) recordings. As I mentioned, Princeton invited her this Saturday to attend a Rossini concert in Richardson Auditorium (in Alexander Hall),

which I think is a good sign. Hopefully she'll meet all the music department people. ACT score: 35. SAT subject tests: Math 2 800, English 710. All in all, far superior to her Class '72 father in every way.

Fatherly exuberance mindlessly included the test scores. They had been baked into the cake, the ACTs ten months ago, the SAT subject tests seven months ago. I had numbed the transgressions from my mind and moved on. Princeton could fill an entire class with the applicants they rejected with perfect scores. Opera was what distinguished my daughter; the test scores merely checked a box. Without thinking, I, dumb-ass par excellence, threw the scores into the email, agog at the prospect of the upcoming weekend.

It hardly needs saying that I was over the moon at the prospect of my daughter going to the university I had attended and loved, where I had found my social and intellectual stride after a four-year Choate battering. I envisioned her neck swathed in an orange-and-black scarf; fantasized attending reunions together. Surely, Princeton hadn't invited her this late in the game if they were intending to reject her. It had all the makings of a recruiting event, and a positive word from my esteemed friend and investor, so revered at Princeton, would surely do her chances no harm.

My daughter, who hadn't spoken to me for some time (a by-product of her parents' marital discord), was about to fly in from Colorado. I could hardly contain my excitement at the prospect of showing her my cherished alma mater and repairing our once-wonderful relationship. Valiantly, day after day, she had fought Lyme disease, getting As in her courses and performing both in the children's chorus and as a soloist at the Metropolitan Opera (from age seven through junior year), all but forsaking a high school social life for the sake of her goals and because she had neither the time nor energy for play. Only because of school absences had she been forced to move to an online homeschooling program, which led to the introduction to Rick Singer, a slope slipperier than any in Colorado. Had it not been for online schooling, we never would have made his telephonic acquaintance. 'Twas a serpent that led to Adam and Eve's ostracism; ours was set in motion by a barely visible bug.

I wasn't able to humanize any of this to my investor, nor was it wise to try. My friend and benefactor, who had put his trust in me, invested millions with me, and used to refer to IDC as his "favorite company," was blistering me to the skies. This deceitful breach not only revealed rotten character, he said, but made him question everything I had ever told him about IDC. He and his wife would never invest in IDC again. His wife was so irate, in fact, that she actually phoned Princeton's president, Christopher Eisgruber, to tell him what a venal lowlife I was, or something to that effect. "You're finished at Princeton," he said, shattering my heart in several places. Princeton, where I had found my stride in life—and just like that, I was about as persona non grata as one can get. ("Persona Non Grata at My Alma Mater"—song title for the movie?)

Far, far worse, my daughter was obviously finished there too, and the weekend there had been magical. Though she'd spent her spare time resting in bed at the Princeton Inn due to Lyme fatigue, she had bonded with the students and teachers at the concert reception and at my class cocktail party. To my delight, she seemed to belong there. While the wife's call to President Eisgruber struck me as piling on (to put it politely), I couldn't blame my friend for feeling betrayed. With life seemingly crumbling all around me, all I could do was listen, take my lumps, and humbly tell him how sorry I was.

Hopefully I could explain myself later, once things settled down. This was (as far as I know) my only true friendship damaged by Varsity Blues but a treasured and important one. I had raised millions from other investors simply because they learned he was in the deal, but it was so much more than business. I truly loved the man. While his primary complaint was that I had included the test scores in my email, I doubt that omitting them would have made much difference. I was redefined in his eyes. Losing this man's respect and friendship was worse than being sentenced to a month in federal prison. I hope he believes in redemption as much as I.

News of Varsity Blues had traveled all around the world, even to my IDC colleagues based in Dubai and Shanghai, who pledged their undying loyalty and friendship and have continued to demonstrate it to this day.

Another Princeton grad, a self-proclaimed financial maven who in our one and only meeting was so impressed by IDC's story that she declared she could raise all the capital the company needed "in a heartbeat"— "You had me at hello," she'd said—called me from Israel where she was traveling. Cited as one of New York City's 100 Most Influential Women, this financial maven, who knew zero about our situation, only the press reports, was in full froth. "My daughter's a gymnast," she berated, bristling with self-righteousness. "When she fell off the balance bar, bruised and bleeding, we didn't help her! She got back on the bar *herself* and kept trying and falling, trying and falling! She *earned* her way into Princeton *on her own*!" This from a woman whose family had reputedly donated tens of millions to Princeton.

Before I could say "Lyme," she shrilled, "I'm going to call my husband," as if my one attempted interjection constituted harassment and that she, even in Israel, needed protection from me. Whoever her husband was, I pitied the poor bastard.

To hype drama and reader interest, the press frequently referred to me as "Big Apple beverage big-wig," "NYC beverage baron," "Chairman and CEO of behemoth International Dispensing Corporation," like I was a billionaire capable of selling my soul and purchasing others.

In truth, for fifteen years, my heart and soul had been dedicated (from a commercial point of view) to a promising but struggling start-up that endeavored to do the world some good. During those fifteen years, we had thrice come within nano distance of being launched into the stratosphere: once with PepsiCo China, once with Coca-Cola / Juan Valdez Coffee / MacDonald's, and finally with the Koch family. In each case, unrelated corporate politics and restructuring did us in, no fault whatsoever of IDC or yours truly.

I, of course, have no objection to being an actual beverage bigwig. It is in truth an ambition of mine but to date remains unrealized. I have suffered all the drawbacks of being a "beverage bigwig" without any of the benefits. I remain hopeful (for good reason) that IDC will become a "behemoth," but as of now, it and I are beverage gnats, albeit possessed of something fabulous. IDC is the inventor of the world's only aseptic tap, The Answer®. It currently has small revenues and as of this writing remains in the red. Over the years, I've put millions of my own money into it and raised millions, based on its legitimate global promise. Micro-tested and validated up the wazoo, The Answer enables delivery of nutritious aseptic beverages in bulk, including milk, to developing nations and disaster areas. It dispenses liquids while protecting the package's remaining contents from contamination even *without refrigeration*! The package is ecologically friendly, saving roughly 50 percent in energy and 90 percent in landfill. A socially impactful innovation if ever there were one. Aseptic packaging innovations by nature take many years to test, validate, and commercialize, and our obstacles had been numerous and daunting, far more than I'd ever anticipated. It's akin to developing a new drug, with lots of money and effort expended up front before the anticipated global results and financial reward.

At the time of my arrest, IDC had not yet knocked down any big marketing doors, and when the news broke, our thinly traded stock price plummeted. Had my equity interest left me awash in bigwig cash, like the *Post* suggested, why would we have bothered with Singer's "side door"? I could have marched in through the front door, holding a big, fat check, as many super-rich parents do, had I been so inclined.

Harvard development people told one couple I know (both Harvard grads) that the price tag for their son was $10 million, though apparently the bar for Jared Kushner's father was considerably lower, in the $2 to $3 million range. Colgate told another friend of mine that they were on the fence about accepting his daughter but that a $300,000 donation toward a building would tip the scales in her favor. We know several mega-rich parents who gave seven- and eight-figure donations to universities to grease the skids for their kids. The affable wife of a billionaire told me on a Colorado ski lift a few years ago that their daughter had gotten into Harvard, Princeton, Yale, Stanford, and a slew of other prestigious universities too numerous to remember. Don't know where the girl ended up going, and I'm sure she's smart and qualified, but who runs the table like that without billions behind them? A prominent Democratic Party donor/fundraiser I know got President Obama to write a letter of recommendation for his son (in lieu of ambassadorship) to Georgetown, thus depriving a more deserving student of admission. Way to go, Barrack! A heterosexual applicant I know highlighted in his college applications that he was gay, resulting in widespread acceptances; not even Singer tried photoshopping along those lines. Dr. Dre, who donated $70 million toward an art building at USC, took a swipe at the Varsity Blues parents by boasting that *his* daughter got into USC *on her own*, without Rick Singer. Should we also assume that Dr. Dre got his medical degree without Singer's assistance? Early on in the relationship, Singer, testing the waters, casually suggested to my wife that he could get our daughter into Stanford for $3 million and Duke for $2 million. Marcia didn't have the luxury even to be tempted. Thanks in large part to some bad breaks, we didn't have that kind of play money to think of something like that. Even if we did, I doubt we'd have considered buying our daughter's admission into a specific college; believe it or not, it's not how we roll. Ours was more a misguided act of desperation than a crass power play. Keep reading and decide for yourself.

Because of Varsity Blues, I had no practical choice but to resign as IDC's chairman, CEO, and heart and soul. Fortunately, I was already in the process of transitioning from wild-eyed visionary entrepreneur (me) to seasoned industry pros from Coca-Cola, Tetra Pak, and Sealed Air—people who, like myself, believed in The Answer's vision and potential. None of them, however, had experience raising money, and when Varsity Blues hit the airwaves, we were in the middle of a critical capital raise. Raising capital for a unique venture is challenging enough, but when your name and face are splashed all over creation as a criminal and cheat ... well, you tell me, would *you* invest with him?

—

Now here's one for the books, an anecdote that should make even those most hostile to me perk up, take notice, and say, "What the f**k! You can't be serious!"

Within days of the news breaking, JPMorgan and Citibank, with whom my wife and I had banked for years, informed us in writing that they were closing our accounts in three weeks. They offered no reason. When we appealed to our branch managers, they hemmed and hawed and consulted their computers before providing the stock answer: "Potential reputational damage." No mention of Varsity Blues, to which they feigned ignorance.

Potential reputational damage! Really? These institutions were among the worst culprits in the subprime mortgage crisis in 2008, which almost led the world economy over a cliff to create the worst global depression since the Great One of the 1930s. Yet not a single banker was awakened by a bevy of pistol-bearing feds, hauled out in chains, and eventually sent to the slammer. Their punishment came in the form of huge taxpayer bailouts and a request never to do it again. I would have taken that plea deal in a flash.

JP Morgan handled millions for Jeffrey Epstein long after it was common knowledge that he was a sexual predator. Same with Russia oligarchs. They continue to bank with the Wildensteins, who during World War II reputedly ratted out Jews to Nazis in return for permission to smuggle their Picassos and Degas out of the country. Many lawsuits remain pending. Yet the House of Morgan had the gall to cite reputational damage with us, like Greg and Marcia Abbott were the equivalent of El Chapo? In response to my request to speak to a decision-maker, one branch manager gave me the phone number of his boss. The number didn't have voice mail. I called the number repeatedly over several days before he finally answered. The bureaucrat couldn't wait to get me off the phone. Could I speak to a compliance officer? "Impossible." Could I speak to his boss? "'Fraid not." Was there *anyone* I could speak to, like maybe Jamie Fucking Dimon? "Sorry, there's nothing I can do. It's outside my purview." Apparently, it was outside his purview but not in anyone else's either.

No wonder no bank executives had gone to jail for the subprime crisis in 2008. Institutions in America, while regulating the hell out of *us*, are structured to eliminate personal accountability, protecting corporate butts through a labyrinth of blind alleys, layers, and regulations authored by faceless people—institutionalizing everything so that no one individual, not even the CEO, can be singled out. Instead, some numbskull checks a box, and *my wife and I* go to prison. This proved to be not only a time-consuming inconvenience but a morale blow at a time when we least needed it. When gluttonous banks refuse your honestly begotten, hard-earned money, how low have you sunk? Fortunately, our banker in Colorado embraced us as clients. Though I currently live in Manhattan, I don't have a bank account here. I am proud to be an entrepreneur and not a suit. Creating something without a support system gives me pride, justified or not, that a suit never should feel.

—

Two Saturday mornings after the Varsity Blues arrest, I was in sitting at my bedroom desk, sipping coffee and opening mail that had accumulated, mostly bills. The hyenas had just ended their unrelenting stakeout of my apartment building. For the first time since the arrest, I felt a modicum of peace.

I opened an envelope that first seemed like junk mail but then jolted me. It contained a picture of my wife and me, the one that had originally appeared on the cover of the New York Post, with gigantic, bold capital letters calling us a spine-tingling racial epithet too offensive and incendiary to put in writing. Under that, in smaller print, was the following manifesto: "I hope you fucking DIE from a slow cancer AND the person who could have saved you was the one person WHO DID NOT GET INTO A UNIVERSITY BECAUSE YOUR FUCKING CHEATING TRAILER TRASH DID!" Then below that the same racial slur in giant, bold caps, followed by "Rot in hell Mother of the Year!!!!!!!!"

My spine twitched with trepidation. Pretentious I know, but briefly I flashed to how Hank Aaron must of have felt in 1974 when he was about to break Babe Ruth's career homerun record and received bags of racist hate mail. I checked the postmark: Denver, Colorado. Offhand I couldn't think of anyone we knew who lived in Denver. We knew a lot of people in the Colorado town where we had lived but nobody who would make a four-hour pilgrimage simply to drop an anonymous, vile hate letter into a Denver slot. Denver was an airline hub, so it could be anyone. Calling my precious daughter "FUCKING CHEATING TRAILER TRASH" made me want to hunt him down a la Liam Neeson (*Taken*) and unleash my "special set of skills" (if only I had any). Neither he nor anyone else knew her valiant story or her innocence in this mess. How could they? The media was serving us up as red meat; Mencken's *Boobus Americanus* was gobbling up the politicized narrative of *Brutus Americanus* without deploying a scintilla of skepticism. "Painting all the parents and children with the same bold brush," as one defense lawyer put it. The government and press in lockstep—not exactly what our founding fathers had in mind.

Why this nutjob had focused on "Mother of the Year" without also mentioning "Father" offended at once my wife, the slur's target, and me for apparently not having earned the parental right to be the slur's target. The cancer reference was especially galling as both my parents had died of cancer. We were both being vilified in the media for white privilege, but racially charged hate mail was another story. I am not using the word here for fear that the media will do what they do best: attribute it to me in order to smear me.

CHAPTER 5

THE GODFATHER, PART IV

By the time I graduated from Princeton, my parents had sold our Ithaca home and relocated to Manhattan—in their midfifties and, like I said, knowing no one. My father had also branched out from ladies' underwear and now made pantyhose exclusively for JCPenney. Using his masterful sewing techniques, he was able to sew a spandex panty onto a pair of nylon hose with a flat seam that didn't show under clothing. This garment reputedly was the first ever control-top pantyhose. By sewing support hose onto the same spandex panty, he also created a total support garment. These two items, while labor intensive and pricey, gradually became the two biggest sellers at JCPenney, not just in pantyhose but throughout the entire company. The separate panty made them uniquely contoured to the asses of the masses and generated brand loyalty throughout Middle America. Ithaca Textiles' pantyhose sales eclipsed those of ladies' underwear, back when women showcased their legs. Dad set up a vertically integrated plant in Wilkesboro, North Carolina, with high-speed yarn-texturizing machines imported from Italy.

Using those machines and the expertise of trained rednecks, he created a special yarn for JCPenney that was more durable than anything in the market, which JCPenney trademarked Flextra®. All they needed to make Flextra a household name was to hire a spokeswoman, one known for her legs, to promote this new wonder yarn. I'm not sure what agency produced Ginger Rogers or why she and my parents instantly hit it off. Not only did Ginger become a family friend and perpetual houseguest, but just like that, she introduced my parents to slews of crème de la crème (i.e., rich and famous) New Yorkers. In a distressed market, Ithaca Industries bought an Upper East Side townhouse between Madison and Fifth and furnished it with faux antiques. This became the company headquarters. Dad ran the business from the first floor and lived and entertained on the floors above, writing off whatever he could (and then some). The Ginger connection enabled my parents to pole-vault overnight—backwards and in high heels—from the Ithaca turnip truck into Manhattan and Hollywood society. Only in America!

The first *notables* I met at the New York townhouse (courtesy of Ginger) were real estate moguls Harry and Leona Helmsley. Say what you want about Leona Helmsley, the "Queen of Mean" with the repulsive lip liner and personality; although the characterizations of her in the papers (even the *New York Post*) were essentially spot-on and she was hardly my cup o' tea, she also saved my father's life, or so goes the urban legend. Just as Hitler was a painter, vegetarian, and ballroom dancer. With Dad stricken with severe pneumonia, Leona moved heaven and earth at Doctor's Hospital (now Beth Israel), where the Helmsleys had given millions, to get him the best emergency medical care money could buy. Years later, when facing a prison sentence for her highly publicized tax case, Leona asked my mother to write her a character letter. Out of historical gratitude, I persuaded Mom to go through the challenging mental gymnastics. I believe Leona had far more difficulty obtaining such letters than I did when my time came.

Dad's near-fatal pneumonia and the fact that someone had made an offer to buy Ithaca Textiles for "high single-digit millions" prompted my parents to sit me down for a come-to-Jesus discussion just prior to graduation. They would only sell the business, they said, if I wasn't interested in it. "If you want it," they said, "it's yours, though you'll have to start at the bottom and earn your way." To say I sensed that they wanted me to say yes is a monumental understatement.

A blank canvas, I was just beginning to think about life after college. Names like Goldman Sachs and Morgan Stanley never entered my mind. Even less, Ithaca Textiles and the ladies' undergarment business, which for me was the Dustin Hoffman (*The Graduate*) equivalent of plastics. ("Nylon. There's a great future in nylon.") With the experience of writing my senior thesis, I fantasized about writing historical biographies, maybe becoming a tweed-clad, pipe-smoking leftist in the tradition of my uncle Sam. I also pondered going to Hollywood and (based on no discernable talent whatsoever) taking a shot at acting fame. I mean, that's where the babes (and the Dodgers!) were. Ginger actually told me I had "movie star looks." Perhaps she could open doors. A young producer friend of mine running Tristar Pictures, sensing the same potential (who forty-five years later wrote me a character letter), kept urging me to get a screen test.

In the end, all the vanity in Christendom couldn't make me forsake my parents' lifelong efforts, not in the wake of Dad's near fatal pneumonia. Like Michael Corleone, family fealty superseded everything. I revered and had always felt a part of their journey, and I was grateful for all that they had done for me. Out of pure duty, I couldn't say no. It was too early to bring our family saga to a premature end. Despite my greenness, I felt they needed me. I liked feeling needed.

"It's not business, Sonny. It's strictly personal."

—

My father started me at $15,000 per year and insisted I learn the ropes as soon as possible, which entailed a year of living in Wilkesboro and shuttling between there and the Cairo underwear plant. Every couple of months, I flew up to New York, where my father introduced me to the buyers and merchandize managers of JCPenney. After a year of this, I moved to the Big Apple permanently. So much for starting at the bottom.

Dad put me in charge of ladies' underwear sales, which were in a state of crisis. Women were changing. Parachute-sized nylon and acetate bloomers (in white, pink, or mint green) were, to put it mildly, out of step with the bra-burning sexual revolution. Even the middle-aged male JCPenney buyers in polyester leisure suits recognized the trend toward printed fabrics, hip-huggers, and bikinis—"fashion," they called it. They wanted to deal with other suppliers and have more choices, which for Ithaca Textiles constituted an existential threat.

I turned my youth and inexperience into an advantage, inundating the underwear buyer with sexy new styles, ideas I plucked from high-end designers featured at Bergdorf Goodman—"knockoffs," we called them. (A harbinger of Varsity Blues cheating? Puh-leeze. My father wouldn't spring for a designer.) Lurking around the ladies' underwear counter at Bergdorf's brought me dirty looks, but in this industry, looking like a borderline perv came with the territory. Imagine the sight of perky young models parading in sexy underwear in my dad's conference room in front of sweating, drooling, balding, polyester-clad buyers. Back in the mid-1970s, that was an accepted industry practice; I'd be shocked if it is today. I never mixed business with pleasure with these models, though the sexy new styles made excellent gifts for the young women I was dating. Had I given them white (or even mint green) bloomers, I doubt *Harper's Bazaar* would have dubbed me one of their top ten "Playboys of the Eastern Coast" (courtesy of an editor I occasionally dated who worked there). As the only "playboy" on that infamous list who actually worked, I didn't know whether to be flattered or mortified. Mine was truly a nonstop job: putting underwear on women by day, removing them by night (or so went the perpetual joke). I out-hustled Ithaca Textiles' competitors and actually increased our underwear turf at JCPenney. As long as JCPenney was our only customer, it was all about turf wars.

JCPenney was the world's largest retailer of *men's* underwear. When their sole supplier, Spring City Mills, was bought out by a conglomerate, its service and pricing deteriorated to the point that JCPenney approached my father to groom a secondary supplier to "keep Spring City honest." Spring City (whose retired founder had a swimming pool shaped like a T-shirt) hadn't covered cotton futures and was raising prices. In return for an entrée into JC Penney's men's underwear business, my father offered to hold prices. We lost 12 percent on each garment made, but it was an investment in the future. Dad and JCPenney agreed on a plan in which at the end of five years, Ithaca Textiles would represent 20 percent of JCPenney's men's underwear pie, Spring City 80 percent. Then Dad put me in charge of managing the transition. My brother, newly graduated from college, had just joined the business. While I managed men's underwear, he seamlessly stepped into women's and did a solid job—without ever visiting Bergdorf's.

One glimpse at me, and the JCPenney's men's underwear buyer, a tough, squat Irishman from the other side of the tracks, with a limp from childhood polio and a perpetual sneer, hated me and the nepotistic privilege I represented—not unlike my Varsity Blues critics. I didn't like him much either. We were clashing archetypes, but once we started working together, we clicked and celebrated our differences. It was a beautiful thing. Though he never went to college, being Catholic, he was a huge Notre Dame fan. Notre Dame's basketball team, ranked second in the nation, was playing Princeton at Jadwin Gym, and he asked me to take him to the game. The buyer salivated at the foregone conclusion of seeing his tough Fighting Irish demolish the "privileged preppy pussies from Princeton," an alliteration he loved repeating in the crowded JCPenney elevator to embarrass me.

He wasn't privy to the powers of my cult or the genius of Pete Carril's Princeton offense. Princeton's jaw-dropping double-digit romp bathed me in blue-collar machismo in his eyes. For all the reasons you might expect, this iconoclastic men's underwear buyer loathed the slick suits representing Spring City's parent company, and together we turned the tables: by the end of the five-year period, Ithaca Textiles made 80 percent of JCPenney's men's underwear, Spring City 20 percent.

In the middle of all this, my father suffered a stroke. Thinking we might lose him and way too young to fill his shoes, I burst into tears at the hospital like a baby. At age twenty-six, I suddenly became the de facto head of Ithaca Textiles and had to handle both pantyhose and men's underwear.

To this day, I believe that the JCPenney pantyhose buyer caused my father's stroke. Corrupt, always with his hand out and cozying up to Dad's competitors, he had no respect for my father's undying loyalty to JCPenney. He also saw me as his pigeon and did his best to intimidate and bully me. He dressed me down in front of our people during a plant visit, undermining my already shaky authority and company morale. After his usual Carter-esque three-martini lunch, he would take a circuitous route back to the office, walking past men's stores like Dunhill and gazing suggestively at the window displays, miffed when I wouldn't take the hint and offer to buy him a natty sports jacket. One day, he upped the ante, sliding a Mercedes Benz brochure across his desk and asking how much I valued our business. Our prices were too high, he suggested, and any number of our competitors would gladly buy him the coveted two-seater. I was terrified, in a panic, with no one to turn to. Compared to the business at stake, the price of a Mercedes was not the end of the world. However, I knew this wouldn't be the end but the beginning. Confronted with this dilemma, I sought refuge in my sense of right and wrong (as I should have with Singer). "I'm confused," I told him. "Are you rewarding the lowest bidder or the highest?"

With that, I walked out of his office, heart racing, palms sweating, but forever proud of the moment. I didn't have the heart to worry Dad or Mom about his, and for some reason, I never got any blowback. Dad returned to the saddle shortly thereafter, the effects of his stroke barely discernable. The corrupt buyer was transferred laterally to a new product line and out of our hair, and I downward back to men's underwear, which by now was purring along quite nicely and not requiring my full-time attention.

My father's business strategy was to put all his eggs in one basket and watch the eggs carefully, but the insular situation with JCPenney and its inherent tensions made me uneasy. We were doing well but always one rogue buyer decision away from oblivion. No matter what the product line, our pricing structure was based on volume. A 20 percent decline would decimate our competitive edge. My inability to do anything about this led to boredom and wanderlust, manifesting in me going out with a growing array of friends to restaurants and nightclubs until the wee hours, burning the proverbial candle at both ends. I lost my edge and plunged into wanderlust, discovering marijuana, then cocaine (which I tried just once, from the summer of 1978 to the autumn of 1981).

Meanwhile, my circle of friends and superficial acquaintances was becoming vast and eclectic. I hung out with preppies; Eurotrash; older people; younger people; socialites; sluts; ditsy models; melancholy heiresses; Wall Streeters with collar pins; up-and-coming media whizzes; writers, actors, and painters; professional athletes (I once double-dated with Willis Reed); multilingual UN diplomats; restaurant and nightclub owners; the princess sister of the Aga Khan; the progeny of moguls, tinhorn dictators, mafia kingpins; and even David Koch. A budding man about town, I was set up on a blind date with Bianca Jagger, former wife of Mick and Far Left activist. The Activist and the Emasculated Underwear Salesman—a match made in Hades—but the spooky coincidence of sharing the same birthday prolonged things like a respirator until I mercifully pulled the plug. Though the novelty amused me, I loathed going to Studio 54 (Trump's Vietnam) night after night, hanging out with Bianca's friends Abbie Hoffman and Calvin Klein. I had nothing to say to them, nor they to me. One rare quiet night, Bianca, her thirteen-year-old daughter, Jade, and I went to see a movie, followed by my first sushi ever. Throughout dinner, Jade kept passing me handwritten notes, to the effect, "Please, pleeeeeeze marry my mother! You're the only normal man she's ever dated!" Normal? Moi?

During this phase of life, which I eventually came to dub my "depressed bon vivant period," I met Bobby Marx (son of Barbara Marx, former wife of Zeppo and current wife of Frank Sinatra) at a New York nightclub. We became a two-man, cocaine-snorting, womanizing brat pack. Come New Year's Eve, I was invited to Atlantic City to celebrate with ... (drum roll) ... the Sinatras. The *entourage* stayed at the Golden Nugget where Frank was performing. Hadn't Johnny Fontaine signed on the dotted line to perform once or twice a year for Don Corleone? Was this New Year's gig part of that arrangement? Early in the evening, while having drinks in the casino sans Frank (who was getting ready to perform), Barbara introduced me to their entourage as the "future president of the United States." Apparently, I had made a good impression, and with all the Peruvian marching powder in my system, I relished the accolade. Could Barbara Marx, showgirl turned philanthropist, also be a seer? (As a felon in his early seventies, I certainly have my work cut out for me if I ever intend to fulfill her prophesy.) At the performance, we sat in the front row with sports celebrities Tommy John and Tommy Lasorda. I boasted to Lasorda that I had more Dodger blue flowing through my veins than he did, which won me a "I doubt it, kid," followed by a bear hug.

Pia Zadora opened, followed by hack comedian Pat Henry, before Frank came out to screams and knocked 'em dead with a host of old favorites and his grand finale "New York, New York": "If I can make it there, I can make anyyyyy God-damn where …" Being in Frank's entourage was a demeaning chore that those chosen few in his generation deemed a privilege, drinking gin and playing gin until all hours while he held court. One needed a stimulant like cocaine just to stay awake.

"In the wee small hours of the morning, when the whole wide world is fast asleep," I found myself having a tête-a-tête with Frank. He was describing a movie kissing scene with Gina Lollobrigida: "Nothing like the taste of stale garlic to make the old dickey go down," he said, tossing back gin, while my dickey equated the taste of stale garlic with the cocaine racing though my system. In the presence of Frank Sinatra, a fearful wave of spirituality washed over me and I went one level higher: *Please, God, no nosebleed! Not now! Not tonight!* Frank carried on: "The Dodgers need a slash hitter like Pete Rose. Somebody tough, with grit …" *Please, God, no nosebleed! Please, God, I promise never to snort blow again.* Thirty minutes or so into our tête-a-tête, with me sniffling and silently praying but still somehow holding my own, Frank clasped his hand firmly on my arm. "When I look at the future of this country and see young men like you and Bobby," Ol' Blue Eyes proclaimed to Ol' Red Eyes, squeezing my arm with a gung-ho patriotic glint, "my faith in America's future is in*tact*!" *Ba-dum-bum.*

I actually honored my promise to God, albeit with a few stumbles, but still couldn't stand myself. The kid from Sayre belonged with this celebrity crowd about as much as did Zelig or Forrest Gump. I felt stuck in my life and, as such, went through serial one-night stands rather than relationships. Under my father's thumb, feeling stagnant and not knowing where I was headed, I had nothing to offer a woman but a good time. A very good time, I liked to think, but then what? On to the next hollow conquest? The more bodies I merged with, the more emotionally depleted I became. (Even Ginger tried to get in on the act—wink, wink—but I did *not* fly her down to Rio.) I longed for intimacy but didn't love myself enough to love anyone. If cowardice is awakening love in a woman with no intention of loving her, in the words of Bob Marley, then back then I fit the bill. No matter what I accomplished at Ithaca Textiles, even flipping men's underwear from 20/80 to 80/20, it would always come with the nepotism taint. T'aint you, 'tis your dad. The more successful I helped make my father, the more I would be branded "rich man's son." My privilege (back then, no one assigned it a color) rankled. I felt myself drifting, dissatisfied, a male slut. As long as I stayed at Ithaca Textiles, working out of Dad's wood-paneled conference room (didn't have my own office), I would forever be plagued with self-doubt, denied the respect I believed I was capable of generating on my own. People dubbed me "The Pantyhose Prince" when I had nothing to do with pantyhose. Just men's underwear, just for JCPenney. My life in a nutshell. Thank God I'd gone to Choate and Princeton, huh?

—

I hate to say that it was Daddy who bailed me out of my life predicament, but when he suffered a heart attack, my life changed forever. Pneumonia, a stroke, and now a heart attack finally brought him face-to-face with his own mortality, and me face-to-face with my manhood. Just like that, this consummate hands-on operator and maniacal one-customer control freak stepped aside and named his oldest son chairman and CEO. I was twenty-nine. Nick, the mercurially brilliant, mid-fifty-something engineer who ran all our plants, was the logical choice. For one thing, he was an adult; for another, he was company president and COO. My father had placed considerable trust in him as we expanded our product lines and opened new plants throughout the union-free South. He even gave Nick 10 percent ownership. However, Nick was no salesman and out of his element in New York; he quaked in the presence of JCPenney buyers and turned to Jell-O in price negotiations. Nick also, I suspect, was bipolar, though to my knowledge the term didn't exist back then.

From his sickbed, Dad rasped like Marlin Brando, "I'm picking the best man I know for the job. And I don't mean just within the company." I was touched; his voice rasped with conviction. How I wanted to believe him, but whatever he saw in me, I didn't quite see in myself. I was determined to prove him right. I used self-deprecating humor to disarm the naysayers, joking that Dad had been misdiagnosed with a heart attack when in fact he had dementia. The worst thing I could do was take myself and my new position too seriously. Remember page 81 of my senior thesis? I don't know how Nick felt inside, but he clicked his heels like a loyal Prussian soldier, and we forged a strong working rapport out of pure necessity.

I am certain that the stress inherent in the one-customer arrangement was what caused Dad's heart attack. The corrupt buyer was gone, but now *all* JCPenney buyers were inundated with suppliers knocking at their doors, wooing them with all the corporate power in their arsenals. Looking to gain entrée into America's largest soft goods retailer, they went over buyers' heads to the merchandise managers and above. America continued to change, and they offered a cornucopia of new styles. Conglomerates playing in numerous apparel arenas used their leverage in one to gain favors in another. We had threats in all directions. And now the old man was incapacitated and the kid in charge. Sound at all like *The Godfather*?

I watched that movie and its sequel a lot in those days, in part to fortify my method acting, which I saw as a key part of the job (as the saying goes, "Fake it till you make it"). While I fantasized about assassinating the heads of our five largest competitors, our real mission was clear: land new customers. I became CEO by day and battery-charging monk (the future Felonious Monk) by night, abruptly ending my depressed bon vivant period. I could no longer afford to squander energy in lightweight pursuits; every molecule was needed for work that was way over my head.

My younger brother (affectionately dubbed Fredo by one and all) continued to grow the women's underwear division. Out of fraternal respect, I stayed out of his hair. Thinking big and beyond, I hired a former men's underwear buyer from JCPenney to run men's sales and a former hosiery buyer from JCPenney to run pantyhose sales. To upgrade our image and signify change, I changed the company's name to Ithaca *Industries* Inc., which came with a catchy new logo: *III*. We had to expand our customer base or perish. The question was, could we survive?

It was a scary, uncertain time as we went to the mattresses. Most of the pantyhose and underwear retail world out there assumed JCPenney had an ownership position in Ithaca Industries, a disqualifying misconception that took us time to dissolve. They wanted to know why suddenly we were calling on them. Was something amiss with the JCPenney relationship? During that discouraging first year, with bipolar Nick freaking out on a daily basis, Ithaca Industries sold the townhouse and moved to a real midtown office a block from the JCPenney building, while my parents moved to a modest rental apartment.

One thing going for us was superb quality; being a significant supplier to JCPenney required it, and Dad and Nick were ultimate taskmasters. Positioning ourselves as the best-kept secret in the industry, we targeted the chains—Sears, K-Mart, Target, Wal-Mart, Mervyn's. Like first-time novelists, we experienced rejection after rejection after rejection. Then suddenly, two years into it, the popcorn began to pop. A small order from Sears! K-Mart! An entire high-end pantyhose program from Evan-Picone! Nike! Ocean Pacific! Mervyn's! Target! Pop, pop, pop! An elderly friend introduced me to the CEO of Avon Products, whom I convinced that his army of Avon ladies could supplement sales of cosmetics and costume jewelry with, in effect, "cosmetics for the leg." Within four years, *III* had acquired more than twenty-five new customers.

"We want to date other people," JCPenney had told us, but now that we had seduced their rivals, we were once again the "It Company." I made sure that everyone at all levels of JCPenney knew all about our successes in the outside world. I took them to lunch at elegant restaurants—La Grenouille, 21 Club, Côte Basque—and casually talked about Nike, Avon, Ocean Pacific, Evan-Picone. To shore up the home front, I presented JCPenney's chairman, who *never* associated with suppliers, with a silver Tiffany statuette commemorating the sale of the one hundred millionth pair of control-top pantyhose, the item my father had originally invented twelve years ago to gain entry into the pantyhose business. The reclusive old buzzard had no choice but to crawl out of his hole and give me a photo op. A picture of me with the chairman appeared on the cover of the *JCPenney News*, read by every single employee nationwide. Buyers, their bosses, and their boss's bosses stopped messing with me. Despite their diversity kick, our business with JCPenney grew robustly in all three product lines. In the corridors of JCPenney, I was actually dubbed Michael Corleone (my first brush with the criminal element). In my early thirties, I had become the Don of Undergarments; buyers whose asses I used to kiss now kissed my ring.

To his substantial credit, my sidelined father never (not even during those first two difficult years) interfered or second-guessed me—with the exception of one dreadful week where he missed the action and, with rhinoceros-in-china-shop delicacy, suddenly wanted to run the show again. Both of us felt unappreciated and came to verbal blows in front of Nick and the board, to the point where I bitterly resigned. Thanks to Mom's peacemaking efforts, Dad calmed down and the boy king was eventually restored. It's curious how people pull together during adversity but fight once things turn successful, though this spat was brief because our bond of love was unbreakable. My looser way of doing things didn't make me a loser in Dad's eyes; it *opened* his eyes. To win his respect on his turf but on my terms was gratifying. His once-little company, the one the union had almost destroyed in 1959, was now the largest private-label producer of pantyhose, men's underwear, and ladies' underwear in the United States. Sometimes nepotism is exactly what the doctor ordered.

Things were moving quickly, and with customer diversity, my parents' long-awaited liquidity event was within sight. We agreed as a family that now was the time to cash in some chips. My brother and I each owned 10 percent, same as Nick, with Mom and Dad owning the rest. We agreed to take *III* public, though the idea of running a public company made me queasy. I saw pitfalls: the burden of red tape compliance and a fickle investor public. Deep down, I wanted two things: money and freedom. Best achieved by an outright sale! When I tactfully expressed my going-public concerns to the investment banker I had chosen, Merrill Lynch, they acquainted me with a new concept: the leverage buyout. The LBO I negotiated with Merrill Lynch proved to be a breeze. Never in my life, before or since, has a business transaction gone so smoothly. It was the early to mid-1980s; the winds of the Reagan revolution were at our backs and zealous investment bankers were salivating over deals and easy to manipulate. I sold the company for double what Goldman Sachs told me they could fetch for it.

One caveat: the investors insisted I sign a five-year employment agreement to stay on as CEO. They were concerned that I was a one-man show and wanted continuity. My father had *truly* been a one-man show, so to be called that tickled me, even though for that very reason I had built a lean sales force and always gave others credit. That's how I turned my youth into an advantage: showing elders, everyone really, humility and respect. Besides providing our family significant liquidity for the first time ever, our LBO created a dozen or so millionaires out of loyal employees living in small southern towns, which made me especially proud. Our family company became a case study at Harvard Business School. With *III* now saddled with debt because of the LBO, running it was less a question of dynamic growth than financial maintenance, not exactly my forte. Perish the thought that my destiny lay in undergarments, but I had no choice; the fact that the investors were adamant I stay on and gave me stock incentives at least confirmed my own independent worth. They took out a $22 million key-man insurance policy on my life, monumental in those days. I was just thirty-three, a New York marathoner in excellent shape, so the premiums were next to nothing. I joked to our new investors that I was more valuable to them dead than alive, which I probably was.

CHAPTER 6

CHARACTER AND CARNAGE

March 13, 2019. New York City. The day after my Varsity Blues arrest, I received a heartening call from someone I hadn't seen in at least a dozen years.

Back in the 1980s, Andrea Jaeger had been the world's number two tennis player. Were it not for the fact that she played in the era of Martina Navratilova, who was transforming women's tennis, she would have been *numero uno*. A teen phenom with braces on her teeth who burned out early, Andrea had taken all her tennis winnings to start a camp for underprivileged kids with life-threatening illnesses. Her camp was based in Aspen, Colorado, an enclave of whiteness and privilege if ever there were one, but a one-of-a-kind place to treat these deserving kids.

Shortly after fulfilling my contractual obligations, I left *III* on excellent terms, then like clockwork fell in love with and married Marcia. Prioritizing romance over fastidious planning in order to indulge my commitment-o-phobia, we eloped and were officially married at sea, by a sailboat captain in the Caribbean whose vessel we dubbed the Love Boat. For our parents' sake, we also had a church wedding in New York four months later in 1987.

Burned out by work and family duty but financially liquid for my age, I sought a different venue from New York. Marcia was game. Though city mice, we shared a sense of adventure, albeit one far more opulent than Larry Darrow's in *The Razer's Edge*, the first book I read once free of family obligations (to discover my inner iconoclast). I began writing my own novel. We found a rustic piece of land with spectacular mountain views twelve minutes from downtown Aspen and built our dream house. Seeing people our ages in such a home was probably enough to turn a classic liberal into a raging Trotskyite, though in the words of one of my letter writers, we "remained unaffected and maintained [our] genuineness and humanity to an inspiring degree." Thanks to Andrea, we also used our property for humanitarian purposes.

Andrea Jaeger had received the prestigious Jefferson Award from Justice Sandra Day O'Connor in the Supreme Court chambers. She was the first female to win the Jackie Robinson Humanitarian Award for "demonstrating a concern for mankind and … exhibiting the qualities of dedication, grace under pressure, personal sacrifice, compassion, hope and dignity that characterize the promotion of human welfare and social reform." Nelson Mandela had traveled from South Africa to thank her in person for her work helping disadvantaged children. Presidents Reagan and Bush had invited her to the White House.

The last time I had seen Andrea, I was clad in a business suit, looking très Wall Street, walking up Avenue of the Americas toward Central Park on a warm spring afternoon. A nun in a light blue habit was passing out leaflets. As I refused a leaflet, our eyes met, and we both shrieked in surprise, then started laughing uncontrollably. I can only imagine what passersby thought at the incongruous sight of a suit hugging a nun like a long-lost sister, each so elated to see the other. (Andrea's journey had led her to become a nun for a brief period, before she shed her habits and moved to Boulder with her companion to resume helping sick children.)

"My God!" Andrea now said on the phone in her high-pitched voice. "I can't believe what I just read."

My eyes welled up from the supportive sound of her voice, after so long. "We screwed up, but it's not all what you think," I said, still not clear in my mind the magnitude of the trouble we were in, beyond news snippets about substantial prison time. I started to rattle off the mitigating excuses—Lyme disease, marital issues, son's addiction—when Andrea cut me off.

"Listen," she sang, "you don't have to explain to me. I know what kind of people you and Marcia are. Were it not for you guys, the Silver Lining Ranch never would have gotten off the ground. It started at *your house*. You changed the lives of at least a thousand children."

That struck me as an exaggeration. "A *thousand*?" I echoed, so happy for any positive recognition.

"At *least*!" she affirmed. "Between the kids and their families, absolutely. You guys don't deserve this."

A wave of nostalgia washed over me. "Remember the time we played tennis? When our eyes met across the net and we had the same epiphany at the same time?"

Andrea giggled, still sounding like the little kid I had known; she knew exactly what I was referring to: "That we were once brother and sister in a past life?"

"I took a game off of you, sis," I reminded her, thinking back at the wonderful children who had visited our Aspen home during the mid-1990s. Seriously sick, disabled kids from poor families and all racial backgrounds, kids with missing limbs, deformed faces, no hair had showed so much wide-eyed spirit and gratitude while we hung out in our super-cool tepee, paddle-boated on our pond, grilled burgers and hotdogs, and, above all, gave them love and acceptance. These kids were inspirations; I felt I benefited at least as much from these excursions as they. Our dream house became their dream house, at least for a fleeting moment, which almost seemed cruel. I wished I could make the magical moment last for them. Our eldest son, barely a toddler back then, had been born with a red hemangioma on his cheek the size of a golf ball. We had to wait until he was five to have it surgically corrected. Visually, he fit right in with the kids. When Andrea finally got the land and mega-funding to build her own log-cabined camp on the outskirts of town, the mess hall had a plaque in honor of "Greg and Marcia Abbott." I never talked about this with anyone ("Character is what you do when no one is watching" ... which I guess cuts both ways with me), but maybe now I had no choice.

"Listen, Andrea," I ventured, "I don't know where this case is headed. I haven't even chosen a lawyer because I don't *know* any criminal lawyers—"

"Why *would* you?" she said, cutting me off. "Would you like me to write you a character letter?"

I didn't even have to ask. Within twenty-four hours, I received via email a two-paged, single-spaced letter on Little Star Foundation stationery, with the full force of Andrea's credentials of having spent years caring for children with the panoply of disabilities.

"In the 1990's," she wrote, "[Gregory and Marcia Abbott] opened up their home to help suffering children of strangers. I saw this ... on many occasions over several years. Children who lost a leg to cancer, children from poverty-stricken families ... who had no hope to attend college because their parents couldn't afford to send them ... received college scholarships paid for by Gregory and Marcia Abbott ... Children ostracized in their schools and communities because of their facial and other health disfigurements found a caring home at the Abbotts. Gregory and Marcia Abbott believed in these children and financially supported [them] ... children who were severely disadvantaged due to health and socio-economic reasons found champions in [the Abbotts] ... The Abbotts did not have a child with Cancer, Cystic Fibrosis, HIV/AIDS or Sickle Cell Anemia but their child had Lyme Disease, a disease that can destroy the health, development and growth of a child ... Many parents with Lyme have their lives turned upside down for years in pain and extremely frustrating situations of confusion of diagnosis, lengthy list of systems, and uphill battles ... [While] this does not make what the Abbotts did right or just in the current college entrance scandal ... [they] behaved uncharacteristically because of the trauma and pain of seeing their own daughter suffer ... [Due to] strain they ... acted out of character ... I have witnessed over many years their being incredibly kind, good, and caring people supportive of thousands of disadvantaged children around the country."

To maintain my sanity, and because they might bear on our fate, I began to collect character letters and stopped watching the news, which was trashing and satirizing the Varsity Blues defendants on a daily basis, even on *SNL*. Tempted as I am to include many of these letters here—dozens of eloquent, heartfelt testimonies from people of all walks of life who have known me for decades and, yes, folks, extolled my character—I don't want to come off as overly self-serving. A smattering of snippets to give you a sense of my criminal character:

"Once Greg Abbott becomes your friend, he is your friend for life."

"Greg Abbott has one of the biggest, most forgiving hearts I know; I would trust him with my life."

"Greg has an enormous, generous heart. There is not an entitled bone in his body."

"When my brother committed suicide ... I immediately embraced Greg as my brother .... He has always been there for me, and I for him. I love and trust him like a brother. I admire his optimism, sense of humor, and loyalty."

"Today, without any doubt I can say that Greg was one of the people who helped young busboy from Serbia become successful businessman."

"Greg is instinctively kind and empathetic. When a close mutual friend of ours (with a young family, who risked his life in numerous trouble spots working for the United Nations) contracted prostate cancer and had go to into debt to pay for his operation, Greg insisted on paying out of his own pocket. He did it out of the goodness of his own heart and out of respect for our friend's courage and good works, and never spoke about it; only the three of us know about it because we've all had our bouts with prostate cancer."

And one from Judge Andrew Napolitano, Princeton classmate, friend of over fifty years and author of nine books on the US Constitution: "The Greg I know is exceptionally selfless. His record of charitable giving to those beset my misfortune and disfavored by nature is well-documented and I am confident is before Your Honor. Yet, as well as I know Greg, I only know of his charity from others, not from him. Charity is in his heart; boasting is not on his tongue ... There is a thread that runs through Greg's life and personality and character. It is the thread of innocence; not in the sense of free from all wrongdoing, but in the sense of guilelessness. He is candidly innocent and openly trusting and he assumes those traits exist in others as well ... [I have] enormous confidence in asserting that the Greg Abbott I know is among the more honest, decent, selfless persons I have ever known. His honesty is so deep, I would entrust all that I own to his care, with no qualms or hesitation."

If you're interested in reading more letters in their entirety, they are in the public record (see Sentencing Memorandum by Gregory and Marcia Abbott, Exhibit B, *United States v. Abbott et al.* 19 Cr. 10117-IT, Document #521). All our letters are there—all, that is, except Andrea Jaeger's.

When her Little Star Foundation board got a whiff that their standard bearer was a friend of someone implicated in the Varsity Blues scandal, they ordered her to withdraw her letter and even stop speaking to me. This hurt and offended me—deeply. After all Marcia and I had done for their cause! Hopefully they will sue for including one-liners of Andrea's letter in this story. It will at once broadcast my gratitude for Andrea's genuine outreach at a most trying time and give others opportunity to behold the Little Star board's pettiness and how they apparently have learned much about fundraising but little about the true meaning of charity.

—

March 30, 2019. While riding alone on the Acela from Boston back to New York after yesterday's preliminary hearing (at which Magistrate Judge

Kelley had, according to the *New York Post*, admonished us to "lay off the weed"), I received a phone call from my daughter.

Two and a half weeks after the Varsity Blues scandal broke, the colleges had sent out their decisions. She had applied to seventeen schools of all varieties, though because of Lyme disease had planned on taking a gap year once she settled on a school. Expecting carnage, which was essentially what she got, she nonetheless was euphoric. Though she'd been blacklisted by the Ivies and many other top schools, four excellent universities had accepted her, two on the West Coast, surprising given that the scandal had originated there. Stanford had wait-listed her. My recently deceased best friend, George Kriste, had turned me on to UC Berkeley. His daughter had been an Olympic-hopeful volleyball player there. I had first toured the campus with my eldest son and fell in love with it. The campus of Elaine Robinson (*The Graduate*), with the Free Speech Movement Café, breathtaking bay views, and the most beautiful college library in America, Berkeley reminded me of what college was like back in my Woodstock era (not that Woodstock had remotely been my thing).

Forgive my faux nostalgia in romanticizing Berkeley, which I gather is nothing like the free-speech Berkley of yesteryear, but my daughter loved it, and they loved her. The number one ranked public university in the nation; hard as hell to get into from out of state. She was over the moon that Berkeley (and the three others) had accepted her *despite the scandal*. A breath of good news for a family desperate for it! In tears, we couldn't wait to tell her mother, who was on a plane back to Colorado. Suddenly my fears of a federal prison sentence abated. As long as my daughter was OK, I could handle whatever the government dished out. She immediately emailed Berkeley admissions that she was going to be a California Golden Bear.

Euphoria soon gave way to sobriety. What if Berkeley and the others hadn't made the connection with our daughter and Varsity Blues? Rather than sit tight and hope for the best, our daughter chose candor. That is the way she is, the way she was raised to be. It took her a few days to write, rewrite, and perfect the letter that was eventually sent to the Berkeley Admissions Committee (with slightly different versions tailored for the other schools).

"On the morning of March 12," she began, "life as I knew it changed forever …" She told them of her horror at seeing her mother arrested by FBI agents, learning that her father had also been arrested, and her devastation in learning about the college admission scandal.

With remarkable clarity, she described the emotional cycles she had experienced over the ensuing days. Referring to her "bouts of fevers and exhaustion due to Lyme disease," she wrote, "I know for certain that whatever my parents did was motivated by misguided love, not venal scheming. I forgive them."

Until March 12, she had known nothing of our efforts to help her. She notified the schools that she had cancelled her test scores with the intent of retaking them. She could not live with the specter of knowing that she might be breaking their honor codes before even arriving on campus.

"When you accepted me more than two weeks after the scandal broke," she wrote, "I literally cried with joy and enrolled immediately. I clung to the hope ... that I had been offered enrollment in spite of the controversy; that you saw I was real ... It is my dream to attend Berkeley, and I understand that in writing you ... I am likely destroying that dream, but I must move forward unencumbered .... I am the same person you chose to admit into the class of 2023, yet I am also undoubtedly changed. I am still the singer who spent eleven years performing at the Metropolitan Opera; I am still a hardworking student who has earned every A on my transcript, every figure in my GPA. My passion for volunteering has long been sincere; my interests in neurology and psychology are genuine. Yet for all that is consistent, I will never again be the person who went to bed on March 11th. I have learned that life is more complicated than I ever thought possible ... I am determined to earn my own way forward in life, and remain fervently hopeful that I may someday earn a degree from UC Berkeley. I will make you proud."

All but one of the colleges rescinded her acceptance, UC Berkeley among them. Just a few weeks thereafter, Berkeley was dumped from the *US News and World Report* university rankings for falsifying alumni donation records and student test scores, but no one was fired or charged with a crime. A year later, Berkeley along with the entire University of California system made the decision to join many other schools in eliminating standardized test requirements on the grounds that they discriminate against disadvantaged students, that high school grades are a far more reliable predictor of college performance.

Does severe Lyme disease not qualify as a disadvantage, even if you're

Caucasian? Isn't a 4.3 GPA while saddled with Lyme a suitable academic measure?

Even the Ivies are heading in the direction of deemphasizing and, in some cases, not requiring standardized tests. After shunning the daughter of a true-blue alumnus (me) without knowing her story beyond lurid headlines and the rantings of a white-collar fishwife, Princeton's dean of admissions now favors a "holistic review" in which subject tests are optional.

The sole college that didn't rescind our daughter's acceptance had already made tests optional. Good for them, though even they didn't exactly embrace her. Her academic adviser canceled their first phone meeting at the eleventh hour in order to take part in a Black Lives Matter march. On the rescheduled call, the adviser insisted she take cancel culture courses to remind her of her whiteness, privilege, and oppressor roots. Rather than allow her to take the science courses that interested her—neuroscience due to her ordeal with Lyme, psychology due to her Varsity Blues trauma—they essentially insisted that she major in self-loathing.

Universities, bastions of self-importance and broadcasted high principle, are no less whorish than banks. They put their own welfare and ideology ahead of the young people they profess to serve. Had I worked in admissions and received my daughter's letter, I would have *wanted* that student to be a part of my school; I would have *begged* her to come. Integrity, heart, and wisdom—qualities no test score can measure—are becoming dangerously obsolete. They should be embraced, nurtured, protected. I am reminded of Colonel Slade's (Al Pacino) stirring speech to the Baird School assembly in the marvelous grand finale of *Scent of a Woman*, laying bare the headmaster's pomposity with the warning, "Be careful what kind of leaders you're producin' here!"

A few weeks after Berkeley rescinded her acceptance, in early May, my daughter flew in to have dinner with me on my birthday. Given our tenuous relationship, this meant much to me. She also planned to attend her old school's prom two days later. After her homeschool isolation, she was excited to bond with old friends and teachers. She bought a dress and shoes for the occasion. The school had known about it for three weeks. While boarding the plane in Denver, she received a crushing text from the friend who had invited her: she was banned from the prom. She called me in tears. Professional Children's School (PCS), where she'd played the lead in the school musical *Grease*, beating out the girl who was playing the lead in *Annie* on Broadway (and where I'd served on the board and got them a fat donation from David Koch), didn't have the guts to call her themselves; didn't consider how their gratuitous snub might wound an already fragile heart. It was all about *them*. Again, I quote the blind but all-seeing Colonel Slade: "There is nothing quite like the sight of an amputated spirit. There is no prosthetic for that."

Although the court officially ruled (in August 2019) that our crime had "no victims," in one respect they couldn't have been further from the truth. Our daughter was a victim of our loving but stupid actions. She, with the well-earned 4.3 GPA and Met Opera résumé—no one took her exams, and no one sang for her in the recordings submitted to schools, though it would have been interesting to hear Rick Singer try that. Her Met Opera photos were official, not photoshopped. Feel free to believe to your hearts' content that we, her parents, were justly punished, but she, the high-achieving, high-principled child, was unjustly punished with rejection and false accusations of stupidity because of us, just as many kids are unjustly rewarded because of their parents. The prosecutors falsely alleged that she had targeted Duke to suit their narrative. She applied to seventeen colleges because (like virtually all college applicants, even the most outstanding ones) she wasn't confident of admission to any one of them. She wasn't going to deprive any student of anything. Once accepted to a handful of universities, she was forthcoming and ultimately punished for it. Hate her parents all you want, but consider what our child might have felt as her prospects turned to ashes in order to burnish the careers of a few prosecutors and fed agents.

CHAPTER 7

"I CAN SMELL YOUR C**T"

March–April 2019. Although I am not shy about asking people to invest in IDC due to its substantial upside, I was paralyzed when it came to seeking a guarantor for my $500,000 bail bond. I was reticent to impose on anyone, strain a friendship, or have anyone think our friendship was based on money. I've never cultivated such a friendship in my life. I know my share of billionaires but have never sucked up to them. While casually explaining my many Varsity Blues woes, including the bail bond, to a friend over coffee, I was bowled over when, just like that, he offered to be my guarantor. A former school administrator, he is hardly rolling in dough; it never would have occurred to me to ask him. I tried to dissuade him, explaining what his exposure was, but he wouldn't budge, insisting that he trusted me implicitly to abide by the conditions of my release. I was too beleaguered to refuse. What a friend, is all I can say!

As stated earlier, I didn't know any criminal attorneys, but as you might assume, I know many lawyers. In fact, the night before my arrest, I had had dinner with a close friend who happened to be a civil litigator and partner at Mayer Brown, the firm that handles IDC's patent work. A few days after my arrest, I reached out to him, and he introduced me to whom he insisted was Mayer Brown's best criminal attorney, Dan Stein, Esq., a Yale Law alum. I liked Dan immediately and still do; we are now friends for life.

I assumed Dan would represent both Marcia and me, and he did as well. He had accompanied both of us to the first preliminary hearing in Boston. However, when Mayer Brown compliance people detected potential conflicts based on the different roles we had played, the firm decided they couldn't represent Marcia. She had been initially introduced to Singer and interacted with him months, hatching his plan before I ever spoke to him. The feds had more phone recordings of her, but so what? As with many marital divisions of labor, she was more involved in the kids' daily educational issues. I had made the wire transfers; that was actually *all* I had done, but without me, the gatekeeper, this never could have happened. At age twenty-six, I had stood up to a corrupt pantyhose buyer who'd threatened the existence of our family business. Why as a grown man couldn't I put my foot down with Singer's scheme when my strung-out wife was looking to me for strength and charity? Was I in moral decline? I wondered how I might have responded to the corrupt buyer had my child been at risk.

Due to our ongoing marital strife and volatile phone conversations over everything from finances to kids to the Museum of Past Hurts, where we couldn't even agree on facts, mistrust abounded between Spouse and me. She accused me of orchestrating Mayer Brown's decision for my own benefit, that I was trying to absolve myself like Felicity's husband, William H. Macy. In truth, I was blistering Mayer Brown for its stance and doing everything in my power to make them relent.

"Throwing your wife under the bus?" she railed. "Going it alone because they have more recordings of me?" She was irately accusatory and terrified of isolation. "Why else would *your law firm* not represent *your wife?*"

"This is normal compliance stuff, just like with the banks," I told her. "As a lawyer's daughter, you should understand." She wasn't buying it; I could feel her seething and trembling over the phone. "Look, I have no intention of throwing you under any goddamn bus! I'm as upset as you are, but Mayer Brown won't budge."

"Well," she lashed, "the judge isn't going to look too kindly on a husband abandoning his wife. She's a woman, you know."

"I'm *not* abandoning you! We'll find another way to skin the cat, I promise." As is my wont, I tried to inject levity. "Please don't make a federal case out of this."

Spouse didn't see the humor, to put it mildly—and I admit it may not have been the best moment for humor of that kind. "You want to go it alone? Fine! It'll cost us twice as much and destroy your family, but since when did either matter to *you?*"

The issue was resolved when Mayer Brown offered to find her a top-notch attorney with whom they could work closely. They chose Arlo Devlin-Brown, of Covington & Burling, whom Marcia ended up liking a lot. All parties agreed, at my insistence, that we submit a joint sentencing memorandum. This would signal to wife, world, and judge that we were in this together. Perhaps we could use this misfortune to pull together and heal. I've always enjoyed an optimistic nature, sometimes unduly optimistic.

—

Meanwhile, let me respond to the question, "What were you doing in a Boston courthouse?" Home of Deflate Gate and the Red Sox electronic sign-stealing scandal in the 2018 World Series, where many careers and livelihoods were adversely affected but no one went to prison? Sorry, but as an avid NY Giant and LA Dodger fan, I couldn't resist a little Boston bashing; nor could I resist it as a Varsity Blues felon. Few will argue that professional athlete cheating hasn't had a wider and more deleterious impact on society than Singer's ACT and SAT fudging, or even Singer's athletic recruiting schemes, yet did Barry Bonds, Roger Clemens, or Lance Armstrong go to prison? Not saying they should, just making a rhetorical point.

Why Boston? Although Varsity Blues began in California, it was being adjudicated in Massachusetts because of an unrelated pump-and-dump case involving a Yale man named Morrie Tobin. To reduce his sentence, Tobin ratted out the Yale women's soccer coach who was allegedly taking bribes. The Yale soccer coach, in turn, in order to reduce *his* sentence, ratted out Rick Singer, who in turn ratted out thirty-three parents and nineteen coaches whom he'd lured into his scheme.

It's how the system works: bullying plea bargains, craven informants. Justice, in the words of Colonel Slade, has become "vessel for sea-going snitches," an ethic that has wormed its way into our hallowed educational institutions. When my eldest son refused to rat out friends during a minor disciplinary issue at Horace Mann, the odious head of the upper school said it all: "If you can't rat out your friends, then they really aren't your friends." Ratting out and smearing is a woke ethic that starts in our schools and now pervades all sectors of society, from students to Supreme Court nominees to Doctor Seuss.

USA VS ABBOTT

April 2019. A few days after our March 30 hearing, Marcia and I were given the paradigmatic Hobson's choice: fight it with a jury trial presided over by Judge Nathaniel Gorton, or plead guilty to the felony of conspiracy to commit mail fraud and honest services fraud and be assigned another more lenient judge for sentencing. I later found out that in all likelihood "honest services fraud" probably had nothing to do with us. It was intended for and generally applied to corruption by public officials, and even that use has been subjected to withering bipartisan criticism. The late US Supreme Court Justice Anton Scalia claimed the statute so poorly defined as to be the basis for prosecuting a public official "for using the prestige of his office to get a table at a restaurant without a reservation." Justice Steven Breyer maintains that three of four Americans can be criminally convicted of that malleable statute.

In any event, we were not keen to be a test case. While neither trial nor plea appealed to us, the decision was a no-brainer: we had to plea.

Justice may be blind in theory, but you know damn well that the judge matters a lot. A George H. W. Bush appointee, eighty-one-year-old Judge Gorton was known to be rigid, prosecutor friendly, a stickler for sentencing guidelines—Judge Roy Bean, the hanging judge, East of the Pecos. Chances were eleven out of twelve that if we took the plea, we would be assigned a judge more lenient than Gorton. There were twelve judges on the judicial wheel, one of them Gorton, so by pleading guilty, we would put our fate in the hands of Vanna White.

Fighting it as Lori Laughlin and her husband (and others) decided to do would entail spending millions this beverage small-wig didn't have, and dragging things out for at least two years. In our system, it costs millions to defend oneself in a case like ours. If we didn't have the $2 to $3 million to throw at Singer for Stanford or Duke, we certainly didn't have it to mount a legal defense against a government that almost never loses a criminal case.

The press also played a part in our decision not to fight. Our defenses were extremely personal, as, if nothing else, this book reveals, and it was becoming clear that our intimate family details (fact and fiction) would be fodder for *New York Post* embellishers and *WSJ* liars for as long as they could milk them. So, by April, after a month of public ridicule, ongoing concern for a child with Lyme disease and emotional trauma, another struggling with addiction, and a marriage on the rocks, we didn't need a lawyer to tell us that there was no choice but to capitulate.

Moreover, the government terrified us. We were told that if we didn't sign the plea agreement within twenty-four hours, we would be hit with racketeering and money laundering charges. The only time I ever laundered money was when I left a spare dollar bill in my jeans.

In a *WSJ* op-ed shortly after our sentence, Alan Dershowitz declared such shakedown practices unconstitutional: "When is a constitutional right not a right? When you're punished for receiving it. If the government arrests or fines you for something you say, everyone recognizes a violation of the First Amendment, even though you've had your say. Yet when prosecutors and courts impose massive punishments on criminal defendants for exercising their Sixth Amendment right to a trial by jury, it's considered business as usual." I later learned that 97 percent of cases are settled with plea deals and that of the ones that go to trial, the government wins 95 percent of the time, with sentences dwarfing the plea. Even if we *were* billionaire bigwigs and money was no object, we did what we did. They had entrapped and wiretapped us, though the recordings were scant. The public and the media were in an uproar. Better to take the plea rather than twist ourselves into pretzels for two or three years. Better to get out of the system as quickly as possible. Life is too short.

Any one of the above reasons was enough for us to take the plea; together they constituted a tsunami.

When Dan Stein received the official notice that Indira Talwani had been appointed as our sentencing judge, he called me immediately. He was elated, by lawyer standards. An Obama appointee and graduate of Radcliffe and UC Berkley Law School, Talwani had a track record of reasonable leniency, with downward departures from the guidelines 85 percent of the time. Well done, Vanna!

Conspiracy to commit mail fraud and honest service fraud carries a chilling maximum prison sentence of twenty years. To raise the stakes for its reading public and my blood pressure, the press broadcast that number as gospel, pounding the nail whenever it could. Our lawyers told us to forget it, that it wasn't relevant. What was relevant was the plea deal we were essentially coerced into signing, in which prosecutors sought a federal prison sentence of a year and a day for each of us. I had almost lost my mind spending *six hours* in a cell! How could I survive a year and a day?

I guess one learns to adapt, but I wasn't ready to roll over and continued to garner character letters. I was actually more concerned about Marcia's flagging spirits. As a rough-and-tumble entrepreneur, I'd taken my share of punches and had mixed it up with all sorts of people, some shady or worse. Marcia was always more selective about the people and experiences she let into her life, and I suspect more traumatized than I by Varsity Blues. The more optimistic I was, the more pessimistic she became, or felt she had to be in order to counterbalance me. Due to the long saga of IDC, she was wary of my optimism. I urged her to begin gathering letters of her own. If nothing else, such validation would cause us to reflect on the good, decent lives we had otherwise led.

May 22, 2019. Plea Day. Our guilty plea hearing wasn't until 2:30 p.m., so I chose to take the 8:00 a.m. Acela from New York, which would put me in Boston before noon. Dan Stein and Marcia's lawyer, Arlo Devlin-Brown, would ride with me. We would meet Marcia, who had flown into Boston from Colorado late the night before, at her hotel.

While tying my tie early that morning with *Morning Joe* on TV in the background, I perked up as Mika Brzezenski said, "Two more parents pleaded guilty yesterday in the Varsity Blues scandal. Two more are expected to plead guilty today." I glanced at the screen just as Mika batted her lashes at her hubby and cooed, "Joe, this is the gift that just keeps on giving."

A *gift?* I get it. It's a story that sells, and sales are the media's bread and butter, but Mika's smug glee incensed me. Reading about gifts is one thing, receiving or giving them yet another, but *being* the gift is an entirely different proposition, the difference between being a cannibal and being on the menu. Fury spiked within me. Mika and Joe, stop posing as high-minded journalists or anything but the suave muckrakers you are. Tell my sick daughter what a *gift* you consider it to be—and while you're at it, show a little courage once in a while and invite some guests on your show who don't always parrot your views but actually challenge you.

For what it's worth, I liked Judge Talwani's vibe at the hearing. I sensed her humanity and a certain disdain for the prosecutors, whom she took to task on a number of niggling legal points. Their self-satisfied, hawk-faced demeanors and millennial, orange-patterned socks made them hard to like. Let's just say that Will Rogers never met our prosecutors!

The lead prosecutor, Eric Rosen—whose cackle laugh and perpetual gloat had created an unappealing image in my mind at the first preliminary hearing on March 30—was not present that day, to my disappointment. I had hoped that Dan Stein (a former colleague and mentor of Rosen) could broker an impromptu private meeting so that Rosen could hear our story straight from the horses' mouths and maybe soften enough to cut us a fairer deal (good old Ithaca naivete or just residual OTL?). Not that I had any valid reason to be hopeful. Rosen had blown off Dan's previous overtures, taunting Dan with such gratuitous cruelties as "How's Infamous Billa doing?"

A chilling, sweaty-palm sense of doom pervaded the air as we pled guilty in the august courtroom. However, when Judge Talwani made a point of declaring that she was not bound by the sentencing guidelines or the terms of the plea, I felt a glimmer of encouragement. She made it clear that she was free to decide however she felt in each particular case. Dan and Arlo took heart in those independent remarks, which seemed pointed at the prosecution, as well as in her recognition that each case was different. She would rule case by case and not apply the single broad brush proffered by the government. Despite the year and a day stipulated in the plea, I believed (as did our lawyers, albeit more cautiously) that once Talwani became versed in our mitigating circumstances, she would give us mere probation and community service. We would have to wait until October 8 to learn our fate, which seemed like an eternity but at least gave us ample time to prepare our sentencing presentation and maybe allow the public outcry to fizzle and other scandals to dominate the news.

After formally pleading guilty, we exited the courthouse through a side door (how appropriate for Singer defendants, eh?), hoping to avoid the press. Not possible. As was once said of Ted Williams's ability to hit a fastball, trying to throw one by him was like trying to sneak the sunrise by a rooster. They spotted us, stampeded toward us, and quickly engulfed us. A camera came within an inch of my face, a microphone within an inch of my mouth.

"Do you want to apologize?" reporters barked over and over, cameras clicking all around me.

I looked for my wife. True to their nature, the hyenas had separated the weak from the herd. One dropped to his knee and was angling his camera up her skirt. As I tore through the crowd toward her, I heard him say, "I can smell your c**t!"

What would you have done? What would you have felt like doing? You, having just pled guilty to a federal crime? You, in a marriage under tremendous stress? So, what would you have done? I felt a protective love for my wife not felt since what seemed a distant past. I wanted to pulverize this urchin for his coarse affront to her. Despite all the trauma between and around us, she'd remained my bride for thirty-two years. I wanted that hyena's Chicklets all over the sidewalk!

It wasn't cowardice that held me back. It was recognition that I was being goaded into the gutter for a photo op. Chicklets on the sidewalk and a smashed camera were what all this was designed to provoke, to make me channel my inner Alec Baldwin and commit public violence within an hour of becoming a felon, thereby creating even more sensational headlines and legal ordeals.

I have not been the most mature person at various stages of my life, and in some ways, I hope I never will be. But for that instant, maturity took hold. Chicklets would not be fed to the hyenas. I merely put my arm around Marcia's shoulder. I say "merely" not to diminish the act but to distinguish the action from the murderous feeling residing within that arm so gently draped, its owner seething with unrealized anger and shame for what our marriage, a marriage begun in joy, hope, and the promise of happiness in family and future, had become at that moment.

I escorted her to the street, where one of our lawyers had flagged a taxi. We could barely open and close the door thanks to the teeming, cackling carnivores. Even when we were safely inside, flashing cameras pressed violently against the window glass until we drove off.

CHAPTER 8

THE LONG, HOT SUMMER

May 22, 2019, to September 12, 2019. To stay sane, I tried to stay positive, not always easy even for an inveterate glass-half-full guy like me. Managing my own traumas—the dawn arrest, stepping down from the business I had founded within a week of the scandal breaking to avoid paralysis, nerve-wracking uncertainty—was the least of it. Nothing rips away at one's innards quite like family ills; "you're only as happy as your least happy child," the saying goes, and all of us were out of kilter. Both boys lived with me in New York, while Daughter lived with Mom in Aspen. A family divided by gender, as I was constantly reminded by Spouse—yang in the East, yin in the West. These were vexing times for me as a father and husband. While I hoped that Varsity Blues would unite our family in common purpose, the most I could realistically expect for the time being was to keep things together with chicken wire and chewing gum.

Our eldest, self-conscious about how Varsity Blues reflected on our family and still traumatized by having witnessed his dad's arrest, recoiled whenever I tried to discuss it with him. He escaped into his coffee start-up by day and quantum physics, complex mathematical theories, and Ted Talks by night. Struggling to process his bottled-up emotions, he sought refuge in his considerable intellect. It saddened me to see this intrinsically fun-loving soul grow introverted. One evening, he brought his girlfriend over; they snuggled on the sofa as pajama-clad yours truly serenaded them on the candlelit piano for nearly an hour with ancient music (The Beatles, Billy Joel, Gershwin) and "velvet frog" crooning. To my amazement, they urged me to continue. Much as I tried to connect with him by watching his

Ted Talks and having him explain the concepts, my attempts at cheering him up rang hollow. The prospect of his dad and mom going to federal prison weighed heavily on his psyche and caused his hairline to recede.

Infamous Billa was, well, all over the place. When rapping at the recording studio, he was content—he loved nothing more than creating music—though recording sessions were usually in the wee hours and caused him to be out of rhythm with nature. Unlike the proverbial rooster, you could indeed sneak the sunrise by him, often at any time of day, since he usually began his nightly sleep just before the crack of dawn. We had long since lost the marijuana battle; without it, he could be monstrous, and he actually seemed to function better on all counts with a little weed in his system. Something to do with wiring and self-medicating. Malcolm is a bona fide artist with corresponding temperament, one that could go wildly amok when life was out of whack—because when life was out of whack, he often turned to wackier stuff. My intent here isn't to get into the complexities of his demons but merely to relate an unfortunate event that happens to be in the public record and therefore reluctantly must be addressed.

It's so disturbing that I can't remember what action, comment, or drug might have triggered it, though I'm certain Varsity Blues was the bedrock catalyst. A few days after our May 22 guilty plea, he was in a destructive state, unlike anything I had ever seen—stomping about the apartment, out of his mind and out of control, a six-foot-four-inch cauldron of rage. The absolute *last* thing I, as his father and newly christened felon, wanted to do was call 911. The *Post* had reporters who did nothing but hang around the precinct, salivating for a scoop. Anything to do with the "beverage bigwig college admissions cheat" and his "blunt-smoking rapper" son was, to repeat Mika's odious words, "the gift that keeps on giving." All I will say is that I had no choice but to call 911—for substance abuse reasons, not to punish. You have no idea how heartbreaking it is when the son you love, who you know loves you, makes you fear for your and his safety. Even more so when the boneheaded system sends him to Riker's Island for a few days, all in the tabloids for the world to see. I've second-guessed that 911 call every day since. He has come a long way since then, getting a courageous grip on his demons and pursuing his musical dreams. Hopefully I learned something too: when bad things hit you in bunches, you wonder what karma you've amassed.

Oddly enough, the child least affected by Varsity Blues, at least on the outside, was the one involved. As long as one didn't bring up the scandal, she was her normal upbeat self who simply wanted to move on with her gap year before attending college in fall 2020. I suspect that she harbored far more turmoil under the surface—Jesus, how could she not?—but she remained with her mother two thousand miles away with a stiff upper lip and spoke with me sparingly.

Both Marcia and I consulted shrinks, for what that was worth. While I spent nights meditating, surrounded by candles and striving for mindfulness, Marcia sought comfort in a chic rosé called Whispering Angel. At her August birthday party, which I flew to Colorado to attend, every guest gave her a bottle of Whispering Angel, except for one couple who gave her a whole case (they are the Caseys, after all). It was funny seeing all the wrapped gifts on the table with the same shape. Normally, she isn't all that easy to shop for. Marcia is a health nut; if she's a junkie at all, it's with vitamins and supplements. I'd never known her to take drugs, prescription or otherwise, or even drink beyond a half glass of wine when out for dinner. Varsity Blues changed things. Once 5:00 p.m. rolled around, the Whispering Angel ritual would commence, which helped her relax on some evenings but caused her anxiety to reach full flower on others. When the calls became tempestuous, I ruminated about suing the bottler of Whispering Angel for false advertising, that his product should be called Screaming Bitch. With our year-and-a-day plea and the possibility of even greater judicial retribution hanging over our heads like a guillotine, it was hard not to be perpetually on edge. The prospect of the draconian multiyear sentence (as the press kept suggesting) could chill even the most persistent optimist. Marcia kept insisting that anything over a year would cause her to commit hara-kiri.

"We haven't told our story yet," I declared, trying to stifle such idle yet insidious talk. "We haven't begun to fight!"

"We can fight all we want. The government and media want our heads."

"And Talwani is a good, fair-minded judge who doesn't like the prosecutors."

"She may hate us even more, for all you know."

I kept repeating my mantra because deep down I still believed in America as a just country, that our punishment would fit the crime: "Mark my words: we will *not* see any jail."

"Maybe I will and you won't. They have more recordings of me."

"And I made the wire transfer. Our daughter was *sick*! Our son an *addict*. Yes, it was wrong. We shouldn't have done it. But *prison?* You gotta be kidding! No way!"

—

While all this was going on, I was besieged by media, not just its yelping, look-up-the-skirt, c**t-smelling members but higher species as well. My phone, text log, and email were ablaze with requests for interviews. My lawyer also received several inquiries. NBC, ABC, CBS, *Vanity Fair*, Lifetime/A&E, independent documentary film makers, and so on and so on. Dozens of requests all wanting to know: would I be willing to be the first parent to tell his side of the story? A clever way to play me, I confess, and I gave it thought. Is it possible to be both genuinely remorseful and chomping at the bit to tell one's story? The press was having a field day excoriating our moral character, besmirching us nationwide with class warfare clichés. And what were we doing about it, what could we do about it, what should we do, apart from amassing character letters, writing our sentencing speeches, and preparing legal briefs?

George Stephanopoulos had the inside track because his twenty-something minion had wheedled his way into our porous hearts. A likeable schmoozer who somehow knew Malcolm (but never exploited his proclivities for a story), he had introduced himself to Marcia, me, and our lawyers at the Massachusetts courthouse at the May 22 guilty plea hearing. He extolled Malcolm as "a wonderful, talented kid," proving once again that one can't go wrong praising another's home or offspring. He ingratiated himself further by finding us a side exit to avoid the hyenas. While that proved a bust, the gesture and the fact that his thirty-two-year-old cousin had actually died of Lyme disease persuaded me to agree to meet off-the-record with his boss.

Stephanopoulos came over to the offices of Mayer Brown. I told him our story straight up, without skirting any wrongdoing (we'd already pled guilty) but also stressing the personal mitigating circumstances. "Well, that certainly provides a different perspective from what we've been hearing," George said when I was done. From George, we learned that the DOJ had notified the media outlets twenty-four to forty-eight hours in advance of their March 12 sting. He speculated that the massive coast-to-coast, crack-of-dawn arrests, when most white-collar citizens might have been given the option to surrender, had been designed to take Robert Mueller off the front page. Unlikely, in this layman's opinion, given that our prosecution was being driven and politicized by the left, the same people who were lionizing Mueller as a hero.

It was hard not to like George. Bright and engaging, he, too, was an Upper East Side parent well versed in the scholastic pressures. We waxed philosophical about why parents put such an insane premium on elite school branding for their children. We agreed that it was detrimental in all sorts of ways. George offered me the opportunity to tell my "unique story" on *Good Morning America*. I was wary of the hard-boiled studio format. A media neophyte, I feared I would tense up and not be myself (which some might think a good thing). I also harbored unrealistic expectations about finding a full-fledged journalistic advocate. Though George is a tiny fellow, he is not, to put it mildly, the sort to fit into anyone's pocket. I kept an open mind and told George I would think about it.

I ignored more than 90 percent of the media inquiries as a matter of course. However, with a burning desire for redemption, I allowed a thimbleful of pursuers to meet off-the-record and got my lawyer, Dan Stein, to paper that they would, in fact, remain off-the-record. As long as Dan felt safe, I felt safe. One ironclad precondition was that any interview we agreed to do could be aired only *after* sentencing. This was critical; the last thing we needed was to be perceived by the judge as grandstanding, as she was the only person whose opinion truly mattered. Once sentenced, whether to mere probation or (God-please-no) prison, I was free to say whatever I wanted regarding any person, any subject. I could opine to my heart's content. I could even write a book, but only *after sentencing*.

Gretchen Carlson and her team from A&E bought me lunch at Sant Ambroeus on Madison Avenue, my regular haunt that some refer to as my "office" (or did before coronavirus). The former Fox News commentator who had sued Roger Ailes for sexual harassment, as well as a former Miss America and violinist at the Aspen Music Festival, Gretchen understood my reticence. She had firsthand experience with how the media distorts facts and demonizes people. That and her sympathy for our particular circumstances, which she said put us in a "wholly different category from other defendants," was her nurturing pitch to me. I told her I needed to think further and consult my family and of course my lawyer.

Then there was VICE, the hip network that wanted to capture me in my "natural habitat" and "humanize" me: sitting on the Central Park bench that my parents had donated to the park's restoration effort, its plaque etched with my children's names (my brother's family had a bench adjacent to it); reading a draft of my sentencing speech to my sons and getting their input; holding an IDC meeting and perhaps getting some free publicity. Somehow, from all these comfortable venues, my true flesh-and-blood persona would be revealed. VICE had originally been interested in filming a segment about this amazing Fifth Avenue rapper. When they learned who his parents were, their interest spiked to an entirely new level. After Infamous Billa's iffy stint with the *New York Post* and his stint at Riker's, how cool would it be to film a sixty-nine-year-old dad bonding with his rapper son (and maybe a few of his rapper friends) to show what a far cry he was from the Upper East Side stereotype.

I suddenly snapped out of my reverie and realized that her pitch was fraught with peril.

Finally, there was *60 Minutes* and Anderson Cooper. His producers found us "sympathetic," our story "compelling." They were intrigued because neither our story nor my persona appeared to fit the media portrayals. The more I became acquainted with them over drinks, the more of a rooting interest they seemed to develop on our behalf. Feeding me red meat—that the only narrative out there was the government's, that the college admissions system is riddled with corruption and hypocrisy—they convinced me to meet with Anderson. I did. I liked him too; I sensed a kind, well-bred, sensitive heart.

I started the meeting as I started this book, describing the FBI raid, and things just flowed from there. When I used the phrase "hyenas with cameras," Anderson said, "My first exposure to the paparazzi was when my brother committed suicide. Once I got into the news business, I met many of them and found that they were just normal people doing their jobs."

I related the c-word incident outside the Boston courthouse. "Was *he* doing his job?" I asked.

"What!" Anderson exclaimed, incredulous.

As the two-hour meeting wrapped up, Anderson said, "Before meeting you, I was prepared to advise you *not* to do this. Now that I've heard your story and gotten a sense of who you are, I think you would be doing yourself, your family, and your country a great service by letting us interview you for a full segment on *60 Minutes*." Anderson offered to fly out to Colorado to meet with my wife and daughter to convince them. Due to an unforeseen scheduling snafu brought on by impending impeachment, it was the head producer who ended up flying out there, but Anderson took part via Skype.

They "loved" Marcia and my daughter, and the feelings were mutual. Anderson proposed doing a joint interview with Marcia and me at our Colorado home. The girls seemed to want the whole thing to go away and not feed the beast. I reminded them that with the trials not commencing for at least another year, Varsity Blues would be around for a while, and that the government and lapdog press were completely controlling the narrative. However, with the girls in a state of trauma and uncertainty about sentencing, I was in no position to push too hard or go rogue.

My media suitors treated me to a plethora of meals and drinks, which I admit had some appeal, although not nearly enough to qualify as a Varsity Blues silver lining. While I did not dither for any purpose other than that the importance of the matter warranted a good dither, I did occasionally wonder whether the cultivation of these relationships, making friends, building trust, might make it harder for them to betray me in the event we decided to go forward.

The rub was that I couldn't find a single friend who didn't deem me hopelessly naïve for considering such a thing, who wasn't adamantly opposed to me doing any media interview of any kind. Liberals, moderates, conservatives, it didn't matter. One friend experienced in such matters defined a journalist as "someone who befriends you before he betrays you." "Don't do it!" I heard time after time from people of sound judgment. A few friends, including my bail guarantor, said that they would never speak to me or respect me again if I was so stupid as to grant an interview. After his experiences with the *Post* and *WSJ*, hadn't OTL Greg learned a lesson?

A Colorado friend told Marcia how *60 Minutes* had sucked in, then screwed over her grandfather years ago, back in the Mike Wallace era. "Even if you have total editorial control, which ain't gonna happen," another friend advised, "people out there will take you apart and quote you out of context. You have no idea how strong the feelings are out there and how many people want you crucified. You're smack in the middle of a political maelstrom. Lay low." Which is what I did, even though the media was destroying us on a daily basis. With one colossal mistake under my belt, I was paralyzed by the avalanche of conventional wisdom.

USA VS ABBOTT

The US Department of Probation was responsible for making official sentencing recommendations to the court. Judge Talwani had already made it clear that she was not bound by the sentencing guidelines or the prosecutors' plea agreement. The judge's own words, coupled with our mitigating circumstances, were the reasons I kept citing to Marcia to keep up her spirits. And then we got some tangible promising news.

On June 12, 2019, Stanford sailing coach John Vandemoer, who had allegedly taken $600,000 in bribes, and for whom the government was seeking thirteen months in federal prison (one more than they sought for the Abbotts), was given a slap on the wrist: a few months home confinement and no prison. Although this decision was rendered by Judge Zobel rather than Judge Talwani, we all saw this as a bellwether. Judge Talwani had a more lenient judicial record than Judge Zobel. Once a week, lawyers for the defendants who had pleaded guilty gathered on a conference call to compare notes, and the consensus was one of strong optimism. "That's great, but Vandemoer is not a rich parent," I prophetically told Dan Stein.

Our scheduled meeting with Probation, after being twice pushed back, finally took place in Boston on July 10. Three hours of probing questions for each of us under the proverbial spotlight. Marcia and I (and lawyers) agreed that any details of our marital discord were irrelevant to the case and therefore off-limits. We would acknowledge their existence and move on. No blame for putting the other into a skewed emotional state; no discussion of who had more recorded phone conversations or who wired the money; no finger-pointing. We would present a united front. We were interviewed separately, and Marcia went first. During the long wait, Dan and I ventured into to the courthouse cafeteria, where IDC's The Answer tap was dispensing milk and cream for coffee. A promising omen? Dan kept receiving texts from Arlo that things were going well.

I can speak only to my interview. With infuriating detail, the probation officer probed me about my life history from birth and everything about finances. She seemed to struggle with the notion that someone with my net worth could experience a cash crunch, but I persisted by talking a lot about the long-term effects of a Ponzi scheme that had victimized me in 2001 and the challenges of IDC, as well as making the important distinction between my own finances and those of the Abbott Family Foundation, which had donated to Singer.

Whether I convinced her or merely wore her down I'll never know, but finally she moved on to the next question: had I ever been a member of a gang? "This may come as a surprise to you," I wryly tossed off, "but ... no." Things loosened up from there. I was allowed to portray myself, wife, and family in an objective light and dispel the scandalizing narrative propagated by prosecutors and press. I was bent on expressing the remorse I truly felt while not letting our crime define us, and I felt I succeeded. In a way, it was therapeutic; I felt safe, like I was talking to a shrink who saw me as human rather than a criminal. Nothing contentious; no gotcha questions. I found her warm and pleasant and appreciated the opportunity she afforded to humanize our lives, to lay out as candidly as possible the pressures I'd been under: Lyme disease; marital discord; estrangement from daughter (attributed to circumstance, not Spouse, whom I used every occasion possible to praise); our son's roller coaster of addiction; financial strains stemming from the 2001 Ponzi scheme; the devastating death of my best friend. One never really knows about such things, but as our interview finally winded down, she asked, "Is there anything else you'd like the judge to know?"

"Yes," I replied, expelling a tired breath. "I'd like her to know, first and foremost, that I am sorry. For the past three hours, I've explained to you the various pressures that led us into making our unfortunate decision, but that does not excuse it. We did what we did *not* for bragging rights, *not* out of narcissism, but out of love and desperation. To bring some relief to a family that desperately needed it. It was wrong. It was stupid. We acted out of character. It is *not* who we are."

"That seems quite apparent," she said almost maternally. "Please email me some of your character letters." She was a good egg, Dan and I both decided.

Over the ensuing weeks, Probation contacted various people in our lives—friends, relatives, doctors, therapists—endeavoring to confirm the veracity of all we had told them as part of its due diligence. By early August 2019, Probation released its report. While it contained nothing regarding our personal circumstances, it concluded that our crime had *no victims* and that there was *no financial gain or loss*. Most importantly, it dramatically reduced our guideline recommendation from level 14 stipulated by the government's plea deal to level 5. In layman's terms: *no prison time*! Probation took this blanket position with most of the other defendants as well.

The government filed an immediate legal petition. With much panache but little principle, it tried to revise the letter and spirit its own plea agreement that it had bullied down our throats. The prosecutors now asserted that the defendants had actually committed "bribery," because "fraud" wasn't doing the job they wanted in court. The judge immediately called for a hearing in Boston, which occurred the following week with just the prosecutors and Probation—an internal governmental squabble.

In its rigorous eight-page brief, Probation eviscerated the prosecution's capricious position, citing legal precedents and employing superior logic. It reiterated that there were no victims and no financial gain or loss, and it made the case that Singer's overarching scheme constituted fraud, not bribery. Honestly, I never felt like I had *bribed* anyone. Bribery is proactive, so pick another word. My first conversation with Singer was only after the "deal" had been crafted. Singer had preyed on Marcia's fears and vulnerabilities, virtuoso serpent that he was. Then, out of left field, I was presented with the opportunity to help my sick, estranged daughter by donating to an IRS-sanctioned 501c3 charity. I knew it was wrong and am genuinely contrite, especially for my daughter but also toward the human community to which I belong—though, in fairness, the only person denied college spots because of our actions was our daughter.

On September 11, just two days before Felicity Huffman was to be sentenced, Judge Talwani handed down her ruling, summarily siding with Probation and shooting the government down on all counts. Going into the sentencing phase, I was feeling extremely hopeful, and it wasn't just based on OTL optimism.

Before we go to the sentencing phase, a few chapters on how a Hydra of stresses—marriage, finances, schools, addiction, sickness, death—got us there. All stressed marriages have one thing in common, a marriage, so let me tell you a bit about ours. It began, as many marriages do, as a love story.

CHAPTER 9

HEAVEN AND EARTHLINK

June 1986. Southampton, New York. Within a few months of fulfilling my five-year contractual obligation and leaving Ithaca Industries on excellent terms, I met Marcia at a Southampton cocktail party. I was thirty-eight years old when that contract expired and was keen to embark on the next phase of my life, as yet unknown.

The cocktail party, like many of its ilk, was teeming with young women more attractive as a group than as individuals, but for me, Marcia stood out from the crowd. She had the brightest, freshest face I had ever seen. While I kept taking down phone numbers simply to end uninspired conversations, my eyes kept wandering back to the natural blonde with little or no makeup in the center of the room. She seemed free of affectations and had no gold digger vibes—in this crowd, unusual. I simply had to talk to her, or at least make the attempt. I was delighted to learn that she didn't want to be there any more than I did. This party represented my past. Little did I know that my future was standing right before me, a vision of long, lush blonde hair, of beautiful legs streaming out of a tight, short skirt (all the things that mattered to me back then), but then the conversation took things beyond. She was far more interested in talking about anything that didn't involve the world of commerce, and the fact that I was commencing a novel seemed to intrigue her. She was a magazine editor, quirky in a way that charmed me and a woman of refinement, intellect (a graduate of Hotchkiss and Duke), and beauty. She had it all, without fitting any mold.

A dark shadow descended upon us—a big, hulking, older dude (late forties, I guessed) swathed in a black leather jacket. I recognized him immediately; I didn't know him per se but had seen him around town over the years and knew his name, which I am not using here. I knew that "Mike" had once been a Green Beret in Vietnam, occasionally inclined to barroom brawls. Before Vietnam, he had been an end on the West Point football team at a time when it was nationally ranked, and after Vietnam, he had become the icon for a cigarette company striving to compete with the Marlboro Man. Mike's picture was plastered on billboards and in magazines, all in all, a colorful character one sees around town. Maybe he recognized my face as well, depending on his level of sobriety, but we had never been introduced until then. He loomed like a monolith, saying nothing but with a presence so oppressive that I finally asked, "Are you two a couple?"

In perfect sync, Mike said yes and Marcia said no. *Hmmm*. It turned out that Marcia was in the process of breaking up with him due to his drinking and cocaine use, but also, I suspect, because they made such an absurd couple.

I finagled Marcia's number and asked her out a few days later. As Marcia and I started seeing each other, Mike took it hard and told people he was going to kick my ass, which he was perfectly capable of doing. Even after Marcia and I married a year and a half later, he nurtured a grudge. Then one day at an accidental encounter at an Upper East Side bistro, we broke the ice and had a conversation, one so amiable, in fact, that I actually invited him to visit our home in Aspen. In the course of our courtship and marriage, Marcia and I had moved there and made it our permanent home. It was a throwaway invite, earnestly said but not expecting it would be accepted. Mike immediately called Marcia and said, "Your husband invited me out to Aspen. I'm coming."

"If we ever divorce," Marcia grumbled to me, "you get Mike."

I don't know whether Mike came out with the intention of winning her back, but as soon as I met him at the airport, the g-forces of male bonding took over. A glib advertising exec, Mike was a self-deprecating narcissist (ponder that one) who prided himself on his Brook and Meadow Club memberships and on being shallow. He hobnobbed with cinema celebrities like Oliver Stone and Christopher Walken, the latter of whom he impersonated with exceptional panache, and had had small roles in *Wall Street* and *Basquiat*, which he performed credibly. Mike was now sober and regularly attended AA meetings, even during his Aspen visit. Once, after I'd had a single glass of wine at dinner, he warned Marcia, "I think your husband might be an alcoholic." Nothing worse than an alcoholic, except maybe a reformed alcoholic.

One day while having breakfast in our Aspen kitchen, we began discussing how we would fare against each other in various sports. Mike had been a tight end on the West Point football team and was a karate black belt, so anything in the realm of boxing or fighting or direct physical contact meant instant and humiliating defeat for me, as I readily conceded. Golf was equally uncontestable given my scratch(ish) handicap. We agreed to disagree on tennis, since it required an equal amount of power and finesse. When it came to basketball, however, sparks began to fly.

"Are you kidding?" Mike scoffed. "I got four inches on you. I'm bigger, stronger. The way I play the game, old sport, it's a contact sport. I'll beat you like a drum. Next subject?"

"I don't know, Mikie Boy," I said, sizing up Frankenstein and deciding he couldn't guard me. If he covered me close, I'd blow by him for a layup; if he sagged off, I'd riddle him with deadly jump shots. In those days, I modestly described my shot from the top of the key as a "layup." I also went to my right but shot with my left, which would further confuse him. Plus, he was hovering around fifty. I didn't think he knew, and most looking at me wouldn't suspect, that I had been on Princeton JV at a time when its varsity was competitive nationally. "Perhaps we can settle it in town in a game of one-on-one?"

"Great, let's get it on!" Mike declared, throwing down his napkin and rising from the table, fuming at my temerity. Just then, Marcia entered the kitchen. "Your delusional husband thinks he can beat me in basketball." Mike snickered. "We're going into town, 'cause he won't listen to reason. Guess I'm gonna have to teach him a lesson."

Marcia knew how I had thrashed all comers in one-on-one basketball, guys bigger, younger, and more athletic than I. In my postgrad adulthood, I had cultivated my one-on-one skills far beyond scholastic levels until one-on-one had become my thing. I thrived on being underestimated, which is easy to do, and too often for good reason. While Mike continued to sniff, snicker, and roll his eyes, Marcia said, "He'll destroy you, Mike."

Such unqualified validation from her was rare, and when it came, it meant the world to me. At that moment, I idolized her. Such compliments would eventually become extinct.

"Are you kidding!" smirked the Big Billboard Man. As he stormed outside and got to the car, however, he suddenly changed his tune. "Ya know," he huffed, opening the passenger door, "someone's going to get hurt. Most likely you, but ya never know. With my movie career, I can't afford to get a freak injury, like an ankle sprain or elbow to the nose. I'm not playing."

I flapped my elbows and cackled like a chicken at the Green Beret. "Movie career!"

"Fuck you. For your sake, I suggest we do a hike."

A few years later, Mike bought a cabin in Montana, man's country, and invited me for some hiking and fly-fishing. After he took me on a ten-mile hike through grizzly bear country (it's a miracle we weren't eaten, I later learned), we received a call from Marcia with the shocking news that Princess Diana had been killed in a Paris car accident. Famished from the hike, we turned on his satellite TV and ate the only food he had in his fridge, a side of smoked salmon that I had brought as a house present. We didn't bother with flatware because there was none. Nibbling with our fingers, we watched the news. For the next several hours, we stayed riveted, switching back and forth between networks. Other than an occasional sigh, Mike sat in melancholy silence throughout. Finally, he folded his arms and wistfully proclaimed, "I could've made her happy."

At first, I was too dumbfounded to laugh. "Mike, you've *never* made a woman happy. What makes you think you can *start* with the Princess of Wales? Because she's dead?"

Three years or so later, we asked Mike to become our daughter's godfather. I came to love his big, warm heart and that he was always himself, warts and all. We told him it was because of his army skills and gun collection, that we wanted a maniac who would protect our daughter. On that score, I'm glad he didn't shoot us eighteen years later after Varsity Blues, but by then he had Parkinson's and had suffered a stroke, which had caused him to mellow a bit.

Marcia and I had moved to Colorado because we each had independently decided we no longer wanted to be part of the Upper East Side / Hamptons parade (the one that ironically had brought us together) but didn't know how to break the news to the other. What a relief to discover we were thinking along the same lines! Our relationship began on a strong spiritual and idealistic footing. We were soul mates—we had to be—as a long and extremely vivid dream I had (right after our first visit to Colorado) illustrates. Although it took place well over thirty years ago, I still recall it as if it were yesterday and can feel it in my bones:

GREG ABBOTT

I was flying like Superman through majestic, pristine winter mountain scenery, over tall, snow-covered spruce forests, craggy peaks, zooming, dipping, with Marcia on my back like Lois Lane. I was strong, adventurous, indestructible, heroic, filled with super powers ...

My sublime, larger-than-life adventure was interrupted by the ringing phone. It was Marcia calling from Galesteo, New Mexico, where she was doing some past-life regression work. Yeah, I know. I'm scoffing, too, but back then we were into that kind of spiritual New Age stuff. She sounded shaky.

"Are you OK?" I asked, glancing at my alarm clock and noting that it was well past midnight.

"It's over eighty degrees here, but I'm *so cold*." Her voice was trembling. "Sorry to wake you, but I just had to call. I don't know what's wrong with me."

I told her about my dream.

"When you go back to sleep," she pleaded, "please fly me to Barbados."

How do you explain such a phenomenon? Mere coincidence, or were we indeed connected on a soul-ular level?

—

Life in Aspen was so perfect that I'm almost embarrassed to talk about it, especially given the publicity over the college scandal and the unrelenting charges of white privilege. I realize that Aspen plays right into the hands of our critics who wonder how people so blessed could possibly cheat, who will hate me all the more simply for having been so blessed in so many ways. I get it, and I also can say that if my circumstances had been exchanged with yours, perhaps I would have been the one to hate your guts (though, honestly, I doubt it).

I'm aware that we were blessed with a wonderful life—the sort of life I never knew existed until I actually lived it. Were I writing my memoires rather than striving to salvage my reputation, I would devote several celebrity-studded chapters to Aspen, to colorful people like the billionaire whose private jet featured a stripper pole; playing golf with Tiger Woods in his prime; my neighbor discussing his flying saucer–like mansion embedded into the mountainside: "I gave my wife an unlimited budget, and she exceeded it!" Or my musical "collaboration" with the late Sammy Kahn ("Let It Snow"). The *Post* butchered the lyrics, so below are the real ones, which, if I do say so myself, capture the essence of the Aspen holiday season:

> Oh, the weather outside's delightful, but the women are truly frightful,
> With implants from head to toe, see them glow, see them glow, see them glow.
> They come to Aspen to find nirvana, every barracuda and piranha,
> Oh, the babes really like to fish, for a Bass or a Trump or a Tisch.
> Oh, they really do make great pets, flying in on the private jets,
> Oh, they boogie at Caribou, with their room temperature IQs.
> Oh, the slopes are great for skiing, but better yet for V-I-P-ing
> But if you really wanna earn some dough, fellatio, fellatio, fellatio!

Now let me talk briefly about the flip side of paradise: where there is money, there are also con men, conspicuous excess, and desperate people who come to reinvent themselves. In the latter case, Aspen was the end of the line, the resort of last resort. If you can't be happy in Aspen, then where? Which may be why a couple of our friends (and others) committed suicide. A Heinz heiress and our landlord while we built our home, after being dumped by her boyfriend, went into her garage, turned on the car, and perished from carbon monoxide. The ranch manager of our illustrious neighbor (Saudi Arabian ambassador to the US, Prince Bandar, whose main house was five times the size of mine), a beloved Swiss fellow with a sweet disposition and kind heart, shot himself in the head over a woman.

A younger golf buddy of mine confessed after a round that he felt like killing himself, not because he'd just shot 90 but because he couldn't afford a time share on a private jet. I tried to console him that such things didn't matter in life, that he was only *thirty-fucking-three* for Chrissake! As fate would have it, this guy was years later one of the defendants in the Varsity

Blues case, determined to fight it to the end—until President Trump pardoned him on his way out the White House.

I am not a superstitious man, but I have come to wonder whether every villain bears the initials "R. S." There's Rick Singer of course, but before him, and the person who shifted Marcia and me from the happy to the unhappy side of the ledger, was named Reed Slatkin. He was to my generation of investors what Bernie Madoff was to his. Beginning in the mid 1980s until caught and shut down in 2001, Slatkin raised roughly $600 million from hundreds of wealthy investors. None of those funds were actually invested, though some were returned to investors to create the illusion of high performance in order to draw in others. I was one of those investors. So were Dad and my friend George Kriste. Here's how it happened:

While skiing in Colorado in 1992, I met Kevin O'Donnell, an affable guy who, after making a sizeable fortune selling software to governments, had moved from Washington, DC, to Los Angeles with his wife and son. His father, Kenny, had been RFK's college roommate and eventually JFK's most trusted adviser, the Tom Hagen of the Kennedy clan. Kevin Costner had played Kevin's father in the movie *Thirteen Days* about the Cuban Missile Crisis (whose Hollywood premier I attended). It was through Kevin O'Donnell that I met Costner and a number of other Hollywood celebs.

O'Donnell and I hit it off immediately. He was smart and positive. We laughed a lot and saw eye to eye on virtually everything. In between ski runs, he was telling me about something called the "internet" that was about to revolutionize life as we knew it. A borderline Luddite, I had trouble grasping the concept. Kevin's teenage son had gone to high school with a geek named Sky Dayton. On his own, working nonstop through several sleepless nights, Sky had discovered a way to crack the code and gain access to the internet. He had founded a company called EarthLink, whose mission was to provide easy access to the public for a small monthly fee. One day, Kevin's son handed the phone to his father; Sky was on the other end. Incensed at being thrust into the awkward position of discussing a harebrained business idea with a nineteen-year-old kid, Kevin changed his tune after talking with Sky, who was seeking investment capital. Kevin realized that he might be sitting atop a gold mine with this internet thing. With the advice and assistance of his money manager, Reed Slatkin—I quickly learned that Kevin never made any financial move without Reed, whom he extolled for having made him millions in the stock market—Kevin contributed the first seed capital to EarthLink and urged me to join him. The whole internet concept struck me as people using their computers like adult walkie-talkies, which I thought was gimmicky but cool. I certainly didn't grasp its world-altering significance. Still, I liked Kevin a lot and was intrigued enough to fly to LA with him and meet Sky Dayton in Pasadena.

EarthLink at the time consisted of a handful of wan, pimply teens with soaring IQs and nonexistent EQs glued to their computers. I had no idea what they were doing, but they were enrapt. Sky, more affable and outgoing than your average geek, seemed mature for his age and extremely bright—impressive really. He explained that people paid roughly twenty dollars per month to subscribe to EarthLink's internet service. He showed me charts of how EarthLink's subscriber base was growing exponentially. The objective, he said, was not to make money immediately but to build infrastructure and lock up as many subscribers as quickly as possible, to put the company in a position to capitalize on the unlimited money-making opportunities that the so-called World Wide Web would provide. Within a couple of years, Sky said, the entire world would be doing business on the internet. Faxing would be obsolete. Virtually all communication and advertising would occur "online" (whatever that meant). People would work out of their homes, and entire new cottage industries would sprout as a result of this revolutionary new means of connecting people. Data mining (whatever the f**k that was) would become a multi-billion-dollar industry. Education would be transformed, as every bit of information on any subject was just a few clicks away. Another company, America On-Line (AOL), had a head start in the space, which Sky explained only validated the concept. The world was certainly big enough for two internet service providers, and Sky was determined to position EarthLink as the cooler, hipper option than the more corporate AOL.

Before I was formally invited to invest, Kevin asked that I meet with his financial adviser, Reed Slatkin, at an Applebee's in the San Fernando Valley, halfway between LA and Reed's home of Santa Barbara. Reed's reputation preceded him; Kevin was constantly raving about his performance as a money manager: double-digit gains year after year, not just for him but for a plethora of successful people I had met who also swore by him.

"Reed's a river to his people," Kevin and others liked to say. It became Reed's tag line. Besides me investing in EarthLink, Kevin thought I might want to invest some money directly with Reed, at least as a trial. Kevin believed he was doing me a special favor by affording me this exclusive opportunity.

I had always been careful with my money, putting very little into the stock market after being burned a bit in the crash of 1987. Though a self-proclaimed mover and shaker, when it came to investing in securities, I didn't trust myself. I had experts make those decisions and explain their reasoning, cautious suits who had backed my father in the old days and earned his respect over time. I was prepared to take a fly on EarthLink based on pure gut feeling—and what if Sky's vision turned out to be even remotely true? It was worth the gamble, I decided.

Reed, however, I found offputtingly cold and not all that interested in me investing with him. We kept things cordial but for whatever reason didn't connect. However, I did join Reed and Kevin to become one of the early seed investors in EarthLink, which turned out to be a bumpy but ultimately successful ride. Extremely successful, actually. It was due to the success of EarthLink that my father and I set up the Abbott Family Foundation, the entity that more than two decades later donated to Rick Singer's Key Worldwide Foundation.

Again, were I writing my memoirs, I would devote several chapters to this swashbuckling entrepreneurial adventure: the ups and downs; the colorful characters; how investors made money hand over fist when the company was losing money hand over fist; how when the company's IPO collapsed and its existence imperiled as it continued hemorrhaging money, I had a fateful impromptu dinner with a friend that led to a life-saving investment by George Soros. I could regale you with anecdotes, like the time someone barged breathlessly into a board meeting to announce that Netcom had merged with Yahoo; while people gasped, I had no idea what that meant until he told us the name of the new company: Netanyahu. Insofar as Varsity Blues is concerned, however, what matters is that the dots to our marital problems and ultimately to Rick Singer began with Reed Slatkin. It is no hyperbole to say that Slatkin proved to be a turning point in my life and marriage.

Over the next three years, without giving him a dime, I slowly warmed to Slatkin. He spoke Mandarin Chinese, shot golf in the midseventies, had a great sense of humor, and enjoyed more respect than just about anyone in the EarthLink community. He was understated, not flashy, and had a no-nonsense impatience for fools, traits one normally seeks in a money manager. Not once did he solicit me. Eventually feeling I was missing out during EarthLink's moonshot, I abandoned my original instincts and began investing with him in late 1996, first a tiny amount as a test. When he performed better than well, I gradually moved more money to him, largely EarthLink winnings but also over time much of my portfolio back east. The more EarthLink grew and gained national prominence, the more I invested with Reed, besotted with the prospect of becoming a master of the universe. Dad, who in his retirement was itching to be involved in something, invested both in EarthLink and Reed, as did my new California friend, George Kriste. Between then and the turn of the new millennium, whenever I needed money to pay bills, I would simply call Reed to liquidate securities and wire transfer the proceeds to my bank. This was normally accomplished within a day or two. Despite our high-flown lifestyle, including flying private, I couldn't spend enough to keep my statement balance from growing. The stock market was roaring, and so was Reed. He was killing it, on a par with Warren Buffet. Even on dismal market days, he managed to minimize loss.

Some of Reed's longtime investors threw him a lavish fiftieth birthday bash at the Biltmore Hotel in Santa Barbara, attended by hundreds of euphoric investors. On a gigantic screen, Kevin Costner, playing crusty catcher Crash Davis (*Bull Durham*), was asked by sportscaster Jim Lampley (also at the party), "Who's the greatest pitcher you've ever caught?" After rubbing his chin and jogging his memory, Costner wistfully recalled, "Slatkin ... Reed Slatkin," then waxed poetically about his legendary fastball. Another spoofy testimonial from Arnold Schwarzenegger about Slatkin's weightlifting prowess, followed by that iconic clip of Anthony Quinn from *Lawrence of Arabia*, where the Bedouin leader proclaimed to his tribe, "I ... am a river ... to my people!" Robed Bedouins and blazered investors cheered in unison; I can't say who displayed more mindless idolatry.

Once the tech bubble burst, my requests for money suddenly took more time to fulfill, a condition that worsened with each new request. My father and George were also experiencing delays. When I talked to Kevin about it, he pooh-poohed my concerns. "Reed is the last person you have to worry about. He's solid as a rock, a river to his people." Kevin was a trusting soul, reflecting his own good, trustworthy character. It is the natural tendency of good human beings to trust others, even more so when it comes to widely recognized experts like Slatkin and Singer.

Deeply concerned but wanting to trust Reed, I visited him at his Hope Ranch, Santa Barbara, mansion. After taking me on a tour of his exquisite garden embedded into the rolling hillside—the Eighth Wonder of the World, people called it—he led me into his office and its battery of computers and traders. He showed me charts and graphs. Not really fathoming his words—I was about as well versed in financial lingo as I was in tech lingo—I focused on his demeanor, which was calm, reassuring. He said that the delays were temporary, that the tech bubble burst had complicated liquidation decisions but that I would get my wire transfer next week. When he drove me back to the airport, I felt nauseous. I asked him to pull over to the side of the road. As soon as I jumped out of the car, I vomited my guts out. Back at my hotel in LA, a wheelchair awaited me. As soon as they wheeled me to my room, I ran to the bathroom and vomited again, violently, endlessly. My body knew what my mind had yet to grasp.

I hired a Santa Barbara private detective with superb credentials (one of his former clients a Koch brother, another Bo Derek) to investigate Reed thoroughly, "down to a gnat's asshole." After exhaustive research digging into every nook and cranny of his existence, the dick came back to me that I had nothing to worry about, that Reed was a "super solid citizen" and philanthropist. The thing about these schemes is that, in retrospect, the reality could not have been clearer. At the time, however, it couldn't have been opaquer.

—

By the turn of the millennium, before doubts about Slatkin began to surface, Marcia and I had two boys. Our eldest was six and starting school, the hemangioma removed from his cheek. Malcolm (the future Infamous Billa) was three, an adorable space cadet. Marcia was in her pregnant glory with our third child—to her delight, a girl.

Our daughter was conceived in suite 609 at the Hotel Carlyle in New York City and born in Cedar Sinai Hospital in LA in late September 2000. At birth, both our boys had weighed over ten pounds, which created a thin wall in Marcia's uterus, or as she termed it, "a womb with a view." Doctors advised her not to have any more children, but she absolutely would not be denied in her quest for a daughter. Given this unmovable reality, she was told in no uncertain terms that she must give birth in a metropolitan area whose hospitals could deal with any emergency that might arise. She needed to be there for observation six weeks in advance of the projected birth date. Our boys had been born in Lenox Hill Hospital in New York, but this time we chose LA due to its proximity to Aspen. With our eldest starting school in Aspen Country Day, shuttling between Aspen and LA was an easy commute for father and son.

Marcia and I began discussing the pros and cons of educating kids in Aspen versus Manhattan. New York schools were technically better, but I was never a great believer in letting one's studies interfere with one's education. A more holistic existence appealed to me. Aspen, while so unreal in so many ways, nonetheless offered an unbelievably healthy and stimulating lifestyle. It also made me incredibly happy. We'd met Andrea Jaeger and hosted her children with life-threatening illnesses, making a tangible difference and adding immeasurable idealistic purpose to our lives. We became bosom friends with Prince Bandar. Our life in Aspen seemed to have so much magic, beauty, and friends and so little stress. I was thriving on all cylinders, like the superhero in my flying dream.

A board member of Aspen Country Day School, Marcia had concerns about its airy-fairy Montessori approach to learning. We didn't want to shortchange our children; we wanted to give them the same quality, rigorous education we had received. Still, I remained partial to Aspen. Kids from Aspen matriculated to excellent colleges; geography worked in their favor, and the high school's baccalaureate program was reputedly outstanding. Moreover, my professional life centered in the LA area. There was EarthLink and my money manager, Reed Slatkin. My still unpublished novel (widely deemed more of a movie than a book) had received excellent Hollywood "coverage," garnering the interest of Edward Zwick (*Legends of the Fall*) and Mimi Polk Gitlin (*Thelma and Louise*). It was Mimi who came up with the novel's eventual title, *Sheer Pressure* (you can still find it on Amazon, so please buy a copy and write me a five-star review). Aspen was a one-hour direct flight away and made perfect sense. Our home was an incredible business asset. New York schools were better academically but also rigid, as I'd heard from my brother, who extolled rigidity as a virtue. In Aspen, we'd have far more freedom to live life with glorious abandon, to take "The Road Less Traveled." We could spend a year traveling the world with tutors, expose our kids to amazing wonders while still garnering academic credits. All that cost money, of course, but, hey, not a problem.

GREG ABBOTT

May 1, 2001. Santa Monica, California. George Kriste, Maryann O'Donnell (soon to be Kevin's ex-wife, and our daughter's godmother), and I sat in an enormous conference room in the LA law office of the law firm Brian Cave, directly across a long table from a battery of Slatkin's lawyers. We'd been sure to get there early. Every seat at the table was occupied by dazed investors; the rest of the room teemed with people on a standing-room-only basis. Many I recognized from Reed's fiftieth birthday bash at the Santa Barbara Biltmore, only now they were stone-cold sober. Ski Dayton loomed in the back, as did actress Anne Archer and her husband, whom I had met through the O'Donnells. A quadriplegic sat slumped and drooling in her wheelchair. Most of the faces there I'd never seen. An aura of distrust filled the packed room; nobody quite knew who was a victim and who might be a Slatkin accomplice. A large speaker rested in the middle of the conference table to accommodate the myriad investors who were listening via phone.

Reed's lawyers announced to the stunned, angry assemblage that Slatkin was bankrupt, that there was no money, that as far as they knew, all Reed's investments over the years had been fraudulent, as were all the personalized account statements we'd been receiving. A classic Ponzi scheme (the biggest of its kind prior to Bernie Madoff)! Those of us who had taken money out from Reed, for whatever purpose, might be forced to give it all back, that the money collected would eventually be distributed to investors pro rata, a process that could take years. From the sound of things, I was finished and would have to sell the Aspen house to avert destitution. Filled with terror the likes of which I'd never remotely felt before, I inwardly resolved to live in rags and sell apples on the street to spare my family hardship.

That night, George, Maryann, and I had an exceedingly glum dinner in Beverly Hills. (Kevin, more entangled with Reed than anyone due to other ventures, and perhaps biggest victim of all, had dropped out of sight.) We dialed Reed over and over: no answer. We shared anecdotes in an effort to determine whether we should have known, whether or not we were at fault for not seeing red flags. We decided that Reed was the Michael Jordan of con men, that we shouldn't be too hard on ourselves. None of us had a victim mentality and generally took personal responsibility for our actions, emotions, and lives, but in this case, what were we but victims? Despite intense exhaustion, I couldn't sleep the entire night and ended up reading the book of Job in the hotel drawer Bible (to lift my spirits).

The next day was my birthday. I flew home in a middle seat, flanked by two morbidly obese guys in tank tops and gym shorts welcoming me back to the real world. In Aspen, my family awaited me in the car and cried out, "Happy birthday, Daddy!" The kids looked so wide-eyed and cute in back, my nine-month-old daughter strapped into her jump seat. I slumped into the front passenger seat, low enough, I hoped, so that the kids couldn't see me sob.

Slatkin's scheme cost me more than a significant, life-altering part of my wealth. My once robust mojo was ravaged to its roots, though I did my damnedest to fight back. For the next eight years, I served as cochair of the Creditors Committee, working to recover lost investor money. By Ponzi scheme standards, we did well; without getting into the complexities of bankruptcy laws, the trustee made the humane decision not to claw all money back, which would have resulted in widespread devastation and suicide. (There were suicides anyway.) Instead, the trustee used a standard money-in, money-out formula to distinguish net creditors from net debtors. That decision gave me room to breathe, though over time I recovered just 15 percent of the amount on my last Slatkin account statement (on which taxes had to be paid).

I could devote an entire book to this intense, fascinating case. I'd love to delve into the considerable work our committee did, the courage and resilience we displayed, to share the praise I (and we) received. But to stay on story, I will simply cite the letter that Rick Wynne, Esq., special counsel to our committee from Kirkland & Ellis, wrote in 2019 to Judge Talwani on my behalf. Yes, I'm being self-serving, but that doesn't mean the laurels weren't earned. Here is a small part of Rick's three-page, single-spaced letter on a matter of grave import:

> I have known Greg both professionally and personally since 2001, and he has shown candor and grace under pressure, generosity towards others, and a sincere and solid moral and ethical base. His actions here are an aberration in the otherwise exemplary life of a good man ... Despite his own financial devastation, Greg spent time with dozens of victims, helping them in whatever way he could. One example stands out, and really shows his character.

> One of the victims was a quadriplegic, a woman who had been injured in an accident. She had Mr. Slatkin manage her settlement funds so she could obtain a secure investment, and was left destitute when the Ponzi scheme was uncovered ... After hearing her story, which was even more heartbreaking than many others, Greg organized a fundraising from Committee members and the wealthier victims to help pay for ... her medical and living expenses. It was selfless and caring, and the sort of person Greg Abbott is and has always been ... a uniquely thoughtful, kind and generous man.

That notwithstanding, I felt utterly worthless, abysmal, a negligent father and husband for taking the magnificent life I had created and squandering it in a bender of drunken optimism. There is no agony quite like knowing you've let your family down, and the spousal sound bites I endured compounded the agony. "Just like your father with JC Penney, you put all your eggs in one basket!" "You trusted an uninsured crook with our money instead of Goldman Sachs or Morgan Stanley!" "You didn't involve *your wife, your life partner*, in investment decisions?" "Chauvinist!" "Gambler!" "Loser!" "Stupid!" Whether uttered with rapid-fire ferocity or, worse, in the course of normal dinner table conversation, these epithets mounted as our relationship ruptured. I was portrayed as a typical rich man's son, a dabbler who'd been handed Daddy's company on the proverbial silver platter, who was born on third base and thought he'd hit a triple. She hadn't even known me back then! Hard to be remorseful when your entire life and self are discredited.

Such was Marcia's way of coping with abject trauma and fear and with the fact that, in the realm of family finances, I had involved her in much the same way that Michael Corleone had involved Kay. To that, I plead guilty, though my actions stemmed not from disrespect but from putting her on a pedestal, from wanting to take care of her and my family—old school. Prior to Slatkin, she had shown little to no interest in finances. Post, her cruel comments, often coming in bunches and preventing me from getting in a word, wounded me perhaps more than I'll ever know. Except to point out that I had been the one to spread Ithaca Industries' eggs across many baskets, thereby saving and growing it, there was no equally pithy response; no value in saying that, albeit late in the game, I had

Slatkin investigated, and the report came back clean. Or that I had saved EarthLink from oblivion after its IPO blew up. Or that I had observed Reed carefully for over three years before giving him a dime. Reed had brought in tens of millions of legitimate investor money into EarthLink and exhibited exemplary conduct as a director. Many brilliant people—money guys far more financially savvy than I—had invested with him for over ten years and swore by him. How good a con man was he? His compartmentalized brain remembered every lie he ever told. Had someone told me at an EarthLink board meeting that there was a crook among us, I would have first eliminated Reed, secondly myself, before focusing on the other directors and advisers around the table.

"No one makes you feel inferior without your consent," said Eleanor Roosevelt, but as much as I tried not to let Marcia's criticism define me, I was verbally paralyzed, not welcoming her invectives but finding it difficult to dispute the vector of her ... observations. All the explanations and nuances in the world couldn't get our money back or relieve the pain. My father, ravaged by throat cancer that was now spreading through this body, had to absorb the blow as well. He was dying. Even my mother, always a pillar of support but shaken by the financial loss and Dad's declining health, got into the act with the biblical adage "A fool and his money are soon parted." Eighteen years prior, while celebrating Ithaca Industries' triumphant LBO over dinner, she had toasted me for having saved my father's life—a cherished accolade lost forever in the Slatkin shuffle.

We sold off our wine cellar and a Range Rover and generally tried to pick up whatever pieces could be located. When the buyer for our car came to the house, he eyed the property and view and began asking me all sorts of business questions. A newly married chiropractor from Basalt, he had managed to save $1 million and wanted to park it somewhere and make more. Assuming I had the Midas touch, he made a snap decision that he wanted to invest with me. Could I get him into one of my deals? He was practically begging. In a flash, I could have snatched his $1 million for IDC, which I had just founded and was in need of capital. Had I been a Reed Slatkin (or Rick Singer), this callow fellow couldn't have been easier pickings. The thought briefly flashed through my mind, before I sat him down on my deck and Dutch-uncled him. Citing my Slatkin experience, I told him that the world is full of shysters and that he had a neon sign on his chest that said, "Sitting duck." I advised him to be more careful before sending him on his way in the Range Rover.

With Marcia now convinced that Aspen bred naivete and that it was imperative our kids be schooled and toughened up in New York, I had no fight left in me to object.

Our family flew back to New York and interviewed with two schools. A whiteout snowstorm sabotaged a second trip and three other interviews. Our first choice was St. Bernard's, which employed the English system and was known for academic rigor. We were strongly influenced by my brother, who had sent his two boys there and sang its praises. During our tour of St. Bernard's, it worried me that the second-grade self-portraits posted in the cafeteria were virtually identical, the only distinguishing factors being hair color, and in a single case, skin color. My brother, a self-proclaimed expert on New York City schools, vehemently insisted that St. Bernard's was the best educational experience Manhattan had to offer.

If you get a thick envelope in the mail, friends told us, it means acceptance. A thin one, your kid is rejected. I was still reticent about going back to New York, but when two wafer-thin letters arrived from St. Bernard's, I went into meltdown mode. *How dare those sons of bitches reject my sons*, I bristled, ripping open the envelopes, only to find two warm acceptance letters. Very St. Bernard's, I soon came to learn.

After a dozen-year hiatus from the big city, I began listening to Billy Joel to get myself into a "New York State of Mind." Such sentiments reached a crescendo upon the falling of the Twin Towers. New York was *my city*, goddammit! Maybe this counterintuitive choice to return was for the best. Moreover, my father, the greatest single force in my life and the one man I worshipped, was about to die of cancer, and I simply had to be at his side.

CHAPTER 10

SCHOOL DAZE

It was a twenty-block walk, exactly a mile from our Upper East Side rental to the St. Bernard's School. My trusted friend and Malcolm's godfather, George Kriste, in town for business, had joined my blue-blazered sons and me as we walked briskly to school up Madison Avenue one beautiful September morning, three and a half months after my father's passing.

Several mothers were milling outside the school on East Ninety-Eighth Street. While George, who at six-nine towered above the crowd, made breezy California small talk, I gave my eldest a hug and offered words of encouragement. His social adjustment had been rocky as he tried to fit into a class of boys who had been together for three years. They had already forged friendships and cliques, and he was having trouble breaking in.

As we then headed with Malcolm to the separate kindergarten entrance, George remarked with incredulity, "My God, these women are uptight. I mean, it's grammar school, and they act like they're sending their kids off to war." His daughter had gone to Harvard-Westlake and UC Berkley, hardly lightweight institutions.

We entered the building and climbed a special flight of stairs to the kindergarten section, consisting of a waiting area between two classrooms. While George did his godfather thing with Malcolm, I grew mesmerized by the sight of a lanky mother on one knee peering at her blinking son. Pointing her long, bony finger straight at her five-year-old's nose, she delivered her motherly advice for the day: "Re-mem-ber, you are a lea-der. Make friends with oth-er lea-ders. Play with oth-er lea-ders. A-void non-lea-ders." She pronounced every syllable dis-tinct-ly, which struck me as moronic as her message. "*Be* a lea-der, be-cause you *are* a lea-der." *Yikes!*

St. Bernard's was a rigorous place, the tone of each class set by a handful of competitive mothers who pushed their little lea-ders to the breaking point with piano lessons, cello lessons, recitals, community service, and a host of other orchestrated activities in a frantic effort to build their kids' résumés. Preteens with résumés—what a concept! The crushing St. Bernard's homework load forced kids to eat dinner early and work straight until after midnight, only to wake up at seven o'clock the next morning and begin the process anew. No time to play, dream, or let creative juices flow wherever they led you. Without creative juices, where would humanity be today? What had we signed up for! Virtually everyone we knew either had tutors or lied about not having them. As the homework load mounted each year, our family dinners eventually gave way to eating on the fly. Child-rearing experts often cite family dinners as one of the most important formative moments in a child's life, but there simply was no time.

New York schools owned us. Between parent-teacher conferences, skits, plays, assemblies, award ceremonies, athletic events, lectures, and the gargantuan amount of homework that too often needed supervision, we had no other life. This is why Marcia took the initiative to sponsor Jane Goodall (whom we'd met at the Aspen Institute) to speak at St. Bernard's, to introduce a bit of wonderment into the culture. With some notable exceptions, we generally liked the parent body, and our social life centered around them.

St. Bernard's essentially went through eighth grade. It had developed a ninth-grade option for the handful of kids not quite ready to apply out, either for academic or maturity reasons. The ninth-grade option struck me as sagacious, yet many parents deemed it a loser's path to be avoided. It also meant your kid was earmarked for boarding school, since the elite local high schools only accepted kids out of eighth grade. The rat race of applying to secondary school by eighth grade was more intense than applying to college. Not even close. Since its founding in 1904, the intent of St. Bernard's was to prepare boys for boarding school, but the overwhelming trend among parents when we arrived was to send kids to one of the prestigious local private high schools like Trinity, Dalton, Collegiate, Riverdale, and Horace Mann and keep them home. This created a monstrous supply-demand imbalance and even more intense competition come eighth grade. I suspect the *real* reason parents wanted their kids to stay home had less to do with love and attachment than with the fact that they could continue to micromanage their kids' lives in this fired-up rat race—rather than allow their kids to learn self-sufficiency away from home (like I had) and make mistakes (like I had). To quote that crooning philosopher Dean Martin: "Good judgment comes from experience. And experience? Well, that comes from poor judgment." Way to go, Dino! Mistakes, while essential to one's growth and character development, are fatal to one's résumé. With so much competition for so few spots, one mistake (a disciplinary demerit, a bombed final, a single B- or C+) might ruin a kid's chance of admittance to a top-flight private high school. No wonder George Kriste found the mothers so uptight.

Like families, each class has its own story to tell. Malcolm's took the proverbial cake, best illustrated by the annual sixth-grade Gettysburg trip. Traditionally, no more than four or five parents volunteered as chaperones. Malcolm's class rewrote the rules; virtually every family sent either a mother or a father, in some cases both, on the trip. St. Bernard's had to hire an extra bus just to accommodate all the helicopter parents. I joked that they should hire helicopters, which no one found even mildly amusing. Once one family learned that another family was going, the dominos of peer pressure took over. Not to go meant you didn't care, which is why I felt I had no choice but to be one of the fifty parental chaperones for forty kids. The only boy whose family didn't go, a black scholarship kid from Brooklyn, wore a black power bandana and, by St. Bernard's standards, behaved militantly during the trip. No wonder: discussions on the trip centered around battles and that eponymous address, never slavery.

Malcolm was a fish out of water, to put it mildly. Though he did reasonably well academically, his best friends were the two black scholarship boys. Other friends came and went. The roughly half dozen uber-ambitious mothers who set the tone for the entire class (and were widely despised for it) were reticent to schedule playdates with Malcolm. He was spacey, physically awkward, and made tangential comments. They feared "space cadet by association," not a good optic for St. Bernard's, yet they were more than happy to have dinner with *us*. The husbands were generally more congenial; it was the strung-out wives who wore the pants when it came to education, scheduling playdates, choosing their kids' friends, and yammering incessantly about their "gifted" lea-ders during dinner while we husbands zoned out. They were like swans, gliding serenely and gracefully across the pond while pedaling frantically under the water; but it was that maniacal pedaling that provided toxic energy for the class. Sometimes they would schedule playdates with each other's kids right in front of us. Highly intuitive, Malcolm knew perfectly well what was going on. He began to develop his own set of complexes and unique identity.

Throughout the school year, many teachers drank ale at lunch in the school cafeteria. Who can blame them for wanting a little nip after teaching these rowdy rapscallions, who actually served them the ale. Priggish school inspectors were appalled and ordered a stop to it. Each year, the chastened headmaster agreed, only to resume the hallowed English tradition as soon as the inspectors departed. *Bottoms up!* Or perhaps *Cheers!* is more appropriate.

St. Bernard's eccentric sense of humor was endearing to many. Of the forty or so kids in each class, I felt it engendered a genuine love of learning in no more than six to eight of them. For the rest, it was about building character, unless it broke you. About half the class, it seemed, developed nervous ticks. Development people made certain assumptions of my net worth, asserting that they expected a mid-six-figure donation. They seemed to know all about Ithaca Industries and EarthLink but nothing about Reed Slatkin.

One night when he was eight years old, Malcolm asked me to lie down with him and put him to sleep. The boys had bunk beds, and his older brother had commandeered the top bunk like a pirate captain. As Malcolm and I lay down in the galleys, I noticed a poster staring down at us: a hideous thug with tattoos and rings all over his face.

"Who's that?" I said, alarmed.

"It's 50 Cent," said Malcolm. "He's a wappah. A vewy successful wappah." The future Infamous Billa couldn't quite pronounce his Rs in those days.

"50 Cent?" I declared, before uttering a corny, OTL dad joke: "He ain't worth a nickel."

Malcolm giggled down to his toes. "I wanna be a wappah, Dad. I love wap music."

While wondering with some alarm how my eight-year-old even *knew* about rap music, I was happy that he was going through this phase so early in life. By the time he was a teenager, I figured, this vile music genre would be long in the rearview mirror and he'd be playing Chopin at Carnegie Hall, or at least singing Sinatra or the Beetles in the shower like the old block from which he had been chipped.

"Dad, can we get a pit bull? I want to take it to school."

He actually meant it, and we discussed it ad nauseum. He felt persecuted and wanted protection. This saddened me to no end, but it wasn't in me to invalidate his feelings. I hugged him close and reassured him that tomorrow would be another day.

Tomorrow came a few years later. Malcolm began composing his own rap songs and performing them under the name Casual T to anyone who would listen. Classmates suddenly loved his music and thought he was cool. His rap recordings were being played at birthday parties and during bar mitzvah season, sometimes even performed live by Casual T himself. Observing this phenomenon, some St. Bernard's parents openly predicted that Malcolm would be the most successful boy in the class, because he was iconoclastic, creative, obsessive, and didn't fit the mold. I sensed that they were patronizing us as a way of apologizing for having once ostracized him. While having dinner with a group of St. Bernard's fathers, the topic somehow turned to hair, something I possessed more of than most of them. One balding father asked me, "Greg, when did your hair become white?" The wisecrack just flew out of me: "The day Malcolm became black." The white-male guffaws didn't subside for at least a minute, but my candid quip told them that I accepted my son for who he was.

One Saturday morning, we awoke early and discovered that Malcolm was gone. We called the cell phone we'd just given him for his birthday but got no answer. His voice mail wasn't set up. After many unanswered calls, panic ensued. The doorman said he had left the house very early. We were about to call the police about our missing fourteen-year-old when Malcolm called to tell us that he had gone to the Apollo Theater in Harlem to audition for something called Amateur Night. "They loved me," he said excitedly on the phone, while Marcia appeared to have a heart seizure. "I was the youngest, only white person there. They want me to perform at Amateur Night." When Casual T got home, he was holding a rectangular green piece of paper containing his audition number, 193. Call me racist if you must (it's the rage these days, so knock yourself out), but I scolded him for his recklessness in venturing alone into Harlem at his age. I also framed his audition number as a memento.

GREG ABBOTT

Did the pressures of educating kids, one an emerging addict, in hyper-uptight Manhattan further erode our marriage? The daily grind, with precious few family dinners, arguably sucked away much of our joy and glittering idealism (not that anyone is entitled to glittering idealism). In the course of raising three kids, while concurrently fighting out of the hole created by a world-class financial predator, every day involved a crisis of some sort. When you're a kid, you don't realize you're also watching your parents grow up. So insidious was the lifestyle deterioration—much like high blood pressure, the silent killer—that we grew further apart as schools took ownership of our lives and consumed virtually all time and energy. Just compare our kids' Aspen toddler pictures, faces brimming with pure joy, to their burdened images a year later in Manhattan. Such abrupt loss of innocence; I wish I could've taken a parental mulligan. Granted, lots of families sail through this meat grinder, so I'm neither whining nor blaming it for our ethical lapse. We own our mistake. I'm merely questioning how healthy such a grasping environment really is. I suspect it has quietly damaged a host of decent souls and families in ways impossible to measure.

—

When our daughter's time came to begin school, I don't know what we would have done without my brother. Getting into a Manhattan preschool was harder than getting into an Ivy League college. Literally. Due to our decade-long stint in Aspen, we lacked the New York connections we might otherwise have cultivated. Masters of the universe paid millions to get their kids into *preschool*! My brother's three kids from his first marriage had all gone to Brick Church, one of Manhattan's premier preschools, located on East Ninety-Second Street and Park Avenue. A stay-at-home dad and antithesis of master of the universe, Brother had dedicated copious amounts of time helping the school modernize its computer system. The headmistress loved him. Between fighting for financial recovery in the Slatkin case, Dad slowly dying of cancer, the stress of launching IDC, our boys' rocky adjustments to St. Bernard's, and my widowed mother being wooed by a gay predator with cash register eyes, we had enough to deal with. Given all the influence peddling I'd witnessed in the New York private school circuit, I felt no guilt whatsoever in leveraging a school connection for the first and only time of my life.

One of my greatest joys in life was holding my daughter's tiny hand

and walking her to school. From the moment she came into the world, she had an aura of pure goodness. I feel qualified to speak not just as a proud father but on behalf of everyone who's ever known her. Even at her preschool age, she extended her heart to all comers—babies, peers, middle-aged adults, social outcasts, the mentally and physically handicapped, and my frail eighty-five-year-old mother. She took care of everyone. "I've never met anyone so wise and selfless at *any* age!" Mom told me in amazement. "You are so lucky!" Her exquisite singing voice was merely an extension of what lay inside.

When it came time for her to apply to girls' schools from Brick Church, it pained me to have schools judge her based on their cold, laboratory criteria. Test scores, manipulatives, and whatever limited info these academic geniuses could muster to evaluate a six-year-old girl struck me as woefully imperfect and certainly couldn't begin to capture her essence.

We confined ourselves to girls-only schools, having read studies attesting young girls perform better in a single-sex environment (in retrospect, a crock). When it came to applying to the next level, little did we know that the very first day our daughter set foot in Brick Church, the headmistress had stamped "Nightingale" (a girls' school, not an epithet of my daughter's musical gifts) on her forehead. One of her jobs was spreading the wealth; making the ongoing schools happy took precedence over making the parents happy. Parents come and go; the schools remain. Nightingale was where my brother's daughter had gone, so with the legacy factor, why not our daughter? My brother fervently disliked the place, so much so that he sputtered incomprehensibly whenever Nightingale's name was mentioned. I never quite fathomed what it was that sent him over the edge. When Marcia and I toured the school, it didn't quite resonate with who we knew our daughter to be. Had she been a field hockey player, maybe; but she was a nightingale, as in the songbird, and as such did not belong in Nightingale. If only Marcia had toughed it out after her recent ovarian cancer surgery and shown the initiative to run the Bruck Church fundraising benefit. If only I were more like my brother and didn't strike the headmistress as an entitled capitalist used to getting his own way, which is more or less what she diplomatically told me when I flew in from Aspen—academic ignorance and bigotry at its finest.

Nightingale lacked the very thing that made St. Bernard's St. Bernard's: a sense of humor. It was hopelessly politically correct, while St. Bernard's was hopelessly politically incorrect—so I guess they had hopelessness in common. Nightingale was renowned for its murderous parent-teacher conferences, in which the teachers along with the marm-ish head of the lower school spent an hour reviewing all your daughter's shortcomings—good old-fashioned negative reinforcement, the polar opposite of how Spence, our unrequited first choice, reputedly operated.

Once our daughter settled into Nightingale, she adjusted and things went smoothly, though I never felt she was thriving as much as treading water. Once after school, as I was in the process of writing a tuition check, she sashayed past my desk and trumpeted what she'd been learning in school, "Daddy, you are a racist, a sexist, and a homophobe," before scurrying away amid giggles. The indoctrination began early. To nurture her beautiful singing voice, Marcia enrolled her in an after-school Broadway music program, where she began learning a repertoire of popular songs and show tunes.

CHAPTER 11

"YOU'VE GOT A FRIEND"

Back in the early 1990s, before EarthLink, I had invested in another potentially earth-shattering venture. I bonded with its founder, a spellbinding New Ager who nonetheless seemed grounded and could masterfully articulate his vision and its massive global potential. The vision was a device that defied the laws of physics, that could dispense liquid pharmaceuticals, such as eye drops, from a large package and preserve the integrity of the remaining contents, thus eliminating environmental clutter and reducing the cost of lots of small packages. Dispense, protect, reseal—hence the name of the company, ReSeal. ReSeal concentrated its sales efforts primarily in the pharma industry, though its founder saw huge potential in liquid foods and beverages. The company had a plethora of patents and no shortage of loyalists willing to dedicate their lives to the cause. After I put money in, the founder rented an entire office floor that remained mostly vacant. "ReSeal will need it soon," he assured me, but the lack of sales continuity suggested otherwise. One day, he'd say they were about to land Allergan; a month later, it was McDonald's. When I asked about Allergan, I got a song and dance that left me reeling. When I tried to discuss my concerns with the founder, he grew defensive. Where he had once pleaded with me to jump in with both feet and help him run the company, he now erected infuriating barriers. He raised money by the fistful, stashing it in different entities, creating a Byzantine structure that inflated the burn rate and raised red flags. I believed in the idea as much as I believed in EarthLink, perhaps more so because it was a product I could see, touch, feel—like pantyhose and underwear. With the sinking feeling that I and other investors were being scammed, I did something I had never done before and will never do again: mount a proxy fight.

With Marcia pregnant with our first, I flew to New York, with her blessing, to do battle. With management controlling 35 percent of the shares and with many other investors either friends with the founder or under his Manson-like spell, nobody gave me a chance of getting the majority of proxies. My father had warned me it would be tough, and boy was he right! The forces against me were downright evil and mendacious. Marcia received anonymous calls in Aspen that I was cheating on her and was a monster, criminal, and liar—anything they could make up to smear me while she was pregnant.

Armed with formidable recommendation letters from the former CEOs of JCPenney and Avon Products, I contacted investor after investor. Many of them reacted like cultists: who was I to attack this spiritual visionary! Pious New Agers told me to go fuck myself. More commonly, though, when I explained myself, investors simply said, "Where do I sign?" They, too, were fed up, and I had the truth on my side. As I made headway, it was clear that this fight was going down to the wire. A ReSeal employee posing as a defector invited me to lunch and slipped poison into my soup, making me violently ill for an entire weekend. I was also rendered bedridden by a massive psychic attack conducted by the New Age founder's murky cast of characters, some of whom were versed in the black arts. (Lest you think I'm full of it, both incidents were confirmed to me without prompting after the proxy fight was over.) I felt drained and battered, a one-man army, not knowing how much longer I could continue.

At the height of my sickness and paranoia, I received an out of the blue call from a lawyer who'd just rolled into town from California, George Kriste. A mysterious, marquee West Coast investor had asked George to fly to New York to help him decide who to vote for in the proxy fight. In my wary mental state, the sonorous radio voice on the other end of the phone sounded too slick, too ingratiatingly friendly. My first instinct was that I was being rolled, that he was just another character coming out of the woodwork to mess with me. But since he'd flown all the way from California and claimed to represent the investor holding the deciding vote, I agreed to meet with him.

George first met with ReSeal management and felt "slimed," as he put it. It took him five minutes with me to make up his mind. Knowing just like that that I had actually won the proxy fight, I expelled a breath, settled back, and relaxed. Imposing but affable at six feet nine, George had succeeded Bill Russell as starting center on the University of San Francisco basketball team, once holding Elvin Hayes to thirty points (until they benched the Big E for the entire second half). Besides bonding over basketball, we discovered that we had mutual friends in Alaska (one of whom later wrote me a VB character letter). A UCLA lawyer by training, George had represented the Native American Corporation in Alaska and made them (but not himself) billions. I liked him instantly but had no idea what beautiful friendship was in store.

When we took control of ReSeal, George became an investor and director. The West Coast investor who'd sent him and cast the victorious vote—the man who later pilloried me upon learning of my involvement in Varsity Blues—supported me to the hilt with investment capital, wisdom, and moral support. The first thing we did was rename the company International Dispensing Corporation (IDC) to avoid the ReSeal taint. When experts we commissioned to conduct a thorough analysis of ReSeal's technology concluded that it was unable to be manufactured, we made the decision to develop our own device, or at least make the attempt. All that investor money, poison in soup, and voodoo—and all we had was the original concept! Most people would have walked. Believing that it was an idea too promising to go to waste, we set out to take the requisite baby steps that ReSeal's grandiose founder had avoided.

—

IDC focused on food and beverage. Using freelance engineers, we managed to develop the world's only aseptic tap, which we patented in all the important countries. Saying that in a single sentence doesn't begin to do justice to this monumental achievement. We landed a plum manufacturer, the same company that made the Coca-Cola fountain syrup valve. They designed a machine to automatically assemble the tap's five parts, with three quality control checkpoints to detect microscopic flaws. We hired a CEO out of Seagram's, who proved to be a disaster. George and I fired him with the gusto he deserved and replaced him with a guy from PepsiCo, who, we quickly learned, had no pull with his old company. He managed to land a small dairy customer but otherwise fizzled as we encountered obstacle after obstacle: microbiological validation, manufacturing infrastructure, educating the industry. Lots of heavy lifting for a device weighing just a few grams. A Jane Goodall endorsement gave us something to talk about but didn't land customers. We underestimated the spadework required. Tetra Pak, the world's largest packaging company after whom we patterned ourselves, was invented in 1943, didn't gain traction until 1968, and didn't make money until 1980, so we had nothing to be ashamed of. The potential was great; on that score, ReSeal's founder had been right. George and I fired the PepsiCo guy. As IDC's biggest shareholder, most active director, and sole fundraiser, I became CEO. We were not in the financial position to attract a top-flight industry rainmaker, and I took no salary. I knew nothing whatsoever about the food-packaging industry, but I had made rain before, so why not?

One evening, catatonic over obstacles with IDC and the Slatkin case, I came home, nestled into a chair in our smallish living room, and sat there in a virtual coma. Through the silence, I heard the shuffling of little feet; seconds later, my radiant daughter with golden curls emerged from the shadows. Saying nothing, she climbed atop my lap. God knows how I looked to her as she cradled my face in her tiny hands and asked, "How was your day, Daddy?"

"OK." I sighed, managing a smile, elated with her featherlight presence on my lap. "How was yours?"

"Wonderful!" she said brightly. She kissed my cheek and then began to sing angelically, peering into my eyes:

> When you're down and troubled,
> And you need a helping hand,
> And nothin', oh nothin' is goin' right.

My mini Carole King soprano did not stop there but sang "You've Got a Friend" in its entirety. Her soft, soulful voice poured out of her, nothing manufactured about it. Tears streamed down my face. It didn't seem right that *she* at age seven was serving as *my* life coach.

She lit up my life; I worshipped her and still do. I walked her to school and sometimes picked her up whenever schedule allowed. On what she dubbed "Daddy-Daughter Days," we frequented the Central Park carousel and ate cotton candy. We ice-skated at Wolman Rink. Come springtime, the rink was converted into an amusement park, where we shot water guns through a small aperture until bells rang and lights flashed. We beat our competitors and won a stuffed animal. My little daughter was the real sharpshooter—Annie Oakley, I called her—so much so that we kept winning and upgrading the size of the stuffed animal until we eventually came home with the ultimate prize, an enormous blue-green blowfish around which I could barely wrap my arms. Soon her bedroom was cluttered with dusty blowfish. Countless times, we went to Build-a-Bear (where we made customized teddy bears), to Make Meaning (where we made customized cakes), America Girl Doll (where we customized dolls), and the Central Park Zoo to see the polar bears. We had lunch and tea at a variety of special haunts. When I put her to bed at night, we played a game called "Hurricane," huddling under the covers while an imaginary hurricane raged outside. Occasionally, we ventured a peek to see if the storm had subsided, only to yank the covers back over us and hold each other tightly. Hurricane became our nightly ritual.

I took her to tennis lessons in the Sutton Place bubble and watched every stroke like it was Wimbledon; to horseback-riding lessons in Riverdale; to opera practice at Lincoln Center on Friday afternoons and Saturday mornings. Once a month, a voice coach came to the house to strengthen her range, but otherwise, she needed no help. I think her musical talent came from Marcia's side of the family. I sang and played the piano, but Marcia's mother put me to shame. Originally from Alabama, she had never had a piano lesson; her relationship with the keyboard was spooky. From the age of four, as family lore goes, she played like a seasoned professional. The designated New York City piano player of Frank Sinatra (him again) was reputedly in awe of her. When my daughter was nine and my mother-in-law ninety, I secretly gathered them at a West Side recording studio to burn a half dozen songs, grandma playing, granddaughter singing. Entitling the CD *Nine and Ninety*, we presented it to Marcia on Mother's Day.

Of course, Marcia and I regularly attended our daughter's opera performances. Over her career, she appeared in approximately thirty Met Opera productions (each involving multiple performances) and sang in six different languages. Over summers, the Aspen Music Festival featured her in virtually all its opera productions. When the sole child part called for a boy, they still picked her. In *Ghost of Versailles*, where Marie Antoinette is symbolically guillotined at the end as a child, it was our daughter's head that rolled. "Daddy, daddy," she chirped, when I picked her up from rehearsal, "I had my head chopped off six times today!" I was so proud of her and let her know it every day.

GREG ABBOTT

While I was sitting on the edge of my bed holding a hunk of brie cheese, my playful angel tried to grab it out of my hand. When I resisted, she climbed on top of me and kept reaching, crawling over me toward my outstretched arm, joyously tickling my ribs. Writhing and giggling (I am extremely ticklish), I blurted, "Cut it out, piggy." To illustrate the grotesque twists inflicted by degenerating marriages, a few years later, that piggy comment was used to illustrate how I used to call my daughter fat. I never called her fat, not once. She *isn't* fat, for openers; secondly, I have never called a woman "fat" in my postforties adult life.

Imagine my despair when my beloved daughter abruptly stopped speaking to me at the tender age of sixteen.

Imagine my despair, as well, when my widowed mother announced that Jeffrey Butler was moving in with her. Jeffrey was the gay man with cash register eyes, twenty years younger than Mom, whom she had met in Palm Beach (where else?). He wrote her unctuous love letters in which he called her "Peaches" and got her back into smoking cigarettes big-time, their equivalent (I hoped) of having sex. She had quit both while tending to my father but now was back smoking like a factory.

"He's gay!" I told my mother. "Everybody knows it."

"He told me that was just a phase. When he was going through a bad financial time."

Resisting the temptation to tell Peaches that I didn't suck a single dick during the Slatkin debacle, I instead expressed my concerns to our family lawyer. He advised me to do everything in my power to stop any cohabitation before it began, that it could lead to common law claims and put our family fortune at risk. Having seen this scenario play out many times, the lawyer gave me the name of a private detective, who (unlike the Santa Barbara dick) unearthed all sorts of unsavory tidbits about Butler's secret criminal life, including having an alias named "Abbott." Clearly, Jeffrey Butler was the R. S. of gay walkers. Presented with an Everest of incriminating evidence, Mom told me to butt out, that it was her life, not mine. Feeling the weight of yet another financial predator and helpless to do a thing about it, I was reduced to referring to Mom's paramour as Jeffrey Dahmer, which made her even more livid. We couldn't have a civil conversation and stopped communicating. All seemed lost, until one day she phoned me while I was driving.

"I have some news that I think you'll like," she said curtly. "Jeffrey died."

How I managed to drive, talk on the phone, and pump my fist like Kirk Gibson limping around the bases after his dramatic 1988 World Series home run still amazes me. I summoned all the faux sympathy I could muster: "Oh, I'm sorry, Mom. I really am. What did he die from?"

"He had one session of chemotherapy." She sniffled. "It killed him."

When I went over to the apartment to console my mother, she blamed me for Jeffrey's demise. So did George Kriste and other friends, only in laudatory jest. It's not as if I had administered the chemotherapy. I felt genuinely sorry for her. She had taken care of my dying father for two years and needed to rekindle joy; but even my kids saw through Jeffrey and considered him a creep.

Eventually, Mom conceded I'd been right, and our relationship grew as close as it had been during my childhood. She loved it when the kids came to visit, especially our daughter, who even at age seven proved to be a warm, comforting empath. She was now a fledgling member of the Metropolitan Opera children's chorus. The Met didn't want another kid, but Marcia had pushed for a thirty-second audition, and the rest is history. At her "retirement party" in eleventh grade, she was dubbed the Dame Judy Dench of the Met children's chorus.

In 2007, we learned that Mom's lungs had spots on them. Her breathing became labored, but she refused chemo and just wanted to die with dignity. Her last words to me: "You've been a wonderful son." When she passed at age eighty-seven, I was holding her hand. I actually felt her spirit leave her body and linger above us in the room. It was eerie yet beautiful. As I rose to call Campbell's Funeral Home to fetch her corpse, I noticed my friend Judge Andrew Napolitano opining about something on Fox News. Mom died with her boots on, or more precisely, with Fox News on—effectively the same thing in her case. I was fifty-seven years old but felt like an orphan.

CHAPTER 12

ALL WORK AND NO PAY

Reed Slatkin was rotting in Lompoc Federal Prison, a real prison with violent offenders, yet his damage had put me in a financial hole that continued to plague. In 2003, I was selected to speak at his highly publicized LA sentencing hearing on behalf of all victims. Practically quoting my speech verbatim, the judge sentenced him to fourteen years, *three more* than the prosecution had sought—a phenomenon our chief counsel Rick Wynne said that he had never witnessed over his entire legal career. A testimony less to my eloquence than to just how evil Slatkin was. Note to our armchair detractors: Reed Slatkin was a *real* criminal who created monumental carnage. Had the judge been swayed by Reed's slick lawyer and given him five years in return for "cooperation," I'm not sure how our collective psyche would have managed. Reed had ruined many lives, and I was determined to do what I could to mitigate that harm for *all* those taken in by him. I worked hundreds of pro bono hours helping victims, a fact the media failed to mention. (I have yet to find a single positive journalistic account regarding any of the defendants. Not one good deed among the lives of thirty-three parents?) As cochair of the Creditors Committee and mouthpiece for the victims, I learned profoundly the importance of justice. Sending Slatkin away for a long time didn't get us any recovery, but it gave us a certain closure, which in turn avoided the illness of the grudge and allowed me and many others to go forward with our lives, however damaged.

—

My attentions focused on IDC; it became my cause célèbre, the way out of my hole and the path to redemption with my family. I threw myself into the multifaceted task, twenty-four seven and then some.

A Wisconsin dairy filled eight hundred plastic bags fitted with The Answer tap with a lab broth, a solution far more volatile than dairy products. They trucked the bags to Seattle, where IEH (Institute for Environmental Health, an FDA processing authority) conducted rigorous sterility tests. With Q-tips teeming with a predetermined cocktail of deadly bacteria, IEH inoculated each spout and then dispensed broth by pressing the tap's button. Inserting one of those Q-tips into one's mouth was lethal, so the scientists administering the test wore protective masks. Such extreme contamination could never occur naturally in airborne fashion, not even in the most unsanitary of environments, only via sabotage. Each day for thirty days, eight hundred bags were inoculated and dispensed. Stimulated by the growth-promoting broth, the deadly bacteria in the spout were allowed to grow, separated from the remaining liquid contents in the package only by a thin silicone membrane. The bag contents were tested daily to see if any of the growing deadly bacteria in the spout would migrate inside the package. The breach of a single package over the thirty-day period meant the test was deemed a failure—an absurdly high standard, I thought, but my opinion didn't matter. Over that month, I lost twenty-two pounds out of sheer anxiety. Every bit of investor money, including mine, was on the line. Being on the East Coast, I had to wait until noon to call IEH in Seattle to get updates and see if we were still alive. The tortuous last five days, I felt like a water-skier in shark-infested waters waiting for the boat to fetch me. When we survived the protocol, the IEH people were amazed. Vindicated and relieved, I remembered being told in Hong Kong, a few years earlier, by a Chinese scientist with a lab coat and an enormous head, that an aseptic tap defied the laws of physics and was "not possible." The IEH PhDs who conducted the sterility tests that proved him otherwise authored a scientific article that was published in the peer-reviewed *Journal of Food Protection*.

We commissioned a "life cycle analysis" to test the environmental impact of our packaging solution. The company conducting the study warned us in advance that we might not like the conclusions and that, no matter what, they were professionally obliged to make their results public. Their independent eighty-page report confirmed what I knew in my gut, that our ten-liter flexible package with The Answer reduced energy and greenhouse gas consumption by roughly 50 percent and landfill by roughly 90 percent, compared to traditional retail packaging.

Armed with these findings, IDC garnered interest from Hershey. The Answer dispensed chocolate milk at the Hershey theme park as a showcase. Hershey invited us to present The Answer at their booth at industry trade shows. We issued a joint press release. Yet IDC was ahead of its time; the industry lacked infrastructure to fill bags efficiently with our larger fitment. We appealed to equipment companies to produce faster fillers that could run The Answer and to create conversion kits to modify older machines. I gave them the same top-line pitch that I gave potential investors: the aseptic packaging industry was approaching $50 billion (the largest player being Tetra Pak); due to the size limitations inherent in single-serve Tetra Paks (one liter and smaller), only 5 percent of aseptic sales took place in foodservice; within a few years, the majority of food and beverage spending would be for consumption away from home (i.e., foodservice); The Answer was ushering in the world's only large-format (three- to twenty-liter) aseptic package; IDC's aim was to become "the Tetra Pak of foodservice"; therein lay our multi-billion-dollar opportunity.

Gradually, higher-speed machines began appearing, all of which could run The Answer. Conversion kits were offered. I raised money in small increments as needed, so as not to dilute investors. While I was generally praised for my efforts, it put me under constant strain. The Answer won the DuPont Award and the FBIF (Food and Beverage Innovation Forum) Award in Shanghai. That and a buck would get you a subway ride. We needed that one major customer to embrace us and jump-start a global foodservice phenomenon.

Suddenly PepsiCo was all over us. Its head of global procurement made a heartfelt appeal to make a presentation at our next board meeting. His mission was unambiguous: to convince our board that PepsiCo was IDC's ideal partner. He took us through an extensive PowerPoint outlining their global plans. PepsiCo China would be the initial launcher—juice, tea, Gatorade, coconut water—and then things would expand from there. The world's largest beverage company in the world's most populous country— not a bad start! Within the PepsiCo community, the project was white-hot. PepsiCo was even thinking of getting into dairy all because of The Answer. I exchanged emails with PepsiCo's CEO, Indra Nouyi, who, according to the head procurement officer, had given this project the quickest green light in company history. When I drove up to their Purchase, New York, headquarters to have lunch with some PepsiCo executives, the company cafeteria was decorated throughout with foodservice package mock-ups of their supreme brands—Tropicana, Lipton, Gatorade—*each outfitted with The Answer!* We visited PepsiCo in China. We took them to Italy to assist in purchasing two filling machines, which they installed in their Guangzhou aseptic plant. When PepsiCo christened its new R&D center in Shanghai, I was the only non-PepsiCo American invited to the ceremony. Unlike with Alger Hiss, I attended. It was rare for a company of PepsiCo's size to be mobilized in such fashion. A supply contract was signed in late 2013. With PepsiCo's approval, IDC issued a press release that PepsiCo would be launching The Answer with multiple iconic brands in China.

PepsiCo was a multiheaded $60 billion company, and not all the heads spoke to each other. The same week as our press release, PepsiCo China (a whole different set of people from the commercial people with whom we'd been dealing) announced that it had entered into a joint venture with Tingyi, a $17 billion Taiwanese company that sold beverages and snacks throughout Taiwan and China under its Master Kong. Tingyi would now be PepsiCo's China bottler. The deal first required Chinese government approval, then a massively complex integration of the two companies. All new projects, including ours, were put on hold. While PepsiCo China's R&D head kept telling me to be patient, it soon became apparent that our PepsiCo project was in trouble. The autocratic owner of Tingyi was now the guy we had to impress, and he was beleaguered. Hs clashed with his PepsiCo counterparts, whom he deemed beneath him. His brother was arrested in Taiwan for business fraud, another huge distraction. The integration of the two companies proved to be a colossal disaster, and sales of PepsiCo's brands took a huge hit. PepsiCo China's overriding priority became salvaging existing brands. It took me a year of wishful thinking before I came to grips with the fact that our PepsiCo project, over three years in the making, was doomed.

Call me any names you want but never *quitter*. From Big Blue, we went to Big Red, Coca-Cola, which was getting into the coffee business. IDC's entry to Big Red was through Coffeecol, the Colombian coffee arm of the Juan Valdez brand in the US, which had a joint venture with Coca-Cola. Coffeecol's CEO and I bonded like brothers, and he immediately took to The Answer. Developing a line of delicious, dairy-based coffee beverages and a sleek dispenser around The Answer tap, Coffeecol showcased us at trade shows in the Coca-Cola booth. I drank iced lattes with sombrero-ed

Juan Valdez himself, the mascot whom they flew up, sans burro, for the trade shows. McDonald's, a Coca-Cola customer also intent on making its own entrée in coffee, informed Coca-Cola and Coffeecol that they were ready to roll with our collaborative product offering. One minor caveat: because they were promoting the Juan Valdez brand rather than their own, McDonald's requested a $15 million marketing budget from the Colombian Coffee Federation to launch the product throughout the world—hardly an unreasonable request given the scope. The president of the Federation balked, his vision impaired by having his head crammed squarely up his ass (yes, I'm still bitter). Even when Coca-Cola offered to split the budget, the penny-wise, pound-foolish Federation blew the opportunity of a lifetime to develop a billion-dollar-plus coffee business with McDonald's. Were it not for that alarming myopia, or PepsiCo's rocky venture with Tingyi, IDC would today be well on its way to becoming "the Tetra Pak of foodservice," and I a "beverage bigwig."

Our technology was needed most in the third world, which lacked refrigeration, so there ensued a period of frenetic global travel—not just China but Saudi Arabia, Dubai, Pakistan, the Philippines, Germany, Italy, the UK, India, Israel, Mexico, Malaysia, Singapore, Brazil, Peru, Poland, Turkey. Constant jet lag ages a man. My colleagues and I visited most of these places more than once. My passport ran out of space and needed an insert for additional visas. (The government should have no trouble finding it when the time comes.) I attracted a world-class team—seasoned executives from Coca-Cola, Tetra Pak, Sealed Air, Scholle—all of whom were willing to put the full weight of their professional reputations behind IDC. An international beverage manufacturer launched a line of juices in China with The Answer. We had enthusiastic meetings with some of the most important food and beverage companies in these diverse countries. *Nobody* said no; on the contrary, the virtues of The Answer intrigued them, and in some cases, they invested in infrastructure in order to move forward. I created the Alliance for Aseptic Foodservice (AAF), uniting manufacturing partners—of bags, fillers, dispensing units—into a turnkey solution with a compelling vision. A $6 billion–revenue equipment company top exec flew over from Italy to meet me for lunch, loved the concept, and became the AAF's first strategic member.

All of the above required money, and the days of me writing a check to cover any shortfall were over. Nobody gave me a chance of raising money from David Koch, whom I'd first met in the mid-1970s as a fellow bachelor around town.

"You're way too small," people scoffed. "No way David will invest in IDC." There's nothing like being told you can't do something to trigger motivation. No harm in trying. Maybe the entrepreneurial venture would appeal to his Midwest sensibilities. We met several times in his office, and David, an MIT-trained engineer, immediately took to The Answer. He interrupted billion-dollar deals to meet with me on a moment's notice. He asked me to send him reams of information, all of which he personally devoured. Finally, he told me what I wanted to hear: "Send me the wiring instructions." My fundraising efforts were over—for life!

Oops, not so fast. Concurrently, as our meetings progressed, something grew amiss with him. He repeated the same questions over and over, making me doubt my own communication skills. His eyes became glassy and unfocused; he blinked incessantly, like he was struggling with something deep within himself. We went over the same material numerous times; he repeated the same stories. Once I sent him wiring instructions, his availability dried up. His secretary began making excuses. Finally, a close friend of David's confided in me that he had Alzheimer's disease and that the family had stepped in to bar him from making financial decisions. I hadn't realized it at the time, but I had watched David Koch's Alzheimer's unfold before my very eyes.

After a few nights churning in bed, genuinely sad for David but also lamenting the big one that got away, I crafted an old-fashioned letter to David's older brother, Charles (the "brains of the outfit"), in Wichita. This was a delicate balancing act, given that I didn't know Charles and was both expressing condolences and asking for an investment. I shared drafts with George Kriste and got valuable input. Apart from offending the second richest man in America, what did I have to lose?

"I don't feel as uncomfortable as I probably should reaching out to you," I wrote, "perhaps because through David I have gleaned so much over the years about your family and its values." I overnighted the two-page letter to Wichita and a week later received a call from the president and COO of Koch Industries, who thanked me profusely on Charles's behalf. After a thirty-minute call, he told me to expect a call from Koch Industries' wholly owned packaging arm, Georgia Pacific (GP).

GREG ABBOTT

That call came bright and early the next day; a high-level GP exec and I spoke for over an hour. I sent him the reams of material he requested. A six-man delegation flew up to New York for a seven-hour dinner meeting, setting in motion a flurry of activity and momentum. IDC prominently presented The Answer at GP's booth at two global trade shows. Under the Koch/GP corporate umbrella, the business possibilities were numerous enough, and their interest keen enough, that they suggested we retain an investment banker to negotiate an investment, perhaps even a buyout. They were tough negotiators. GP struggled with the small investment (by its standards), while IDC kept focusing on the billion-dollar potential. This dance continued unabated for two years, over numerous meetings, dinners, and cigars in New York, Las Vegas, Chicago, Atlanta. Koch Industries' entrepreneurial culture or not, they still behaved like a big, cumbersome company; yet they were fully engaged.

—

In the middle of all this, my life was shaken to its core. While hiking in the hills of Carmel, California, with his wife and daughter, George Kriste (my best friend for twenty years and go-to guy in all matters of life) dropped dead of a heart attack. It was unexpected and shocking for a man of his vigor. As I said in his eulogy in Pebble Beach, "It doesn't seem right that it was his big, wonderful heart that ultimately failed him when it had never, ever failed anyone else." I wept on and off for weeks. I felt rudderless, listless, in agony from the tremendous void. Even now, I sometimes impulsively dial his number out of sheer muscle memory. I could always count on George for that jolt of positive energy. I felt free to be myself and bounce crazy ideas off him (like writing to Charles Koch), knowing that I was safe from judgment and gossip—and also, due to his good counsel, safe from myself.

His widow wrote to Judge Talwani: "My husband and I were married forty-five years. He had a strong moral compass. He was a commanding and convincing presence. I believe Greg would have reached out to his best friend before allowing himself to become entangled in what occurred. And while I am certain George would have successfully counseled Greg not to fall prey, I know as well that he would have defended the essential goodness of Greg Abbott to the end." Beautiful sentiments, though I'm not sure even George—"a six-foot, nine-inch Jack Russell on speed," as I nicknamed him—could have stopped this loving dad from "helping" his sick daughter, any more than Bloom could have stopped Bialystock from producing *Springtime for Hitler*.

—

Two months after the Varsity Blues sting, the World Packaging Organization's panel of judges bestowed on The Answer its ultimate honor: the WorldStar President's Gold Medal, as the world's most significant packaging innovation. It is no exaggeration to say that WorldStar is to packaging what Oscar is to film. With zero political clout and without showing up at the black-tie award gala in Prague (I couldn't; the government had my passport), IDC beat out more than two thousand entries, including behemoths Nestlé, Coca-Cola, PepsiCo, Tetra Pak, and Unilever.

A German supplier of natural ingredients, who'd invested millions in equipment around the world to support The Answer, told us they were on the cusp of landing several major branded customers that could "blow [their] projections out of the water." IDC was on the brink of breaking into the enormous Pakistan milk market. My contact at GP, the man who made the original call, flew to New York to buy me dinner right after I pled guilty, to express support and reenergize negotiations. It was a beautiful gesture when I most needed it. A month later, however, his GP division lost its largest and most important customer and was thrown into disarray. People were laid off. Just like that, they had to shelve our discussions. Yet another Herculean effort stymied. As if to underscore all this, David Koch died in August 2019 of multiple illnesses, while Bill Maher and Robert Kennedy Jr. made tasteless jokes about it on TV.

This was basically how IDC was positioned when the damned Varsity Blues scandal forced me to resign as chairman, CEO, and director. Some investors have marveled at my tenacity, grit, and ethical commitment, that I've never taken a dime of salary while minimizing shareholder dilution over all these years. Others, frustrated by the slow pace of sales, began to see me as a dreamer. One or two others, solely due to Varsity Blues, have even gone so far as to call me a con man (though never to my face), which couldn't be more untrue. I willed this opportunity into existence and defy anyone to identify a single entrepreneur whose level of drive and sacrifice exceeds mine, and who isn't a dreamer. I'll pretentiously go with the words of Nelson Mandela: "A winner is a dreamer who never gives up." Once IDC finally catches a break, which it will, all that chatter will die of natural causes.

CHAPTER 13

THE VON TRAPP FAMILY ON CRACK

Addiction can tear a family and marriage apart. It is almost impossible to separate the child you love from the addictive behavior you despise. I first became aware of Malcolm's extreme high-THC marijuana use while he was in high school, Saint Ann's in Brooklyn. I've spoken to several Saint Ann's graduates, dropouts, and parents who've told me about its lack of structure. Though intrinsically cut from Saint Ann's artistic cloth, Malcolm needed structure; he was not ready for its freewheeling, self-starting, amazing education. He skipped classes and ambled around Brooklyn Heights smoking weed. He ignored homework assignments and didn't study for tests. By midsophomore year, he was enrolled in PCS, which graciously made an accommodation for him—the first rapper in school history—which is why I can't come down too hard on them for barring my daughter from her senior prom. It was misguided, in my opinion, but I forgive them.

Strangely enough, all three of our kids attended PCS, each with a vastly different professional path. Ironically, the most academically motivated among them was the only one not to graduate. She had to withdraw due to unsustainable absences caused by Lyme disease. In case you haven't noticed, we are not exactly a cookie-cutter family. We hardly planned it that way; it took us by surprise. We have a moneymaking opera singer; a serious hip-hopper with an Instagram presence; a powerful though not all that melodious baritone (our eldest); a dancer (Marcia can curl her feet and prance around on her toes like the ballet dancer she once was); and a cheesy, lounge-lizard piano player—not exactly a family musical act you can take on the road. The von Trapp family on crack.

Malcolm never smoked crack—one positive thing I can say about his tumultuous high school years. It took a Herculean effort just to get him to school in the morning, yet his academic performance was more than decent. Marijuana proved a gateway for street Xanax and opioids, which caused extreme mood swings and even violence when he came off of them. Once he overdosed on Percocet and something called Lean (a combination of codeine with promethazine, hard candies, and Sprite), a frightening experience that mandated we call 911 (a different call from the one referred to earlier). The medics revived him with a Narcan shot. More than once, we had him removed from the apartment for substance and mental health reasons and taken to New York Presbyterian and Bellevue Hospitals. Our daughter grew so frightened that on some nights she would sleep in our room with Mom behind a locked door, while I slept in our daughter's room with the door open to keep an eye on our erratic middle son. In therapy, he made mincemeat of shrinks. Anxious whenever his birthday, holidays, or summer vacation approached, he typically went on pill benders, which is why many of those special occasions were spent in rehabs, something he later cited against us to prove we didn't care about him.

Over the course of our kids' educations, we likely spent more on rehabs, therapists, alternative treatments, and sober companions for Malcolm than we did on tuition for all three kids combined. We sent him to places called Four Winds, Cumberland Heights, New Vision Wilderness, Serenity Springs, Serenity Point, Swift River. These places only work if the patient wants to get sober, though I question their stated success rate and wonder if the rehab industry isn't a racket. We hired sober companions at great expense to be with him every waking and sleeping moment. He wasn't allowed to go to the toilet without a sober companion (or minder, as they are also called) standing watch, which filled me with guilt and anguish. He went through seven minders, one of whom said he preferred six years of Navy Seal training to two months as Malcolm's sober companion. In retrospect, hiring minders was tantamount to flushing money down the toilet. The only benefit was that they bore the brunt of his behavior and gave us a modicum of illusory relief.

I accompanied Malcolm to Mexico to try ibogaine, a hallucinogen that, while banned in the USA, was known to produce excellent results overcoming addiction. We were that desperate. Of all the treatments—rehabs, sober companions, shrinks—ibogaine had the longest-lasting sobering effect. For eight months after returning from Mexico, he was clean.

Changing his stage name from Casual T to Infamous Billa (a tag devised by his brother), he produced a prolific amount of rap songs, some of which revealed exceptional talent. His early work was grating; constantly we argued about its raunchy, copycat content—bitches, hos, cop killing, drugs—though gradually the themes grew softer and truer to his roots. His songs reflected the battle raging inside him, but the more he rapped, the less inclined he was to use hard drugs. When free of their effects, he was delightful, which is why neither of us gave up on him. Thanks to Marcia's nimble vision and a filmmaking friend, Malcolm rap-narrated a short film on elephant poaching, titled *Let Them Live*, which played throughout Kenya and on the jumbotron at the Shanghai airport. *Let Them Live* was nominated for an award at the United Nations, a ceremony that Malcolm attended in blue blazer and tie. Later, he disavowed the film, claiming that the poachers had no other means of making a living. His drug-induced moods were mercurial, cycling from pleasant to oppositional to pleasant, from the castle to the shithouse and back.

Constantly, my wife and I second-guessed ourselves, wondering whether we should have sent him to a therapeutic boarding school or cut him loose until he hit rock bottom and was willing to embrace treatment. We were flailing.

Out of sheer frustration, I suspect, Marcia began laying full onus on me. After all, Malcolm looked more like me and had matching genitalia. I was deemed a substandard role model, evidenced by Slatkin and IDC; chastised for not being a "drill sergeant"; called an array of names, none flattering. That's what addiction does to families. Our household was on constant edge due to the scourge of addiction. There was no rest as I tiptoed around eggshells, anticipating Malcolm's next mishap or the next free-floating spousal tongue-lashing. Depending on which internet article one reads on male teenage addiction, one can find scientific data blaming the mother as much as the father. I don't believe in finger pointing when it comes to such complex subjects. Like divorce in New York state, addiction should be a no-fault proposition. It is a disease. Persistent love and acceptance, not shame, is what gets people clean, I guess ...

Back in 2003, when we were just settling into New York, I enrolled in a night school stand-up comedy class—way beyond my comfort zone. I had always admired men like George Carlin, Robin Williams, Chris Rock, and Mel Brooks, how they could go on stage totally exposed and expand awareness though laughter and lines that stay with us (e.g., "Politicians should wear sponsor jackets like race car drivers; then we would know who owns them," said Robin Williams). Nothing penetrates our consciousness quite like humor. I consider comedians of their caliber society's greatest philosophers and truth tellers; they make us think and uplift us more than virtually any tycoon, educator, tech geek, or politician. When Robin Williams hanged himself, I felt I'd lost a friend, and the world a great soul. After Slatkin, in the hyper-intense pedagogical environment we'd signed up for, I craved laughter. Witty quips came easy and cheap, but big, old-fashioned belly laughs were nonexistent.

On the morning of my first stand-up class, Marcia informed me that she had to undergo a serious medical procedure. Posed with that *dilemma* (pardon the black comedy), my comedy career ended before it began as I accompanied her to the hospital.

At the same time, Marcia's miniature dachshund was dying, fading so fast that vets said it was a matter of hours, that she would likely pass before her owner's procedure. There's something amazingly supernatural about dogs. Like great comedians, they have much to teach us. They're the angels of earth, the most loyal, loving, intuitive souls on the planet.

The dog clearly sensed her mistress's malady. On the day Marcia went to the hospital, her little black, long-haired animal, all but pronounced dead, began to perk up. After Marcia's successful operation, the pet stayed alive for another fifteen months to look after her. I have forever been haunted by this miraculous story and wonder if there's a way to engender the same powers of unconditional love in the human race and society in general, or at least be cognizant of what might be possible within the recesses of our higher selves.

—

Shortly after our three young kids were enrolled in New York City schools, my assistant's husband contracted a debilitating illness, one that for years went undiagnosed. They went from doctor to doctor, none of whom could figure out what ailed him. They took stabs at diagnosing him, prescribing various medications, but his mysterious condition worsened. He grew weaker and in time had to quit his job. Sometimes my assistant would come to work with rosy optimism; her husband seemed to be getting better, was showing more energy and better spirits. Then, like the rock of Sisyphus, his health rolled back down the mountain. Eventually, he was unable to leave the house. Noise and light bothered him; he suffered crippling joint pain, acute memory loss, inability to focus. Finally, one doctor told him he had chronic Lyme disease. He put him on an extreme protocol of antibiotics to blow out the corkscrew-shaped spyrochetes that had ravaged his nervous system, but by then, it was too late. Incensed that the medical community had taken so long to recognize Lyme as a legitimate disease, my assistant railed at the institutional prejudice that had ruined her husband's life. Eventually, she had to quit working for me and devote full time to nurse her husband. She became a Lyme activist. Last we talked, she said that her husband spent his days curled up in the fetal position on their bed, blinds drawn to block out light, muffs over ears to block out noise. A human vegetable.

This was my introduction to Lyme disease. A couple of years later in 2016, we received the chilling news that our daughter, then a high school sophomore, had contracted it.

By that time, my wife and I were so much at odds—over everything written above and more as disagreements mushroomed—that one day, without warning, my daughter abruptly shut me out of her life, for reasons that had nothing to do with how I treated her. Just like that, she wanted nothing to do with me and wouldn't tell me why, no matter how much I persisted.

Even when it came to her medical care and education, I found myself on the outside looking in, a veritable pariah verbally brutalized and/or frozen out on a daily basis. Only when I put my foot down did my wife hand me a printout from a German medical lab. Of twenty different blood measurements taken from my daughter, seventeen were positive, four of them off the charts! Shaken as I was, the more I tried to involve myself, the more resistance, and even blame, I encountered from both women in my family. No matter what tack I took, it exacerbated the stress, and stress was the last thing our family needed. Besides attending the Global Lyme Alliance's gala and speaking with her Lyme doctor (who told me our daughter's blood levels were among the highest he had ever seen, but also, thankfully, that she was steadily responding to treatment and would likely be cured within two years), I was shut out by an invisible wall. Compared to the fairer sex, Trump knows nothing about building walls.

Through the eyes of her tutor, who saw us over many "bleary-eyed, pajama-clad" evenings: "When [the daughter] was in eighth grade, so began the steady escalation of marital distress that came to define and rule the household over the next several years ... [The daughter] was ... only exposed to her mother's point of view, which fueled an estrangement between father and daughter. [Her] relationship with her father was held hostage by the exploding marital trauma. In the end, Greg would have no relationship with his daughter [and] take all of the blame for what happened to his family ... Greg agreed to transfer Rick Singer funds ... thinking that perhaps [his daughter], with the relief of high scores under her belt, might again speak to him, laugh with him, answer his calls, say I love you."

Eavesdropping through my daughter's bedroom door at bedtime, my only source of information on her, I could hear her sob and confide to her mother about her ailments, social isolation, addicted brother, and insensitive father. It tugged at my heartstrings and made me feel less than a man. Knowing I'd been scapegoated didn't relieve my sense of inadequacy. Cupping my ear and trying not to creak the wood floor, I learned about hair loss, extreme exhaustion, blurred vision, joint pain, burning muscles, menstrual irregularity, and brain fog. I heard how she once got into a taxi and was terrified when she forgot where she lived! Luckily, she was able to summon up the Metropolitan Museum and make her way to our nearby home from there. She worried that she had Alzheimer's disease. She felt stupid and incapable and worried about her future. Even the normally supportive PCS classmates teased her at school for being spacey. For some reason, neither Spouse nor Daughter wanted me to know any of this. Blundering into the bedroom, or even broaching these things later, would have been an unmitigated disaster. With no option but to play the long game, I was fed a steady diet of revisionist history concerning my relationship with my daughter and my entire life. The history of Ithaca Industries was rewritten to portray me as a privileged caretaker. My business "lack-umen" had been encapsulated by Slatkin; "narcissism" by IDC; fatherhood by the "piggy" comment. Our dream was crumbling.

Due to unsustainable school absences resulting from Lyme, we reluctantly pulled our daughter out of PCS early junior year. Marcia had researched numerous online programs before settling on Laurel Springs,

USA VS ABBOTT

which, unlike PCS, offered AP courses. Much as I'd like to claim I was intimately involved in this process, I was little more than a nodding figurehead. I was essentially told to butt out and make money.

Without a brick-and-mortar school, our daughter needed a college counselor. The ex-wife of someone who later became one of the defendants (she herself was not charged) innocently introduced Marcia via phone to Rick Singer to possibly fill that role. He'd been doing this for twenty years, Marcia told me, and was loosely affiliated with Laurel Springs; the Laurel Springs people seemed to hold him in amiable regard. Indeed, one of their top administrators had *keyworldwidefoundation.com* in her email address. Had it not been for online schooling, our paths never would have crossed. Neither Marcia nor I ever met Singer in person; nor were we ever on the phone with him together. As I've stated repeatedly, my contact with him was limited to three phone calls spaced over several months. During the early months of 2018, well before making his telephonic acquaintance, there were no rumblings of any kind, so I assumed things were purring along.

In early April 2018, after a series of tumultuous episodes, Marcia and I began living apart. She took our daughter with her to Aspen.

And that's as far as I will go on that topic. All marriages are challenging; it's inherent in the institution and how we learn about ourselves. One offense leads to another until one forgets the original why of it all. There's enough blame to go around to nullify all blame. I can be a pecker at times, she a henpecker. She takes the "fun" out of "dysfunctional." I put the "greg" in "egregious." Plunging down the rabbit hole of ages past has no direct bearing on Varsity Blues, which is why we didn't include the juicy details in our Probation interviews or joint sentencing memo, and why I am drawing the line here. That said, had we been in better communication, I doubt this ever would've happened.

In June 2018, two months after our separation, Marcia flew our daughter to a Swiss clinic for alternative Lyme treatment. A Lyme expert and health advocate accompanied them. Her letters to the judge (one for Marcia, one for our daughter) are worth reviewing to give the reader a bit more insight into our psyches during this period.

She described our daughter on good health days as "vibrant and charismatic ... a brilliant young woman," yet good health days were rare.

Our daughter "fought to perform simple math problems ... was increasingly worried about how she would be able to access her intellect to achieve all her goals as a young woman ... Young people with Lyme become isolated. It is impossible for them to focus for long periods of time. Due to the lack of recognition of Lyme disease, young people are not given proper respect or the extra time they need in order to function in the world at large and in the educational process. Sadly, both their friends and educators lack understanding for their plight and often tease and make fun of them."

She had high praise for Marcia: "Having had experience in this field for a decade, I was impressed to see how knowledgeable Marcia was about her daughter's diagnosis. It's rare to see a non-medical professional be Lyme-literate. I noticed what a dedicated and loving mother she was ... an obvious person of quality. Intelligent, kind, and earnest."

The health advocate summarized our predicament: "After meeting with quite a few parents of sick children, I've observed similar traits. They are isolated and frequently find themselves in situations where need supersedes judgment. They are desperate to make their children well. They have tried every treatment 10 times over. Still, they are not able to achieve wellness for their sick children. This puts these parents up against the wall where they often will accept any solution for what ails their family. So, when parents are at the end of their rope, overly exhausted, in their search for healing they can be vulnerable to predatory situations, both medically and personally. They are willing to investigate grey areas because they've usually run through all the black and white ... I've often seen that it's incredibly easy to get a hook into families when pain and vulnerability spill out in every direction."

A couple of months prior to our separation, I began getting inklings of unrest in the college counselling process. Because I was largely out of the loop, I can only surmise what transpired in those first few months by piecing together tidbits I remember of phone conversations with Marcia. (FYI: The feds are equally in the dark. The phone recordings of defendants they obtained by wiring Singer in the middle of the game amounted to highlight reels, like ESPN showing three or four key plays rather than the whole game. They didn't show the three-yards-and-a-cloud-of-dust conversations of how the ball advanced to the red zone, revealing how Rick

Singer enticed his pigeons like a drug peddler *before* he had the feds tap his phone to entrap us to reduce his own sentence.)

My first recollection is Marcia telling me of Singer's loose connection with Laurel Springs, that he was in the process of advising our daughter on which AP courses to take in the summer, which in the fall, and how to position her applications. Singer wanted his assistant to edit the college essay. The assistant's work was so inauthentic that our daughter rejected it and went with her original draft. From all I can glean, what started as a normal counselling relationship eventually devolved into Singer bringing our daughter's weaknesses into sharp focus. It's a jungle out there, Singer conveyed to my wife; one needed an edge in order to compete. Not even the Metropolitan Opera and a 4.0+ GPA were enough to cut it these days, and Lyme disease was a major liability. Besides making standardized tests problematic, no school, despite their high-minded pretenses, wanted to take on a sick student.

Not long after that, Singer, testing the waters, suggested to Marcia that for $3 million he could squeeze our daughter into Stanford; shortly thereafter, he told her of a possible opening at Duke for $2 million—if we acted quickly. No athletic recruitment scheme was ever broached because opera was our daughter's hook. Opera was the centerpiece of her essay; she had real, official photos of her Met performances, not forgeries; glowing recommendations from the Met itself, not fake letters. Suggesting a monetary donation was no red flag; it's how the game is played all too often by those who can afford to play it. Photoshopping your kid's head onto a water polo or rower's body was another story, but Singer was too savvy to play that game with us.

"He's a bit of a bully," Marcia confided over the phone. "He insists that no top-flight college wants a kid with Lyme disease."

"You mean they discriminate because of illness? Isn't that illegal?"

"I'm just telling you what he tells me. That any ACT score under 33 will doom her to a mediocre school. Things are getting more and more competitive each year. Without killer scores, she's unlikely to get into *any* top school."

"After all she's been through ... working so hard against such obstacles."

"He's really quite pessimistic." Marcia sighed, clearly distraught. "It's so depressing."

"What about extra test time?"

"Even triple time is useless once brain fog sets in."

"No, I mean multiple days," I said hopefully, grateful just to be involved. "We know from her tutor that she tests well when over a period of days, right? Well into the thirties on the ACT, well into the seven hundreds on the subject tests, right? Don't the ACT and SAT have provisions for multiple days? They must."

"She *has* that approval, but Singer says multiple days is a liability, that colleges take a dim view of that sort of thing. It's been abused by too many people."

"But we have doctors' and lab reports! How many days would she need?"

"Three, maybe four *per test*. Not just the ACTs but two subject tests, Math II and Literature."

Reality suddenly dawned on me. "You mean ... nine to twelve days just for testing?"

"For *one go-round*. Most kids take the tests several times. Suppose, like most, she doesn't do all that well the first time? Then it's nine to twelve days all over again. Do you really want to put her through that, in her condition?"

"I hate those fucking tests," I muttered. "I mean, she has a 4.0 *and* performs at the Met ... *with Lyme disease!*"

"That's why Singer keeps suggesting big donations. If only you weren't such a failure."

I ignored the gratuitous dig. "Isn't Singer supposed to be her advocate?" It struck me that Rick was running roughshod over Marcia. Surely college admissions hadn't changed *that* much as to marginalize a student with 4.0+ GPA and a Met Opera résumé. I had never donated to any school that my kids weren't attending, or of which my wife or I weren't an alumnus. Just a few years earlier, our boys had gone through the college admissions process like everyone else, guided by their so-so PCS college counsellor, and had fared just fine: Dartmouth and Bard. Neither of them had quite our daughter's credentials. "Look," I offered, wanting to relieve Marcia's burden but wary of ruffling her feathers, "do you mind if I speak with Singer?"

"It'll only rile him up. He's very touchy and seems to be losing interest, like we're not rich enough to afford his services." Yet another dig. "I don't want him to drop us."

"Perhaps he's the wrong guy."

"This is no time to find someone else. He's connected to Laurel Springs. He claims he has experience dealing with sick children."

The conversation ended as it had begun, with uncertainty and no direction.

No doubt Singer readily sensed the stress was Marica was under dealing with a sick daughter. No doubt he sensed her fear-based nature and insecurities and was able to glean a marriage in tatters. That's what predators do: keenly observe and exploit the weak points of their prey. We were already divided, so all he needed to do was conquer. Once he learned through Marcia that we had a family foundation and probed a bit more, our financial benchmark was established. In mid-March 2018, Marcia phoned me with Singer's take-it-or-leave it "accommodation," as he put it: in return for our family foundation donating $50,000 to the Key Foundation, our daughter would take the ACT test in a single day in a West Hollywood facility, arranged for by Singer during her West Coast college tour, whereupon a proctor would do the rest, if necessary. It sounded like a compassionate, one-off arrangement; it never occurred to me that this was Singer's MO.

In discussing the morality of such a move, Marcia and I gave more weight to our daughter's physical and emotional condition. We rationalized it given the circumstances. From her standardized test tutor, we knew what she was capable of; we simply wanted her tests to reflect that—nothing more, nothing less. Valiantly, she had fought through a plethora of autoimmune symptoms to get As and never miss a performance at the Met Opera. She used her musical gift to sing for the elderly and homebound. Her social life and play time had dried up to nil. When she wasn't doing schoolwork or opera, she was in bed nurturing her aching body and fragile emotions. Lyme disease, the isolation of online schooling, and family fracturing sent her into frequent bouts of depression. Throw on top of that the normal stress of schoolwork and the college application process, and we decided to spare our sick, emotionally fraught daughter the added burden of having to take the ACT over a three-or-four-day period, then repeat the marathon with each of the two subject tests.

Had we thought her condition permanent, we would have prevailed on her to rethink the college process, but doctors in New York (and Switzerland), noting her steady progress in response to treatment, indicated that the prognosis was excellent for a cure, that she should be all better after taking a gap year. Our daughter didn't want to postpone anything. She had worked too hard and suffered too much to delay her college dream, to spend another isolated year in the pressure cooker called home without knowing her future. She needed to feel joy, interact with friends, believe in herself and the arc of her life. None of her obstacles were enough to stop *her*, but combined, they were more than enough for us to ease her burden.

So, to relieve my own guilt over the state of our family, I consented without much resistance. I had yet to talk to Singer and didn't consider the odds of anything backfiring; it didn't occur to me that he was an out-and-out scammer. I hated those tests. Profoundly. I reflected on my own history—testing like a monkey and still graduating from Choate and Princeton cum laude—and said, "Fuck it." More than anything, I was grateful to be in a position to help my estranged daughter. In an odd way, Rick Singer was my only link to her. Hopefully, after a happy result, an enormous pressure would lift and our loving daddy-daughter relationship would return. Marcia and I agreed that for the sake of our daughter's pride and self-confidence, she must never, ever know.

One of my letter writers, a former movie mogul whose own daughter had suffered from Lyme disease for ten years, described it as "a chronic disability that can ruin a life … When I tell you that our daughter's condition devastated every aspect of her and our family's life, I am not overstating the situation. Maintaining school work and some semblance of a normal life is almost impossible in the face of the daily pain, fatigue, and clouded thinking that is caused by the disease. And the one thing that every parent learns is that stress of any sort exacerbates the condition. Stressful situations are to be avoided at all costs."

But stressful situations abounded, pervading every nook of our lives, clouding our judgment and compelling us to circle the wagons out of love for our daughter, one of our few remaining areas of common ground. "Our marriage was dysfunctional to the point of paralysis," I later said to the court at our sentencing hearing. "Shame on us for not rising above it for the sake of the daughter we both believe in and adore; and for the sake of our own character and integrity that brought us together …"

I spoke to Singer for the very first time in late March 2018 (roughly a week before our marital separation), to make his acquaintance and confirm wire transfer details. I remember it as a cordial conversation, in which the topic of tests was all but avoided. If we spoke of any side benefits, it was in passing; mainly he boasted about the good works of his Key Foundation. Far from seeming a predator, he struck me as kindly, understanding of our daughter's plight. I assumed he was throwing us a lifeline, not a harpoon. When the ACT score later came back as 35, I was frankly uncomfortable.

I had somehow expected something in the 32–33 range, more reflective or her true ability sans Lyme—still good enough to qualify her for virtually any college in theory.

A few months after the wire transfer and ACT result, I learned from Marcia that Singer was demanding another $75,000 donation for help on the SAT subject tests. This took me totally off guard; I somehow had assumed the original $50,000 was to cover everything. When I called Singer, he was immoveable to the point of hostility. I tried to negotiate the donation down to $50,000 as before, but he was downright aggressive. The ACT was one test, the SATs two, he barked; I was getting a great deal. I had no fight left in me and suddenly loathed the guy. Marcia was right; he *was* a bully. But we were already down the seedy path. Might as well finish what we started and be done with it. Rationalizing this as our family foundation's last hurrah where our kids' education was concerned, I held my nose and wired the money. As I did every evening, I lit a meditation candle and sent prayers to my daughter. If anyone deserved a break, it was she. I knew it was wrong, but never in my wildest dreams did I think it rose to be a crime against my country, worthy of federal prison.

Several weeks later, when I learned from Marcia that the College Board had delayed releasing the subject test scores, I grew concerned and called Singer for our third and last conversation—the one the feds taped. Once Singer assured me that the delay was normal and there were no worries, I asked him the fatal question of what my daughter had gotten on the subject tests prior to the proctor, thereby incriminating myself and giving the feds what they needed to charge me with a crime. That was the last of it until my arrest seven months later.

CHAPTER 14

SENTENCING PARADE

September 13, 2019, a Friday. I was feeling superstitious, on edge. Felicity Huffman was to be sentenced that afternoon, the first of a string of sentencings over the next six weeks by Judge Indira Talwani. Ours, scheduled for October 8, would be her fifth sentencing, which both my lawyer, Dan Stein, and Marcia's lawyer, Arlo Devlin-Brown, deemed a plus. We would have the chance to gain insight into Judge Talwani's thinking and make whatever adjustments needed to tailor our joint sentencing memorandum, letters, and speeches.

Friday the thirteenth notwithstanding, I liked Felicity's chances. Marcia was more pessimistic, due in part to her perpetual need to offset my optimism, the same optimism that had invested with Reed Slatkin and thought IDC's success was just around the corner. I let the lawyers do the talking. Judge Talwani had given us a window into her thinking: siding with Probation that our crime had no victims, that there was no financial gain or loss, that the amount donated to Singer's foundation was irrelevant in terms of the guidelines—all tremendous blows to the prosecution. As I stated previously, Probation had reduced our criminal designation from level 14 stipulated by the plea agreement to level 5, which in practical terms meant no jail time. Talwani had stated on the record that she was not bound by the terms of the plea agreement and would decide each case on an individual basis. This, coupled with our mitigating circumstances, bode extremely well, we all generally agreed.

The above legal developments were not generally reported in the media. The Fourth Estate's sole focus was that a rich and famous

Hollywood actress was about to be sent to the gallows for abusing her fame, wealth, and power by paying a whopping $15,000 to a dirtbag. Every cable news network had a banner at the bottom of the screen alerting viewers that Felicity Huffman's sentencing hearing was coming up at 2:30 p.m. Eastern. Network talking heads, in tones they hoped sounded portentous, kept saying that Huffman's sentence would be a bellwether for the other defendants. I was one of the viewers, anxiously reclining on the same bed where the fed SWAT team had arrested me. I got my news a bit quicker than most, courtesy of the *60 Minutes* people attending the hearing, who were texting me with up-to-the-moment developments. They still wanted to feature us in a segment. It also seemed to me that over the past few months, they had developed a genuine affection for, and rooting interest in, our family. Call me out to lunch, but that's what I believed then, and that's what I believe now.

Their texts preceded the ticker tape reports running across the bottom of my TV set. First, the prosecution tore Felicity to shreds with brutal bloodlust. How could they be so vindictive toward a woman who'd expressed public remorse, whose crime and outlay were relatively small! Then Felicity's lawyer spoke in her defense, lifting my spirits, a process that continued while Felicity delivered an eloquent, tearful speech of remorse. Throughout, she handled herself with impeccable grace and said all the right things, which most of the media acknowledged, though some cynical voices dismissed everything she said on the grounds that she was an actress and therefore could fake anything. As one who's spent his life in the arena trying to manifest positive results, I have little time for cynics.

Now it was Talwani's turn. My spirits went up and down as my *60 Minutes* friends texted me the essence of her deliberations. On one hand this, on the other that ... It sounded like Felicity was about to get probation, until the judge sentenced her to fourteen days, 250 hours of community service, and a $30,000 fine. Talwani spoke kindly at the end: "I don't think anyone wants to be going to prison," she said to Felicity. "I do think this is the right sentence here. You move forward, and you can rebuild your life after this. You pay your dues ... Ms. Huffman, I wish you success moving forward."

The *60 Minutes* folks called me immediately after to express their surprise. The whole tone of the hearing seemed to be pointing toward probation, they told me, but ultimately Talwani couldn't do such a thing without inviting public outrage. Imagine the woke outcry if Felicity

Huffman, one of the two faces of this celebrated national case, got off scot-free. The TV talking heads, including Judge Napolitano, declared it a symbolic slap on the wrist, a political sentence to throw the media and public a bone, but I was bummed. All the TV commentators seemed to think that Felicity was the least culpable offender and that others would likely get stiffer sentences. Despite all the legal rulings in our favor, it appeared that Talwani felt she had to do *something* in way of prison. Felicity paid only $15,000 and did it once; the Abbotts paid $125,000 and did it twice. To me, the message was painfully clear: my wife and I would be going to federal prison for some amount of time. Probably nothing like the year and a day the prosecutors were seeking, but I kept remembering the claustrophobia of my mere six hours in a jail cell and felt chills of dread.

Our lawyers weren't so sure we were headed to prison, and I was ready to be convinced. Yes, they were disappointed, but they continued to believe that our extenuating circumstances were more powerful than Felicity's—or anyone's. Felicity, they pointed out, had done a blog on parenting and was specifically targeting Julliard, where she surely had connections given her Tinsel Town credentials. This meant that some other aspiring Julliard student, theoretically at least, could have been denied a spot. Every case was different, and because Felicity's was the first and most high-profile, the public hysteria might die down in the weeks ahead and give Talwani some leeway. They also tried to mollify us with the fact that Felicity was headed to "Camp Cupcake" in Dublin, California, that if—God forbid—we were sentenced to time, it would almost certainly be in the same sort of facility.

Our lawyers counseled us not to get too worked up about the next two sentencings, which involved fraudulent athletic recruitment schemes and larger sums of money.

To get his son into USC as a fake water polo recruit, Devin Sloane had bought a Speedo and swim cap on Amazon. He sewed the Italian national water polo team insignia into the cap. Because his son didn't play water polo at his high school (or anywhere), Sloane and Singer concocted the story that he played on the Italian national team during summers. He hired a Hollywood photographer and graphic designer to stage a close-cropped water polo shot in his own pool. Not to be snarky, but if the posing son didn't know about the scheme, then he wasn't college material. The photograph was given to Singer, who gave it to the USC water polo coach, who rejected it because there was way too much torso showing. Back to the pool they went, and this time the photographer and graphic designer produced a photo that was water polo worthy with a more submerged body. For all this orchestration and for paying $250,000, Sloane was chastised by Rosen for having shown a "breathtaking disregard for basic principles of good parenting and common decency." Talwani sentenced him to four months in prison, five hundred hours of community service, and a $95,000 fine. When I compared Sloane's active machinations to my three short phone calls with Singer, or to Marcia's sympathetic circumstances in dealing with childhood illness and a crumbling marriage, I didn't feel that either of us belonged in his category. Our cases were dramatically different. I don't know how many defendants sought out Singer with unethical intentions, but we certainly did not.

Still, I resisted the urge to judge fellow defendants or believe their press. I especially loathed the cruel depictions of Lori's daughters as airheads. I mean, Elle Woods (*Legally Blonde*) was an airhead too, and look what a brilliant law student *she* turned out to be! Lori's daughters weren't built like rowers, but wasn't coxswain within the realm of possibility? Based on firsthand experience, I was growing to regard all media reports and prosecutorial allegations with skepticism, if not outright disdain. I felt compassion for *all* the defendants, not because we were innocent but because of the malicious forces marshalled against us. I also felt for the people truly offended by our actions, not the prigs in my circle but poor and middle-class kids who'd busted their butts to get into college. I wanted them to know the sort of person I was, that I understood their outrage and the duty that comes with privilege; that I appreciated that we are all one human family with shared values. As I continued gathering letters of support and writing my own letter and speech for the judge, I had never felt more introspective.

As the adage goes, "new money solves problems with lawyers; old money solves them with drinks." I tried to solve them with drinks with my lawyer. Pontificating over drinks one evening that America, land of the free, is the most incarcerated nation on earth (a notion that was just entering my consciousness), I told Dan Stein that I didn't believe in prison for anyone except hard-core, violent offenders: financial criminals like Slatkin, predators like Singer, pedophiles like Jeffrey Epstein. There had to be more creative ways of making a point regarding Sloane's almost comical effort. How about requiring him to wear a Speedo whenever he went out in public for the next four months? (In my case, that would have been tantamount to home confinement; I eat Italian and therefore don't dress Italian.) For victimless crimes, I suggested (as a second glass of wine arrived), why not a more proportional approach? Vilifying people of means doesn't help people of color who've been unjustly incarcerated, correct the flawed college admissions system, or solve the galloping wealth gap. It means warehousing more people at taxpayer expense rather than looking at injustice squarely in the eye. Incarceration is the lazy man's out and only exacerbates injustice. Vengeful bloodlust does nothing to help heal or reform a nation in desperate need of both. I recalled how the people of Charleston responded with mind-blowing forgiveness after the mass shooting of their loved ones, and proclaimed them to be the greatest spiritual leaders we have in this country. Listening to me opine, Dan reached across the table and gave my shoulder a patronizing pat, like his client was cracking from all the stress. Maybe he was.

The next defendant to be sentenced, Stephen Semprevivo, had paid $400,000 for positioning his son, a recreational tennis player, as a tennis recruit at Georgetown. Like Sloane, he received a four-month prison sentence, as well as five hundred hours of community service and a $100,000 fine. Both the Sloane and Semprevivo verdicts were irrelevant to our case on matters of law, our lawyers emphasized, but clearly the judge was taking all cases very seriously and seemed to believe we had all pled guilty to significant felonies.

The sentence we were waiting for was that of Gordon Caplan, who until his arrest had been cochairman of the law firm Wilkie Farr & Gallagher. His offense involved test scores, not athletic recruitment, and therefore was more relevant. Our lawyers believed that Caplan, by virtue of being a lawyer, would and should be held to a higher ethical and legal standard. Fed recordings had him saying that he didn't care about the morality of cheating, only about getting caught. Prosecutors, seeking the same punishment for Caplan as they were for each Abbott, argued that Caplan never hired Singer as a college consultant but approached him solely to cheat. I don't know if that was true; the prosecution alleged a lot of things in our case that were patently false. When Caplan got one month of prison time, our lawyers, while offended in a professional sense, were happy for us. They had expected a higher sentence, yet for some reason, Judge Talwani didn't hold Caplan's profession, and the ethical standards that supposedly went with it, against him. Apparently, the primary distinction was between test scores versus bogus athletic recruiting. A one-month sentence, it now appeared, was our likely cap, yet Caplan had none of the family pressures that had besieged us. With the human factor squarely in our corner, our lawyers felt that probation was still well within the realm of possibility.

All the speeches of remorse sounded the same, almost canned, which I guess is not surprising. What else can one say except how "ashamed" and "sorry" one was for letting down one's family and society, how one had learned a life lesson and would be a better person hereafter. Five days before our sentencing hearing, the *New York Times* carried a story titled "Parents Paid to Open College Doors. Now They're Spending to Limit Prison Time." It discussed how defendants were hiring outside consultants to write their letters and speeches to the judge, "using their resources to boost their own chances of getting a lenient sentence, by marshalling the best possible experts and the best possible arguments." The article went on to say that Judge Talwani had expressed "impatience ... even incredulity" at some of the arguments and materials presented to her. To Semprevivo, she issued a warning for us all: "I maybe should say to you, before I get nine more of these [ghostwritten letters]: I don't feel I need an expert report from a criminologist to tell me how to rule here, particularly where it's the same criminologist that's going to be probably presenting for everybody in LA."

Two LA criminologists had contacted me, but I gave them short shrift. Given all we'd been through as a family, the decimation of my personal and professional reputation, and most importantly the anguish of my daughter, I wanted my words to ring authentic. With a burning desire for redemption, I needed no surrogate to speak for me. The *Times* article actually acknowledged this at the end: "Gregory Abbott, who is scheduled to be sentenced next week ... began his letter to Judge Talwani by assuring her it wasn't written without outside assistance. 'Despite the several consultants who solicited me, insisting I needed them,' he wrote, 'the following words are totally my own, as they should be.'" The *Times* account is spot-on accurate; for once, the media got it right. A number of syndicated publications picked up this article but cut out that last section on yours truly. Surely oversights in each case.

On the Friday before our Tuesday sentencing, I received two promising omens.

Atypically clad in suit and tie, I was sitting at the bar of the Mark Hotel, killing time on my laptop before a meeting scheduled at the Union Club in a couple of hours. My dress shoes were scuffed and lacked luster; they hadn't been shined in years because I rarely wore them. I would be wearing them on Tuesday and wanted to show the court all the respect I could muster. Not that Judge Talwani would notice my shoes; it was more about my own mental state. Upstairs was a shoeshine throne, along with restrooms, gym, and hair salon. The shoeshine guy was not at his post. Assuming that he was temporarily indisposed on the men's room throne, I took my position on the shoeshine throne and began fiddling with my cell phone. Riveted to texting, I heard some doors open and close but paid no attention. When a male voice distinctly rang out, "Would you like me to do those for you?" I looked up and did a double take. Was I really staring at Sir Paul McCartney?

"Um … that would be lovely," I said, jabbering giddily. "I mean, since you offered. Actually, just having a photograph of you simulating the act would be enough. I want to show my friends how far I've come in life."

Sir Paul guffawed, then said kindly in almost a whisper, "Actually, I have a policy of not doing such things. I hope you understand."

"Of course," I said, wanting in the worst way to tell Sir Paul our Varsity Blues story and get his deific empathy ("Help, I need somebody / Help, not just anybody / Help, I need someone / Help!"). "I just thought you could use the money."

Sir Paul let out a jolly-good laugh that made me feel jolly good. He headed down the stairs, then suddenly stopped and turned back. "You know, with you sitting up there looking like Lincoln, I probably should fall to my knees and shine your shoes. But I'm in a bit of a hurry, mate."

This brief brush with greatness elevated my mood. It was a sign, I decided, as the Taiwanese shoeshine guy emerged from the men's room.

The other omen came in an early-evening phone call from my lawyer, Dan Stein, and was more concrete. "I just got off the phone with Rosen." Normally even-keeled, Dan sounded out of breath and could barely contain himself.

Still upbeat from my Sir Paul encounter, my adrenalin surged. "And?"

"He read our sentencing memorandum. He said it's the best he's seen, by far. He even called some of it 'compelling,' which for him is saying a lot. He said it's too late in the game to recommend a lesser sentence than eight months but that at next week's hearing, he'll just make a few perfunctory statements and sit down. The judge will get the message." (Rosen's original year-and-a-day sentence recommendation had recently been pared down to eight months. The government, bludgeoned in all legal rulings, was making widespread downward adjustments in order to appear more reasonable.)

"Maybe I'll end up liking Rosen after all."

"Sounds promising to me," said Dan.

CHAPTER 15

SHOWTIME

October 8, 2019. Boston courthouse. Whatever happened to Eric Rosen, Esq., the government's prosecutor, between the Friday call with Dan Stein and the following Tuesday's sentencing hearing, God only knows. Perhaps his grandstanding boss, US attorney Andrew Lelling, lit a fire under him in order to grab more headlines. Or perhaps Rosen simply reverted to the gloating, unprincipled self he'd always been in this case. Either way, he didn't keep his word to Dan but rather, in a courtroom packed with press, went after us with a vengeance.

"Judge, the Abbotts are the only defendants before the court who engaged in the college entrance exam scheme more than once," the prosecutor began. "In fact, they did it twice. They used the fraudulent scores in an attempt to gain entrance for their daughter to Duke University in place of another deserving student." *Lie number one*: Unlike many other defendants sentenced, we did *not* target a specific school. Our daughter applied to seventeen universities, including Duke, her mother's alma mater. She also applied to her father's alma mater and couldn't have gone to both places. Rosen kept repeating Duke in his speech in an effort to accuse us of depriving a worthy student of a spot. It was dishonest, and he knew it.

"The Abbotts are among the more culpable defendants for a number of reasons … Every parent who participates in the scheme is obviously brazen, but the Abbotts rank up there as … some of the more brazen amongst them … For the Abbotts, they wanted to win, to crush the competition. They bought their daughter a 35 on the ACT, a score in the top 1 percent, nearly a perfect score. They weren't trying to get her in the ballpark; they were trying to win the game … And then they did the same thing on the subject tests. They weren't going for decent scores. They wanted the nearly perfect scores, an 800 in the math, a 710 on the literature." *Lie number two*: There was never any discussion about "buying" a specific score, only about being in the ballpark, to use Rosen's terminology, though when it comes to baseball, I doubt he knows his derrière from second base. We did *not* gun for 35 on the ACT or 800 on the Math II SAT, and frankly, I was uncomfortable when I saw those scores. If Rosen was right and we were going all out, how do you explain the 710 on the Literature SAT, a score my daughter likely would have surpassed had she had the necessary extra days? Her own testing tutor had written that she exceeded that mark in several practice tests. The scores, while doctored to spare her a twelve-day ordeal, were otherwise random; we wanted them to reflect our daughter's true ability sans Lyme disease. We didn't pay more because we wanted stratospheric scores, like there was some kind of sliding scale. We paid what we did because Rick Singer arbitrarily set the price based on what he could squeeze from vulnerable and divided parents.

"[Marcia Abbott] called the College Board, threatened legal action. She lied about her scholarship, attempted to shift blame to the College Board for missed opportunities." *Lies number three and four*: there was no evidence whatsoever that Marcia threatened legal action or lied about any scholarship, as her lawyer, Arlo Devlin-Brown, debunked in scrupulous detail when it came his turn to speak.

"What about Greg Abbott? … he paid the bribe money out of his own foundation … that could have gone to real charitable purposes and instead was earmarked for self-promotion." *Lie number five*: I wanted to help my sick daughter—*period!* To characterize that as "self-promotion" is obscene and, where I come from, deserving of a back-alley whuppin'.

"And after his arrest, [Mr. Abbott] gave a statement to the *Wall Street Journal* denying all responsibility for crime that he pled guilty to weeks later." *Lie number six*: As discussed early on, I did not speak to the lying *Wall Street Journal*. Not a word.

Insisting that our "willingness to shoot for the moon displayed a remarkable callousness that is not present with … other defendants," Rosen reiterated that the Abbotts each merited eight months in federal prison, twice the sentences of Sloane and Semprevivo, who paid much more money and were proactively involved in elaborate athletic schemes.

Not only did Rosen betray his former colleague and mentor, he mischaracterized us in an unethical manner, lying at least six times and, worse, ignoring all the mitigating factors that had tormented us as a family, which more than forty letter writers and several physicians affirmed. So much for our "compelling" sentencing memorandum. So much for judicial integrity and his constitutional obligation to seek truth—and therefore, in this layman's opinion, Rosen's moral fitness to practice his profession. In strictly human terms, which is all I feel qualified on which to opine, I would argue that Rosen's lie-riddled address to the court was at least as self-serving and villainous an abuse of power as our ethical breach with Singer during a period of extreme vulnerability.

—

Our lawyers were more than equal to the task. Both pointed out the absence of aggravating factors in our case: we didn't involve our daughter; we weren't involved in any athletic recruitment scheme or photoshopping; we played by the rules with our two sons because they were in a brick-and-mortar school that had a college counselor; we allowed them to pursue their own paths based on their particular skills and interests; we had no role in setting the price that Rick Singer quoted us, but rather Singer set his price based on what he gleaned the foundation could afford. They argued that the government overstated the significance of us doing the scheme twice; that the ACTs and SATs were part of "a single course of conduct that occurred over a relatively compressed period of time."

"At the very time Rick Singer entered Mr. Abbott's life," said Dan Stein, who spoke first on my behalf by mutual agreement of our lawyers, "he had just separated from his wife of thirty-one years, and they were barely speaking to each other. His daughter had moved to Colorado with Mrs. Abbott, and Mr. Abbott was not speaking to his daughter at all at the time. He said in his letter that the only connection he had to her at the time was through Rick Singer. Their son's addiction … was spiraling out of control. Their daughter was suffering from a … debilitating … mysterious illness that was a cause of great stress in their lives. Mr. Abbott's closest friend had passed away a few months before … Based on my many discussions with Greg, I understand that he was in a place where he had let everybody down. The people he loved the most were hurting, and he wasn't able to help them [during] a time of true desperation. Now, of course, Greg should have decided not to go along with Singer's scheme. We have suggested in our memo ... [that] had Mr. and Mrs. Abbott been speaking to each other, if he had the counsel of his friend, perhaps he would have made a different choice ... that he simply felt as if he was trapped ... I say all this, Your Honor, not to excuse his behavior ... but because ... this offense was not born out of greed or narcissism or a sense of entitlement, but was truly born out of a sense of desperation from a family that was rapidly spinning out of control ... I think there's also value in a legal system that people see as one where you admit your crimes, you plead guilty, you take responsibility, it doesn't necessarily lead to the jailhouse; that there's also opportunities for mercy and for redemption ... Mr. Abbott's history and characteristics are ... worthy of leniency ... He paid for the surgery of a friend who wasn't able to afford it. He championed the cause of the victims of a Ponzi scheme, including raising funds for ... a quadriplegic. In reviewing the letters submitted on Mr. Abbott's behalf, I was struck by how many of them spoke of the same traits, and these were letters written by people from all walks of life, who spoke of his big heart, his trusting nature, his loyalty, honesty, and generosity of spirit. One friend wrote that he trusts Mr. Abbott with his life." Dan concluded, "I frankly see them as ... the least culpable of defendants."

It took all my inner fortitude not to lose it when Dan was speaking. The same was true once Arlo Devlin-Brown, following Dan and speaking on Marcia's behalf, got going:

"I want to start with something that the government has said, both in a filing and I believe in a few sentencings ... They've said that, 'Prison is the great equalizer. Everyone behind bars, rich or poor alike, suffers in the same way.' Sickness and addiction are also great equalizers ... Of course, people with money can get better health care. But money doesn't shield a mother who's finding clumps of her daughter's hair in the bathroom because her autoimmune system is attacking itself. It doesn't help when a boy that you raised and love causes you to fear for your safety at times and you go on these up-and-down roller coasters of relapse and sobriety. Those are the things, Your Honor, that, no matter how wealthy a family, can break a family ... It split apart a thirty-one-year marriage ... divided the family literally, with Marcia in Colorado with her daughter and Greg with his sons in New York .... Some of [the government's] rhetoric I find really beyond the pale. Marcia Abbott was not in Colorado feeling a, quote, 'air of invincibility,' quote, 'looking to ... crush the competition.' She was trying to homeschool her daughter with the assistance of an online program, while traveling all over the place trying to get someone, anyone ... who could find out what was really going on with her daughter and fix it ... The same thing with the government's sentencing brief ... the Abbotts were accused of exploiting their daughter's Lyme disease. This is a girl who dropped out of school, where she [was] doing very well, and was now being homeschooled by her mother with the assistance of an online program ... Her Lyme disease doctor found her situation very serious and made a recommendation about extra time before Rick Singer ever entered their lives. So, Marcia Abbott was focusing mostly on her daughter's medical care trying to give her homeschooling. Her daughter was committed to wanting to go to college. And Marcia Abbott wasn't—nor Greg Abbott—gunning on Duke. And I find—again, this is a little distressing, that the government seems to be trying to convert this case into one where there was some particular school and some identifiable student that was going to be harmed ... Her daughter applied to many colleges ... Their daughter was committed to trying to live as normally as possible and apply to college and see where it took her. And her parents wanted to support that. [They] didn't, unlike some parents, seek someone out for corrupt purposes."

Arlo went on to describe "a very disturbing incident" in which the government adjusted call transcripts to attribute to Marcia things she didn't say, "hearing what they want to hear and interpreting the calls the way they want to interpret them." As for the government's reprehensible claim that Marcia threatened to sue the College Board and lied that our daughter had a scholarship, charges designed to lump her with other more aggressive defendants, Arlo methodically destroyed the prosecutor's allegations point by point by quoting the actual call log and citing examples where the government altered call transcripts to suit its own unethical narrative.

In recommending no jail time, Arlo concluded, "This was a family that was under extraordinary pressures, extraordinary pressures from addiction, from sickness, from splitting up. These are things that can devastate any family, and it can weaken the fiber of your otherwise strong moral fences ... This was not a crime driven by narcissism, or privilege, or desire to brag. It was born of sickness and addiction and the despair of a mother."

—

Having delivered eulogies for my parents, spoken to a judge and packed courtroom at Slatkin's sentencing, and recently given George Kriste's eulogy in front of more than five hundred people, I was not unaccustomed to speaking before crowds in emotion-packed situations. Even though I had practiced my speech countless times, I knew that deep feelings would well up when I least expected them and cause me to break down. I had learned not to be embarrassed by these honest emotional surges but to pause and ride them out. (There are several places in the official transcript of my speech that state "pause in proceedings.") Though this was the first time speaking on trial as a defendant, with prison on the line, I was less nervous than expected. I tried to look the judge in the eye but not overdo it—to address my remarks solely to her and forget about everyone else in the court, to have a private conversation with her. Everything in my speech, from explanations to remorse, I still fully feel in my heart:

"Your Honor, I grew up to romanticize the American dream, where anyone regardless of background can carve out a good life by virtue of honest, hard work. My parents, children of immigrants, grew up during the Great Depression and couldn't afford college. But they were smart and worked themselves to the bone to make a better life for themselves and their family. I was the first in my family to go to college. My parents taught me the virtues of hard work and sacrifice; honoring a handshake even when it works to your detriment; taking away something positive from both victory and defeat. To treat everyone with respect and humility, whether king or pauper. To strive mightily but never put money and success on a pedestal, as they are hollow without personal integrity. These are the values I have tried to live by and instill in my three children—values which in this tragic instance I failed to uphold.

"I grew up to feel natural empathy for others and know what it's like to struggle and to suffer. Like many parents, I'm guilty of trying to spare my children pain, even while knowing that my most valuable life lessons have come from looking pain in the face. Our daughter *has* looked pain in the face. As you know, Your Honor, she was, and is, suffering from chronic Lyme disease, as well as the trauma of having her parents and family in turmoil. Through physical and emotional adversity, she earned As in her courses and was a soloist at the Metropolitan Opera, while suffering the headaches, fevers, dizziness, joint pain, fatigue, brain fog, rashes, loss of hair, loss of stamina, and loss of memory that come with Lyme disease.

"Culpable and contrite as I am, I can state without reservation that I was not propping up an undeserving student for my own narcissistic ambition but trying to help my earnest, talented yet sick daughter, who in the realm of testing had the deck stacked against her. I offer this not as an excuse but as an explanation for my serious ethical breach. To understand my terrible mistake, one needs to know my wonderful daughter. She is as authentic as they come. She worked as hard as anyone: performing in over thirty opera productions, singing in six different languages, earning excellent grades—while under the debilitating yoke of Lyme. Despite her pain, she resolutely worked through her illness day after day, all but forsaking any social life for the sake of her goals and because she had neither the time nor energy for play. Because of unsustainable school absences, she had to switch to the isolation of online schooling, which was when a well-meaning friend introduced us to Rick Singer for college counselling. Had it not been for online schooling, our paths never would have crossed. Regretfully, had my wife and I been in better communication and not two thousand miles apart, I am certain this aberrational scenario never would have unfolded. Once Singer revealed his true nature, we should have walked away; unfortunately, our marriage was dysfunctional to the point of paralysis. Shame on us for not rising above it for the sake of the daughter we both believe in and adore; and for the sake of our own character and integrity that had brought us together in wedlock in the first place. I will never get over the anguish of knowing that I hurt my own innocent daughter.

"That is not to say that my daughter is the only victim. I can imagine the affront to every teenager who worked hard and made sacrifices to achieve his or her college dream, and their parents who raised them to play by the rules and didn't have the means to game the system in the myriad ways it's done. Believe me, I have seen it all in Manhattan—from nursery school to college. I myself have been offended by the sense of entitlement and the dizzying lengths parents go to promote *their* agendas for their children, concoct résumés, buy board seats, and pony up to schools that marginalize those families who can barely afford to pay the tuition. I've always tried to keep my distance from the culture of strung-out parents and stressed-out kids. I share the same sensibilities as most people and, strange as it may sound, identify with the public outrage over my own actions. It took the travails of having an addicted teen; a marriage in dire crisis after thirty-one years; an estranged daughter afflicted by Lyme disease; and acute business pressures for me to act desperately, simply to bring a modicum of relief to our existence. Throughout my life, I have shown integrity and taken the right path under pressure, but in this perfect storm,

I buckled. I accept full responsibility. To every single soul demoralized or offended by my actions, I deeply apologize for betraying the American dream I so revere and violating our sense of shared values. While I truly believed Rick Singer that I was being generous and helping disadvantaged kids, by having my foundation donate to his IRS-sanctioned foundation, I also knew that my daughter would be getting some kind of help that was outside the rules. I didn't know exactly how, and frankly, I didn't want to know. Yes, I was under pressure, yet there are millions of people with pressures who still play by the rules. To all those souls who struggle every day to put food on the table and to get their kids access to college, I apologize for any sense of resentment or inequity my actions provoked and humbly ask forgiveness. I want them to know that I am not, nor ever have been, a schemer, but was acting out of love for my sick daughter. Still, it was wrong, stupid, and I feel genuine remorse—not because I was caught but because taking this shortcut diminished me in my own eyes. I cannot imagine myself ever again forsaking my moral compass that otherwise has served me well for sixty-nine years.

"Your Honor, many dear friends have tried to console me that the system is flawed and that I, in my particular situation, did what many parents would have done to help their child. My response to them has been unwavering: a parent's first duty is to teach his child right from wrong, and in this case, I set a miserable example. Our daughter has handled this ordeal with inspiring grace; she is a beacon of innocence and virtue in this debacle who deserves empathy, admiration, and respect. Though not proud of my own actions, I am incredibly proud of her and believe more than ever in the aphorism that we have as much to learn from our children as they from us. She has forgiven us. She is uniting us. Our family is healing. Your Honor, all I ask is that you see me and especially my family as the decent human beings we are rather than the media stereotypes we are not, and know that I am truly sorry on every conceivable level."

For some quirky reason, perhaps nerves, Marcia didn't go to the podium like the rest of us but delivered her speech standing at the table at which we all were sitting. Like me, she had written her speech herself; unlike me, she delivered it with grace and restrained emotion. She had read online articles about how judges deplored long speeches and emotional displays, deeming them self-pitying and manipulative. While I believe the emotional cracks in my speech were seen as genuine by Judge Talwani, I also believe that Marcia's speech was true to who she was and well received.

"I have spent many months not only regretting but analyzing my actions, because it is not enough to say, 'I was in error' … I've never knowingly been around criminals, nor have I even imagined breaking the law, yet neither of these things protected me. My husband and I were both motivated by good intentions and concern for our daughter, but this does not excuse our choices … I've always known that acting out of fear and anxiety leads to negative results, yet unquestioningly acting out of strong maternal love can equally lead one down the wrong path, especially with judgment clouded by fracture and illness … I ask the forgiveness of all who were hurt by my mistakes. Throughout my life I have witnessed people leapfrogged over because of connections, gender, money, or politics. I promise you, that was never our aim when we reached out to a college adviser.

"Finally, I ask forgiveness of my daughter for my wrongheaded choices made at an extremely vulnerable time. Everyone who knows her has always had faith in her intelligence and work ethic, but no one could rely on the unpredictability of her illness. She worked through a fog of illness, maintaining a high GPA and, when rested, scored well on tests and practice tests. My interaction with Rick not only diminished her achievements but her valor in persisting through adversity … Your Honor, I stand before you today extremely contrite and remorseful. Each day, I regret my mistakes, yet I remain committed to a giving life, to do all I can for my daughter's recovery, my family's unity, and to continue to contribute to my community and to the world at large. Thank you."

As she sat down, a hush fell over the courtroom. The time had come to hear from the only person whose opinion mattered.

—

As she openly deliberated from the bench, Judge Talwani appeared to struggle. Not just my opinion but that of Dan, Arlo, and my media chums in attendance.

"A sentencing," said the judge, "is a very difficult thing because there are … different factor[s]. There's the individual people in front of me. There's the larger societal concern. It's a somber time for me and a difficult set of decisions. And I join the defendants in some concern about almost a sense of glee in some of the quotes and statements in the government's memorandum, because this isn't a time of glee or 'Got you.' These are sad events when we're doing sentencing, and I am faced with figuring out what to do in circumstances where people are people and may well be very, very decent people but people who've committed a crime."

This promising start was followed by lengthy back-and-forth logic regarding the guidelines, in which she "diverged from the government" regarding its sentencing methodologies while acknowledging that we had pled guilty to "serious felonies" and had, after all, "done it twice." This latter fact our lawyers did their best to minimize, but it loomed over the proceedings as our biggest vulnerability. Whether the judge herself considered our acts "serious felonies," or whether she was simply citing our guilty pleas as the determining factor, I'll always wonder. "Mr. Abbott noted in his letter that was filed that he didn't understand he was committing a felony, and I think that may have been the case with a lot of the defendants here." She looked straight at me. "Ignorance of the law isn't a defense."

What could I do but nod politely? I'd been aware of that preposterous truism for years. I was also aware that there are more than four thousand federal statutes, many containing thousands of subset regulations of which, according to the law, every citizen was expected to be cognizant. Is there a single judge in the United States who isn't ignorant of many aspects of the law?

I was aware that US Supreme Court Justice Stephen Breyer considered the "Conspiracy to Commit Honest Services Fraud" statute so ridiculously broad as to define three of every four American workers as criminals. I was aware that one of Charles Koch's pet political causes was to rectify this conundrum by placing the burden of proof on the government to prove criminal intent. Breyer on the left, Koch on the right. Holding government accountable—what a novel concept! Sound at all like the US Constitution? All that said, this hearing wasn't about guilt or innocence; that had been established back on May 22 when we took the plea. It was about sentencing and hopefully sweet mercy. The judge had declared that she had enormous leeway. As I sat at the edge of my seat, I hung on every promising word she uttered.

"The government argues that the Abbotts eagerly participated in the case, and again I don't find that ... I don't see any eager participation.

I don't have the direct involvement of the child, and maybe I should elaborate a little bit why that is important to me ... The issue when the child is knowingly involved ... is being put in the way of a subject to federal felony charge, and that's a danger, and that did not happen here ... I'm quite cognizant of the difficulties that this family has been undertaking and having to deal with, and I do take your point that addiction and illness are matters that are making things much more difficult here than in some cases."

Then, after a suspended pause, Judge Talwani rendered her decision: "I don't see any reason to sentence these two defendants at the level that the government is seeking, and I will impose, instead, a one-month sentence on each of them."

As I plummeted into numbness, Dan and I looked at each other; his eyes gleamed brotherly compassion. I leaned over and whispered heartfelt thanks for being such a passionate advocate, then looked over at Marcia at the other end of the table. Her eyes were frozen in the direction of the judge, who hadn't yet finished. I wanted to wrap my arms around her and tell her that everything would be OK. What's a month in the course of a lifetime?

"I don't think it is needed for specific deterrence," the judge added, "and I don't think it is needed for rehabilitation. But I am, nonetheless, imposing it." The rest of the hearing, involving $45,000 fines, 250 hours of community service, and one-year supervised release for each of us was a blur to me as I sat in a stupor while our lawyers handled the details. I think both sides felt they had lost.

My stream of consciousness went something like this: All that work writing letters and speeches and assisting Mayer Brown in the sentencing memorandum; all the effort obtaining letters of support from friends of all walks of life, from all over the world; all the emotion, public humiliation, and life adjustments of the past seven months; all the legal fees, strategy sessions, and late-night phone calls; all the morale managing of Marcia and the kids; and especially all the dashed hopes and dreams of our magnificent daughter who had done absolutely nothing wrong and just about everything right—and it boiled down to a decision based on politics and headlines. If not for deterrence or for rehabilitation, then on what basis other than politics and headlines?

I was not indulging in self-pity or bitterness, nor denying wrongdoing, but just being, for want of a better term, philosophical. Far from being blind, justice was doing a little peek-a-boo around the kerchief to gauge public opinion. Maybe I'm wrong, but I believe our speeches caused Talwani to waver and struggle. This was quite obvious as she dithered. Both our lawyers told us upon adjournment that they thought she was on the verge of declaring a recess due to her quandary. As with Felicity Huffman, I don't believe Judge Talwani wanted to incarcerate us or thought it was legally or socially necessary. I believe she meant it when she called us "very, very decent people" and admonished the prosecutors for showing "glee." I don't think she liked Rosen and weasel-y minions any more than I did. She is a thoughtful woman who was moved by the "difficulties [of] addiction and illness" we'd been dealing with and even acknowledged that incarceration wasn't necessary for "deterrence" or "rehabilitation." But she imposed it nonetheless.

Why? Yes, we had pled guilty to a felony—but, *let's get real*, at gunpoint, because (as I outlined in considerable detail earlier) it was the only sane option available. Legal minds can differ about the legal characterization of our offense and the constitutionality of our plea agreement. For what it's worth, a prominent lawyer who once served as New York City deputy mayor opined to me in no uncertain terms that it wouldn't survive a Supreme Court challenge. When the law becomes so abstract and unrelatable—conspiracy to commit mail fraud? conspiracy to commit honest service fraud?—that the person being arrested doesn't know what he's been charged with while being hauled out of his home in manacles, humiliated in front of son and building, something isn't right in America. Despite her previous statements about judging each case on its individual merit, despite her own judicial rulings siding with Probation that there were no victims, that the amount of money paid to Singer's foundation was irrelevant to the guidelines, that we were good people under multiple stresses, Judge Indira Talwani was not immune to political or media pressure, or even to her own possible prejudice against real or perceived wealth and privilege. Judges, like defendants, are only human.

I appreciate that Judge Talwani struggled.

—

As Marcia and I returned to our hotel room, I was impressed by her calm. Despite all the emotional water under the bridge and some latent resentment that I'd been dragged into this, I was far more concerned about her state of mind than my own. Thankfully, she was composed, relieved that the suspense was over.

Our phones vibrated all night with calls and texts, the first from our daughter, who also was glad it was over and relieved by the manageable sentence. Our sons were less verbal but equally compassionate. Our friends—who'd never been near a prison—had mixed reactions. Some declared it a victory, saying that a month was nothing, especially when the government had originally sought a year. Others were shaken that we were headed to federal prison and offered their shoulders to cry on. Their support meant the world to us, but we were way past self-pity, in warrior mode. The yoke of uncertainty under which we'd been living for the past seven months had finally lifted, other than our prison assignments. The judge had agreed to allow us to stagger them. Marcia wanted to go first and get it over with. Wherever we each ended up going, she would go on November 6, I on January 3. It was time to buck up, embrace our new reality, and see it through until the sun once again shone brightly in our lives, which it surely would.

While Marcia was taking a shower and I lay on the bed, I received a text. I didn't recognize the number, but in that moment, the words moved me to tears: "Thinking of you. You're one of the coolest and greatest guys I've ever met. This is just a blip on your life's body of work. Best, Louis."

I had no idea who Louis was and for the moment was content simply to receive the sentiments, even if they no longer rang as true as they once might have. As best I could, I wanted to offer Marcia solace and support, to spend a calm night with room service comfort food (burgers, clam chowder, a glass or two of Whispering Angel) before we went our separate ways the next morning. She needed to get back to our daughter, and I to the boys, the same yin-yang separation, but perhaps through our shared ordeal, pulling together during this trying year of humiliation, uncertainty, friction, and torment, we could transform adversity into something positive and unifying or the sake of our family. Rekindle something precious.

On the Acela ride home the next day, I called the mysterious Louis. He was someone with whom I once had a business relationship. I hadn't seen him in fifteen years, and he laughed when I sheepishly asked his identity. Back when I'd known him, he had lived in Princeton, where he'd homeschooled his four kids using the mother lode of university professors at his disposal. He had since moved to Vermont, yet had a Chicago area code for business, hence my confusion. We talked for thirty minutes and vowed to stay in touch. His heartfelt outreach after so many years meant a lot to me, and I told him so.

The doorman gave me a bear hug when I arrived at my building, not exactly a common sight on Fifth Avenue. As I stepped into the elevator to go up to my apartment, an older female resident, with a prim-and-proper perm who'd been widowed a few years ago, was already inside the cabin. We'd always enjoyed a cordial elevator relationship. She frequented the opera and had seen my daughter perform at the Met. I hadn't seen her in months, so in a chipper voice said, "Hi. How are you?" She turned away from me. Had something gone awry in her life? "Is everything all right?" I asked, forgetting my own problems for a moment as the lift ascended.

"Let's just keep our distance," she said icily, trembling with scorn, holding back tears.

After that douse of cold water (a prophetic douse given that coronavirus was just four months off), I got to my apartment and found a small parcel sitting on my desk. I checked to see who the sender was, but there was no return address. *Too light to be a bomb; anthrax perhaps?* I tore open the box to find a red MAGA hat with white lettering (a bomb of sorts) but no card of any kind. I winced until I took a more careful look. My anonymous gift was identical to Trump's hat but for one small difference—hopefully a really big difference, actually. It read: "MAKE AMERICA GREG AGAIN." All I wanted was to make Greg Greg again. Perhaps this little keepsake, whatever the sender meant by it, represented some food for thought, especially when my time to do time came in January and I would have plenty of time to think.

PART II

CHAPTER 16

86702-054

December 30, 2019. Waymart, Pennsylvania, Canaan Penitentiary. I had self-surrendered at the Canaan Federal Prison in Waymart, Pennsylvania, to serve my thirty-day sentence—actually twenty-nine, since the March 12 arrest counted as one. Though I was to serve at the satellite camp down the road, each incoming prisoner had to register at Canaan's main facility, the much larger maximum security penitentiary. I had put in for Otisville, the much cushier "Club Fed" in the Catskills, with reputedly its own tennis court, piano, private rooms, and once-a-week steak dinners. Otisville is where every northeast white-collar offender wants to go, the Princeton of prisons. But it was full. I could have gotten in; all it would have taken, according to a prison consultant and others in the know, was greasing a certain influential rabbi with a $10,000 "donation." Did I really want to begin paying my debt to society by bribing the Rick Singer of rabbis?

My court-ordered surrender date had been January 3, but I had cleared my early arrival with the prison, wanting to get it over with. Since sentencing, I had spent the months writing the first draft of part I; suffering through another heartbreaking Dodger playoff loss; trying to assist IDC from the sidelines; emailing my wife in prison; spending quiet time with kids and friends; and being the only resident in my building snubbed by holiday parties. When Princeton played Dartmouth in a battle of football undefeateds at Yankee Stadium, I watched with friends (Dartmouth parents) from the enemy side, uncharacteristically apathetic about the result and of no mind to face my classmates across the stadium. I reckon

I would've been embraced, given all the support I'd received elsewhere, but felt too squeamish to test it. I meditated nightly and watched the movie *Gandhi* in an effort to prepare myself for prison. I was determined to experience this month as life enriching, to make the days count rather than count the days.

For the past thirty minutes, I had been alone in a holding pen, freezing in the prison smock they'd given me. The disposition of my street clothes was an open question: would they be destroyed or saved in a cardboard box for my departure a month from now? Prison policy was to incinerate them. When I politely implored the correctional officer (CO) to make an exception, given the shortness of my sentence, I got little more than a smirk. I'm sure you'd agree that the request was not unreasonable, but the guard seemed perplexed, if not annoyed. I had come in jeans, a T-shirt, and old sweater, but the parka wasn't cheap. That they felt perfectly justified in destroying my personal property made me understand right away that, as long as I was serving my sentence, I was not Greg Abbott. I was 86702-054, property of the Bureau of Prisons (BOP).

When I'd called the prison before Christmas to ask a few basic questions pertaining to my early arrival and what I could bring, they told me to bring absolutely nothing. No phone, computer, or even contact info, all of which would be destroyed. They strip you of everything. Just bring enough cash to put on my prison commissary account (as my wife had done at Dublin). To be safe, I had brought $700, about twenty-four dollars a day, surely more than enough to buy necessities for a month. My wife, whose term preceded mine, was helpful here. The first week was the most critical and costly: sneakers (an absolute must, considering the painful boots they give you); two pairs each of sweats and thermal underwear (also absolute musts unless you want to freeze); radio gizmo with earplugs to watch TV; laundry detergent; phone and computer minutes; water bottles. Beyond these necessities, all you needed in subsequent weeks was to fill in with random processed snacks, cheap for good reason. Whatever was left unspent of my $700 at the end of my stay would be refunded in the form of a debit card.

When I arrived that morning, Canaan wouldn't accept the cash. *Government at its finest*, I thought, glancing at the row of photos on the reception area wall: President Trump, Attorney General William Barr, BOP Director Kathleen Hawk Sawyer, two extremely white men in suits and ties, and the Canaan warden whose egg-bald head and enormous ears reminded me of a garden gnome. Hard to muster any genuine respect for authority, but I would fake it. When I informed the CO that the prison had *told me* to bring money, that my wife's cash was accepted at her prison, he grimaced. "Didn't you read the handbook?"

In fact, over the Christmas holiday, I had cracked open the handbook for a few seconds before shutting it forever. Handbooks depress me. Typically, they are written badly by drones who believe we the people need to be told how to operate an airplane seat belt. Wading through a swamp of regulations that I would never retain was not how I chose to spend the few precious days before prison. Perhaps my cavalier attitude had been a mistake. The max pen guards were handbook personified, and verbally abusing inmates, I would learn soon enough, was the crux of their job description. Given the alarming characters they had to deal with on a daily basis at the max security pen, one couldn't blame them for an attitude that applied equally to campers. Regardless of our crime, we were all "filthy animals" and "maggots."

My trusty friend who had driven me (the same stand-up guy who'd guaranteed my bail bond) would need to take the money and wire it via Western Union into my commissary account. I had given him my inmate number, 86702-054, and conveyed a sense of urgency since commissary was in two days and thereafter only once a week. All I had was my smock! Using Western Union to transfer money to a federal prison was not exactly in the wheelhouse of this St. Paul's and Harvard alum, and I hated to burden him further. What a mensch he was! He had picked me up at 4:45 a.m. and driven through freezing rain and thick fog two and a half hours, through ice forests reminiscent of *The Nutcracker*, to Waymart—a gesture I will never forget. As soon as we said goodbye and he headed back to New York, I felt terribly alone and uncertain.

Finally, a pair of COs entered the office of my holding pen. "Well, if it isn't Phil Donahue."

"Most people say I look like Steve Martin."

He looked his white-haired, sixty-nine-year-old prisoner up and down. Due to the year's stresses and distractions, I hadn't worked out much since March 12, 2019, which my armless smock did little to conceal. "How many years is your sentence?"

"One month." Sounded smug even to me.

The guards looked at each other before erupting in guffaws. "Congrats! You set a new record! What's the fuckin' point of serving one month?"

"You said it; I didn't." One month still felt like an eternity, given how slowly the first hour in the tiny cell had gone.

"What the hell did *you* do, step on an ant?"

"My crime was victimless. I was part of the Varsity Blues college admissions case."

"What sport?"

"It was for test scores. My daughter was very sick, and I was very stupid."

It didn't take psychic powers to surmise that the guards were flabbergasted that my crime had landed me in a federal prison camp just down the road from murderers, rapists, pedophiles, Somali pirates, terrorists, arsonists, violent drug traffickers, and evil Ponzi scheme financial rapists.

"I told my kid that he can't go to college until he first serves in the military," the second guard informed me, as if I were Rick Singer himself. I wondered whether Singer could have used the CO's brawny torso to transform a string bean into a high school All-American footballer with perfect 800 SATs.

"How much did you shell out to get your kid into college?"

How I hated this when-did-you-stop-beating-your-wife question. "More than I wanted," I parried. "It was a charitable donation, or so I was led to believe."

The banter abruptly stopped, as the first guard dove into paperwork and his colleague left. Much as I felt the urge to connect with him while he pushed his pencil, to convey that I was different from the characters he normally interacted with, it was best to keep my mouth shut unless spoken to. I actually cared what he thought of me, but then he too departed, leaving me alone again.

In the Bible, Canaan is known as the Promised Land; here it is known, in the words of a fellow inmate, as "the asshole of Pennsylvania," or more commonly as "Beast of the East." The Canaan maximum security prison houses 1,400 inmates (requiring six hundred armed guards) and is considered one of the most dangerous penal facilities in the United States. It averages 250 assaults and two murders per year, and those are just the official counts. Roughly 70 percent of the current inmate population will die there, either due to life sentences, long sentences that outstrip a prisoner's life, sickness, or murder. Its address, 3057 Eric J. Williams Memorial Drive, is named after the young CO who was stabbed to death more than two hundred times by an inmate serving a life sentence. As recently as July, 2019 (five months ago), a seventy-six-year-old inmate was murdered, and five COs were hospitalized for airborne exposure to a synthetic drug they were trying to confiscate during cell searches. Canaan was also the scene of one of the USA's largest institutional outbreaks of salmonella poisoning, when more than three hundred prisoners and guards became violently ill from eating chicken. (During my stay, we ate some iteration of chicken several times a week; chicken and starch were the prison's dietary staples. I got grossed out and constipated, but nothing else, and lost my spare tire.)

One thing Beast inmates and campers shared, if they stepped out of line, were the 260 SHUs (special housing units), their version of solitary, though each SHU can accommodate two prisoners (and unlimited mice). Apart from one small, frosted glass window, there is no glimmer of the outside world. SHU dwellers spend twenty-three hours a day locked in a dank cell with no bars. Not exactly designed for rehabilitation. Though aware that I would soon be transferred to the satellite camp down the road, I had Googled Canaan too many times and read about too many atrocities not to be uneasy. Behind bars, freezing in a smock, there is not a gigantic leap to paranoia. What if the COs screwed up my incarceration like they did the commissary money? What if due to some overbooking snafu, there was no room at the camp and I had to spend a night or two in a SHU with a Beast murderer or rapist? Based on my Googling, such things were known to happen from time to time.

But then things got moving. The two COs returned to usher me from cubicle to cubicle: fingerprinting, DNA swabbing, and primitive medical and dental exams that boded poorly in the event I got sick. Shivering in my paper-thin smock, I was escorted to an adjoining warehouse to get outfitted in Canaan prison greens and heavy boots, the camp uniform. Each green button-down shirt and matching pair of green pants, as well as the heavy green winter jacket, was affixed with a patch containing one's inmate number. Brock, a soft-spoken African American camper in his thirties from Syracuse, New York, serving fifteen years for drugs, had the prison job of procuring uniforms and bedding. Sporting humungous biceps, he couldn't have been nicer as he brought me different uniform sizes to try on. Normally a large, I opted for XL, assuming I would be wearing sweats and/or thermal underwear underneath. Shivering from cold in my bunk, and the shower logistics, loomed as my biggest concerns. "Thirty days, piece of cake," Brock assured me—amazingly gracious, I marveled, given the length of his own sentence, a year longer than Slatkin's simply for nonviolent drug offenses.

Each camper was given a fluorescent yellow ski cap that could be seen for miles from one of the Beast's guard towers. With my ill-fitting boots instantly causing blisters, but glad to be in warmer clothing and heading away from the Beast to my ultimate destination, I was led outside to an idling van. I climbed into the back; the vehicle was crammed with other campers in prison greens and fluorescent yellow ski caps being shuttled to and from their prison jobs. Were there were an Ivy League for prisons, I mused, Canaan would be Dartmouth due to the color green and its isolation.

"The feds are liars and criminals," a fellow camper said as soon as the door closed. He was peering straight at me as if he read my mind, which he kind of did; I felt an immediate kinship. He introduced himself as Anthony and offered me his fist to bump. They all knew my name and why I was there.

"You're the closest things to a celebrity we have here, Mr. Abbott."

I was also the oldest guy in the van. "What about Paul Manafort?"

"They transferred him out last week. What's Felicity Huffman like?"

"I don't know her," I said, "nor Lori Loughlin."

"What's going to happen to Lori and the others who are fighting it?"

Anthony answered for me: "She's toast. The feds have too many resources; they'll never allow themselves to lose such a high-profile case. The fix is in."

"I hope you're wrong," I said, "but I fear you're right."

"Ninety-five percent of what goes on in our *in*-justice system has nothing to do with the law," Anthony (a former chief of police, I soon discovered) threw in.

—

I had somewhat rosy expectations as to what I was about to experience at the camp, based largely on my wife's description of her one-month "vacation" in Dublin, the women's Otisville of the west. The ladies in charge there had liberally deducted time from her thirty-day sentence, which she attributed to their fear of publicity. Once Marcia casually dropped the name *60 Minutes*, each of the three days she had visited

USA VS ABBOTT

Boston for preliminary, probation, and sentencing hearings, plus travel days, suddenly counted as time served. So did the final weekend of her scheduled stay (people cannot be admitted or discharged over weekends). They also counted the Friday she was discharged at 7:30 a.m. as a full day. As a result, my wife's sojourn was twenty-two days. Based on the same philosophy, Felicity had served only ten days of her fourteen-day sentence. I assumed I would be treated the same. Due to the short duration of her term, my wife was not assigned a job; they began processing her out as soon as she was admitted.

At Dublin, the female inmates had enjoyed a Thanksgiving dinner with all the succulent trimmings, "as good as one gets at home," Marcia said. They had a beauty parlor; the wearing of makeup was encouraged to boost inmate self-esteem. There was a large food prep area with microwaves and other cooking implements where one could prepare one's own meals if so desired—though my wife said the mess hall food wasn't all that bad, on a par with airline food. Come evening, the lady inmates made treats like lollypops and popcorn. They had their own rooms with private bathrooms and showers. They could walk into town and join friends from the outside to window-shop (prisoners were allowed no money) at the Prada outlet store, as long as they returned to camp for the bunk counts.

The inmates pretty much ran the camp themselves and took pride in its cleanliness and appearance. They decorated the Christmas tree with creative aplomb, as if they were at home. They gave one another neck and shoulder massages, though with the exception of one openly gay couple who held hands everywhere they went, there was not a smidgeon of sexuality. Any untoward advances were not tolerated and typically resulted in the offender being sent to the SHU for an extended period.

According to Marcia, many of her fellow inmates were accomplished, educated, cultured women victimized by zealous feds and a system that exploited gray areas of the law and exerted no discretion. Many of the white-collar offenders hadn't been aware that they were breaking the law, and it wasn't because they were stupid. One was a Stanford grad, another a Harvard grad. Two had master's degrees in education. My wife described one inmate as a more beautiful version of Beyoncé. Some had multiple luxury homes around the world. My wife opined that 90 percent of the ladies didn't belong there, that none was remotely dangerous, and no societal purpose was served by their imprisonment. They belonged with their children.

One young Mexican mother had been forced by the cartel to drive a truckload of meth across the border to keep her son from being murdered. My wife related stories she'd heard of how the feds resold one-third of the drugs they seized at the border back to the cartel at twice the price, a corrupt little dance that apparently had been going on for decades. She described the camp culture as a paragon of sisterhood, the antithesis of Tina Fey's *Mean Girls* high school. On the day she was released, December 6, 2019, her prison mates sent her off into the world with a full makeover. When I picked her up, attire aside, she looked ready for an Upper East Side ladies' lunch.

But this wasn't California. It was fucking cold, middle-of-nowhere, butt-fuck (hope not) Pennsylvania, the last thing I could ever have imagined.

A couple minutes later, the van arrived at the Canaan camp. No bars, walls, or barbed wire fences but nonetheless exceedingly bleak through the freezing rain and dense fog. The two metal buildings that comprised the place were barely visible from the van. I was ushered into the dormitory, which was organized like an open barracks: a rectangular grid of eighty double-decker metal bunks (twenty rows of four). Total inmate capacity was 160, though during my stay there were roughly 130 nonviolent offenders all rooming together—still a sardine tin by almost any standard.

Parallel to each pair of bunks was a tiny desk flanked by two narrow lockers, one for each bunkmate. This roughly forty-inch open area between bunk and desk constituted the entire personal living space for two inmates. Prison etiquette mandated that no one set foot in another's personal living space, even to dart through it to get across the building to the facilities. Shortcuts, no matter how benign or expedient, were strictly prohibited, one of the many rules that inmates scrupulously obeyed.

"Broadway" was the sole thoroughfare for inmates to traverse the building and gain access to bathrooms, showers, phones, TV rooms, drinking fountains, and laundry room. Smack in the middle of the grid and considerably wider than the normal space separating bunk from locker, Broadway was as busy as its New York City counterpart, only noisier and more crowded, or so it seemed if you happened to call Broadway your prison address, as was the case of 86702-054. All newcomers were assigned there.

"Good luck sleeping," cackled a snarky inmate on his way to the toilet. My bunk was at the very end of Broadway, less than ten feet from the brightly lit, open bathroom and phone bank, and within earshot of everything else on that boisterous side of the building—universally acclaimed to be the worst location in the camp due to all the inmate traffic (with the exception of the upper bunk, which during my stay remained mercifully unoccupied). Was I being singled out due to my privilege and short sentence? Every inmate literally passed by my bunk several times a day and night—to piss, shit, shower, shave, socialize, do laundry, watch TV, call loved ones …

A newcomer can't possibly know the things he needs in a prison camp, but as I stood there in bewilderment, the necessities—and the humanity of my fellow inmates—began materializing before my eyes. With Anthony taking me under his wing and seemingly directing traffic, I felt like a visiting dignitary as one inmate installed a wafer-thin mattress and quickly made my bed. Others deposited items on my desk: toiletries; loaner sweats (until I could buy my own); towels; prison T-shirts and boxer shorts; toilet paper; laundry bag, extra green uniforms marked 86702-05; Tupperware food bowl and plastic spork. Each time I looked, another food offering appeared from an anonymous source: packets of mackerel, tuna, salmon; crackers; bottles of water; apple; pastry; packet of ramen noodles … This was more than enough to tide me over until commissary in two days, assuming my friend wired the money in time. During my tenure, I made sure to make similar offerings to all new prisoners.

Gesturing at the pair of black plastic sandals at the foot of my bunk, Anthony said, "Wear them at *all times*. Don't go anywhere in this building barefoot or in stocking feet. This place is a Petri dish, which is why we bump fists and don't shake hands. If one inmate gets sick, we all get sick." (This was before anyone knew about the coronavirus.) "Unless you have a heart attack or worse, forget about medical treatment. Last year we had a hepatitis C epidemic, and they didn't do squat."

I mentioned my propensity for kidney stones; I had had at least ten in my life.

"They'll give you ibuprofen and tell you to lie down and drink plenty of water."

I couldn't conceal my alarm. "Have you ever *had* kidney stones? The pain is excru—"

"Worse than childbirth or gunshot wounds, I know. Just don't get 'em."

Nervously, I began guzzling a bottle of water to hydrate. My first of over a dozen kidney stone attacks had been in the early 1980s, in the office of Calvin Klein when I was pitching them on a pantyhose program for Ithaca Industries. My insides felt like they were about to explode (extremely frightening, given that I had no idea what was happening). Assuming I was about to die, I was rushed by ambulance to Bellevue Hospital, where I vomited from pain in the emergency room. Nothing less than constant morphine could relieve the unspeakable agony until I passed my "designer kidney stone." I imagined how moaning and projectile vomiting would go over with 129 hygiene-obsessed convicts living in close quarters, as Anthony took me on a tour of what was to be my home for January 2020. The former chief of police of a small Westchester County town (an ethnic version of Chief Brody in *Jaws*) serving several years for a tax offense, he seemed more like Canaan's mayor as we made the rounds. Along the way, he introduced me to passing inmates, all of whom clearly respected him as one of the camp elders. My reputation had proceeded me; most referred to my sentence as "bullshit," though in the blur of assimilation, I couldn't remember anyone's name. That would come.

My biggest concern was alleviated upon seeing that each stainless steel shower stall was private, with its own dressing area. One could shower for as long as one wanted! The prison consultant had told me showers were limited to three minutes; rather than pay his $250 bill, I should've sued him for emotional damage. One could also drop the proverbial bar of soap with impunity, though Anthony quickly tempered my optimism: "Always wear your sandals, even inside the shower. And rinse out the stall with scalding water before you set foot in it. Many inmates are animals. They piss and shit in the stalls. They jerk off. They hock up phlegm and spit all over the place." As if on cue, someone from one of the stalls hocked phlegm with gusto, noise amplified by the reverberating acoustics. Over the course of my stay, I would become so accustomed to that vile sound emanating from the bathroom and shower echo chambers while I tried to sleep that I dubbed it the "Canaan National Anthem."

Anthony led me past three TV rooms: one for blacks, one for Latinos, one for whites. He let the shock register on my face before smiling. "Relax. Different folks like different programs, that's all. You can watch TV anywhere you want; just bring your own chair and don't mess with the dials. And realize that when it comes to TV watching, you're a peon. There's reverse seniority: the longer your sentence, the more TV say you have."

"As it should be," I said reverently.

"You're here for a short time, so stay in your lane and keep your head down. And never trust an inmate"—Anthony flashed me a no-nonsense glint—"not even me."

We stuck our heads inside the laundry room. A Latino inmate complained to the "mayor" in Spanglish that three of the four washer-driers serving the camp were broken and that the one that worked leaked profusely and required constant mopping. (Over the course of my stay, nothing was done to fix the three broken washer-driers.) While he moped and mopped, the "laundry ranger" seemed to preside over several bags of laundry. As soon as we left, Anthony advised, "He does laundry for several inmates. Do *your own* laundry and steer clear of bartering and the black market. If the guards decide to crack down, guess whose high-profile ass goes to the SHU. You got a target on your back, pal."

Suddenly it was 11:00 a.m.—lunchtime. Like wildebeests, we joined the herd heading out of the dorm to the main building roughly fifty feet away, which housed a dining hall as well as a library, classrooms, a music room (no piano, sad for me; only guitars and bongos), a gym, a medical station (where inmates picked up prescriptions at 6:00 a.m. and were chastised for faking illnesses to avoid work duty), a barber shop (no scissors), a commissary, a visitor's room, and the CO offices. Lest you think our lunch hour unduly early, dinners were served at 3:00 p.m., though occasionally at the chicer 4:00 p.m. hour, depending on the whim of the inmates who worked kitchen duty. They gave you twenty minutes to eat and then herded you out as quickly as possible so they could clean up and dispense with their chores. One didn't mess with the mess hall guys; they handled your food, or at least what passed for food.

As Anthony and I took our place in the chow line, I perused my fellow inmates. Overall, they struck me as a defeated lot with no purpose beyond getting through the day. Virtually every day of my life had been marked with some kind of purpose and hope, and now here I was. Around two-thirds were Caucasian, the rest black and Latino, with a handful of Arabs and Asians thrown in. Anthony gave me the same rough two-to-one breakdown between drug-related versus white-collar crimes. Most were serving multiyear sentences—two to twenty—all for nonviolent offenses. They'd come from much harder places and didn't want to be sent back, so generally were on their best behavior. Before I got too comfortable over this, Anthony said, "There hasn't been a fist fight here in well over a year;

we're overdue, so keep a low profile." When we got to the stack of trays, Anthony advised me to check mine for cleanliness. It was riddled with water droplets, so I picked another one.

Each inmate had his own regular dining seat, and it took Anthony a bit of finagling to find a permanent place for me. One never sat in another inmate's seat, any more than one talked in the middle of another's backswing. Prison and golf, I quickly observed, were remarkably akin. One learned the etiquette before one learned the game, and inmates were quick to chew you out for any breach. Like golf, prison etiquette was extensive and rooted in basic common sense and courtesy. No cutting chow or laundry lines; no entering an inmate's personal living space (apart from Broadway); no shaking hands; no *not* washing your hands after using the bathroom; no venturing anywhere in bare or stocking feet; no using the toilet without spraying the seat with the sanitary solution on hand and wiping it down before and after use; no shutting your metal locker loudly; no inappropriate touching or nudity (which could land one in the SHU). Perhaps prison etiquette was even more pedantic than golf: no Fox News at night; no MSNBC or CNN in the daytime. No TV news whatsoever on weekends. No sitting in another's chair in the TV room. No entering the main building wearing anything but your prison greens (unless you're working out in the gym). No asking a fellow inmate why he was there (though virtually everyone volunteered, since it was the easiest ice breaker). No missing a bunk count; no talking during bunk counts, or any behavior, like skipping work duty, that might cast a bad light on the camp and cause the COs, camp director, or warden to go on a disciplinary rampage. Normally, the COs turned a blind eye to shoddy bed making and much of the camp's black market economy, and the veteran inmates wanted to keep it that way. They were as persnickety about etiquette as any blue-noser at the LA Country Club—which, trust me, required a far more elaborate "conspiracy" to gain admittance than Canaan. When it came to black market goods, especially pills, cell phones, and food smuggled in the back of the building at night, one classic golf adage said it all: keep your head down.

Anthony had plunked me down in a group of middle-aged and older white men. They were talking about the First Step Act, a prison reform bill that President Trump had signed a year ago, but which the "Deep State" had yet to implement. For those inmates over sixty who had exhibited good behavior and taken certain self-improvement courses, their sentences would be cut by one-third. My fellow diners were abuzz with speculation that the camp might lose a quarter of its population at any moment. As I feathered my way into the discussion, they were curious about my case and mystified by my demeanor. There was no way to disguise all the affectations that seven decades at Choate, Princeton, and life in the privileged lane had osmosed into my persona. On that score, I was an oddity, but it worked more to my advantage than against me.

All black and Latino inmates sat together at the far end of the room, but racial tension was nonexistent. Segregation is hunky-dory when conditions and neighborhoods are identical.

My first prison meal consisted of slop that could have passed for rattlesnake or squirrel but was declared chicken; dried out rice that assaulted the esophagus like rock salt; and carrots so overcooked that they had a plastic man-made consistency. "On a par with airline food," my wife had said? I didn't know what airline she was referring to; I certainly had never taken her on any such flight. For IDC, I had traveled to many third world countries and had never been served anything so unappetizing or mysterious, except maybe in rural China.

I kept my disgust to myself. A couple of inmates a few seats down were praising the Canaan fare compared to that of the tougher places they'd recently come from, places like Fort Dix and MDC Brooklyn, where the meat had bubbles and came in colors one had never seen before and couldn't begin to describe. These were soft-spoken, articulate gents—former doctor, former CEO, each serving five years—and their gratitude shamed 86702-054 into silence. With my small plastic spork (not even Hannibal Lector could use it to inflict damage), I played with my slop, moving it from one side of the indented tray to the other like an anorexic girl pretending to eat. While rummaging for edible morsels, I couldn't help but think about the infamous salmonella chicken outbreak, or fantasize about the packets of tuna in my locker.

"Most people gain weight here," said a sixty-ish guy directly across from me, "because all the starch." Terry was the inmate in charge of the library, a plum job and a hub where I hung out a lot during my stay. He gestured toward a morbidly obese man in the chow line clad in a T-shirt and shorts despite the freezing winter weather outside. The only camper not in uniform for obvious reasons, though he could have been outfitted for a license plate. "That guy weighs five hundred and fifteen pounds. Weighed only three hundred twenty-five when he came here a year ago."

"How does he fit into his bunk?"

"One learns to be resourceful."

"What's he in for?" A taboo rookie question, but I received no looks.

"Hard drugs, like all the guys from Maine. We got seven of 'em. Nothing much else to do up there." Terry chuckled darkly. "Sort of like here."

CHAPTER 17

GREGOR

Perhaps the worst part of prison was waking up and realizing that I was there. A Hollywood pitchman might describe the depression I experienced as *"Groundhog Day* meets Kafka's *Metamorphosis"* (in which the main character—Gregor, to add insult to injury—wakes up to discover he's been transformed into a giant cockroach).

Awakening as a giant cockroach at 5:30 a.m. to the blaring prison loudspeaker ("Pill line, pill line, p-p-p-p-p-p-pill line!"; or on snow days, "Landscape crew, landscape crew, landscape crew, report for duty immediately, you filthy animals!"), I wasn't sure I had slept at all. Certainly not the deep REM sleep essential for rejuvenation. The mattress was too thin to cushion the bunk metal, and there were no pillows on which to rest one's head—or suffocate a snoring inmate. Physical comfort wasn't the half of it. I slept with one eye open, in a state of limbo between sleep and consciousness, aware on some level of all that swirled around my bunk. Sandals clomped incessantly as a steady stream of prisoners traipsed by to piss, shit, shower, shave, or shoot the breeze. Lest you think I'm overly repetitive, try living with it day after day, night after night. My locker was unlocked and rife for pilfering. Not that I had reason to distrust anyone I had met so far, other than that they were criminals and many of them poor. Not many could afford to return from commissary looking like Santa, as I had, with a bulging laundry sack of goodies (mostly water) slung over his shoulder.

My friend had wired the money in the nick of time. From behind the protective plexiglass at 6:00 a.m., the forty-ish Caucasian inmate responsible for dispensing commissary items had asked me, "Are you the father of Infamous Billa?"

A *New York Post* reader, I assumed warily, recalling how that rag had trashed my son. "Yes, I am the *very proud* father." I made sure to emphasize the italicized words. "You from New York?"

"Pennsylvania. I listen to your son's music on YouTube and *love* it! He's amazing!"

So, Malcolm's gangsta rap has reached the gangstas, I thought happily, which gave my spirits a sixty-second lift before returning to real time.

In anticipation of the 5:30 a.m. loudspeaker, I went to bed early in the beginning, shortly after the 9:00 p.m. bunk count. Layered in sweats and thermals, I thankfully wasn't cold. Veteran inmates were less fastidious about retiring, and my bunk vicinity was where the action was. Many stood a few feet from my bunk, conversing and laughing without regard for the fact that someone might be trying to sleep. Nocturnal loudness clearly wasn't part of prison etiquette. Each time I was about to nod off, a toilet flush would reverberate. Several times a night, shitters and showerers would sing the "Canaan National Anthem" from their echo chambers. I had long ago assumed my sense of smell was shot with age. To my wife's dismay, I was never able to detect the pungent pot emanating from Malcolm's room. Sleeping ten feet from Canaan's glaringly lit, open bathroom, which on one occasion backed up into the shower and laundry rooms, I can report that my olfactory senses experienced an acute reawakening.

Then there were the phones, four for 130 prisoners, all within spitting distance of my bunk. Inmates wanting to talk to loved ones first had to nail the voice recognition required to get connected. The slightest deviation from the original recording one had set up required repeating oneself until the super-persnickety computer was satisfied. It was frustrating enough saying "Greg Abbott … Greg Abbott … Greg Abbott" over and over to call my family but utterly infuriating listening to others try to connect while I tried to sleep.

During one of my very first nights, I kept hearing over and over, "José … José … José …" José had wisely kept it simple but still couldn't crack the code. After roughly fifty "Josés," I arose from my bunk long enough to ask him, "Would you like me to take a crack at it?" José rolled his eyes in a beleaguered fashion, whereupon I fell back into my bunk and began counting "Jose's" like sheep. Meanwhile, his fellow Latinos gathered outside their TV room (twenty-five feet from my bunk), elevating the dorm's decibel level the later it got. A mariachi band couldn't have been more unsettling. The Latinos kept different hours from the rest of us, but it was hard to begrudge them, given that they were laughing and having fun. No big whoop if my sleep wasn't REM. It wasn't as if I had an important business meeting to attend the next day. The world was functioning just fine without me, a stark reality that perhaps bothered me more than anything else during those first desolate nights. I pined for my family every single night.

Then there were the harsh lights glaring down from the ceiling twenty-four hours a day, cruel and unusual punishment that forced any aspiring sleeper to wear his yellow ski cap and pull it down over his eyes. Blocking florescent lights with a florescent cap—all because fifteen months ago, a camper had escaped to meet a hooker in a local motel. Such an event in Waymart had all the subtlety of a ticker tape parade. To make matters worse, in making her escape, the hooker backed into a cop car. The whoremonger was unceremoniously sent back to the tough prison from whence he came; meanwhile, the rest of us were still being punished for his transgression. Whoever he was, I cursed his memory. I cursed lots of people—Singer, Rosen, Slatkin, the lying *Wall Street Journal*—during those first few desolate nights.

Observing veterans, I learned to combat the lights by draping an extra blanket over the length of my bunk and extra towels over each end, creating a kind of pup tent. That cut the glare but not enough to dispense with the cap over eyes. The extra blanket and towels were held in place on the vacant top bunk with library books I had borrowed. With apologies to Emily Dickenson: "There is no frigate, nor friggin' weight, like a book." According to the vaunted handbook, pup-tenting was forbidden, but the COs looked the other way so long as the tent was folded up and out of sight during daytime.

The cherry on the sleepless sundae was the densely tattooed guy from Bangor, Maine, stationed one bunk up from me on Broadway. His loud, wake-the-dead snores riddled my prone body with tremors that put me on constant edge until all I could think of was the wood-chipper scene in *Fargo*—a lovely prison bedtime image, no? Even the inmates in the far reaches of the dorm bitched about him, but what right did *they* have to complain? This guy was practically on top of me! I tried all sorts of earplugs; all were useless.

GREG ABBOTT

With 129 roommates, I was reminded of when my kids were young and I used to growl in Scrooge-like jest, "I *hate* sleepovers!" Still, I looked forward to bedtime as an opportunity to work hours off my sentence without being conscious. Each wake-up meant one day less remaining on my sentence; but it also meant *Groundhog Day* meets *Metamorphosis*—"déjà vu all over again".

—

I did not attend a single 6:00 a.m. breakfast. I'm not crazy about breakfast food, and lunch was at 11:00 a.m. After my first commissary purchase, I had plenty of food items in my locker for any hunger pangs or chow line abominations that might arise, so breakfast was jettisoned in favor of emotional maintenance. I hauled myself out of bed, slipped on my sandals, and made my zombie-like shuffle to the bathroom (the only time I praised God for its proximity) to brush teeth, wash face, and un-dishevel hair alongside other cockroaches; then shuffle back to the bunk to slip on a green uniform over the thermal underwear I had slept in. While I dressed, fellow cockroaches scurried about. We didn't speak or brush antennae; our mutual annoyance was a given. I was invading their thoroughfare; they were invading my personal space.

Once dressed, I went to the library to answer the paltry number of emails on one of their five antiquated computers. Surfing the internet was not possible. Signing in involved a fingerprint scan and entering 86702-054 along with another nine-digit serial number. There were precious few people on my email list. We weren't allowed to bring contact lists, and you could only receive an email if that notified person first responded to the laboriously complex prison protocol. Once logged out, I returned to the dorm to call my family or a friend. Each call was limited to fifteen minutes, and each minute punctuated with: "You are speaking to an inmate at a federal prison." How nice for my kids to hear, though it turned adult stomachs too. Once you hung up, even on a voice machine, you were locked out of the phones for thirty minutes. The same policy applied to email. They did whatever they could to isolate you.

At loose ends, wanting to seize the day but with nothing to seize, I ambled back *again* to the library to peruse the ten-day-old *Wall Street Journal* on Terry's desk and bitch. "Three times this rag made up quotes from me out of thin air. Stupid stuff I'd never say. Even threw in the F-word. Never spoke to them once."

"Fake news," said Terry, a vehement Trumper who then told me about his ten-year tax case. "The feds seized my home and emptied my bank accounts, so I couldn't afford to mount a legal defense."

"Gee, you don't sound Cuban. What was your defense?"

"To challenge the legitimacy of the IRS." Rather than protest the obvious, I half listened to Terry's history lecture on the IRS as he dug in on esoteric legalities, conspiracy theories, and the Illuminati. "I'm gonna win my appeal. You watch."

During the first couple of numb, sluggish mornings, I read random passages from a book by Joe Torre, as told to So-and-So, about the Yankee dynasty in the 1990s, reliving game situations long familiar to me. It was all this sleep-deprived, brain-dead cockroach could process. When the book vanished from the library one morning, I was fucking livid. As St. Bernard's headmaster had once quipped to me about his faculty, "The pettier the issue, the bigger the stakes."

It took me a couple days to break through my lugubrious inertia and haul myself down the hall to the gym. My workouts consisted of riding the stationary bike for forty-five minutes while watching ESPN (though the gym was too noisy to hear the commentators) and doing push-ups. There were no barbells, which could double as weapons; Canaan took no chances. Serious workouts were more of the improvisational *Rocky IV* variety and out of my league: balancing a giant log over one's shoulders to do squats, or over one's abs to do inclined sit-ups; loading baskets with cinderblocks for various sorts of unorthodox lifting. Getting my endorphins flowing after months of Varsity Blues paralysis elevated my spirits. Between emails, phone calls, shooting the breeze with Terry, and workouts, perhaps prison life wasn't so monotonous after all—until I glanced at the clock and saw that it was 8:30 a.m.!

Our entire physical universe could fit on the head of a pin, or so it seemed; just the dorm, main building, and the short, wind-blown walk in between. The lack of space was counterbalanced by ... the surplus of time. With snow blanketing the ground, freezing temperatures, and wind gusts (I think I saw the sun thrice during my stay), neither the icy basketball court nor walking trail were viable. The short walk between dorm and main building often teemed with seagulls, who flew over from a nearby garbage dump to get whatever prison fare certain inmates fed them—a negligible culinary upgrade, I suspect.

Even more discomfiting was the sight of the Beast, a chilling vista one couldn't escape whenever one returned to the dorm. Only from that distant vantage point could one grasp its enormity: a gargantuan concrete monolith, adorned with swirling barbed wire and seven guard towers, and a circumference of over one mile. What saddened me most was the humungous Old Glory flapping proudly above it. I became more incensed after reading in several books that the United States has 5 percent of the world's population and 25 percent of the world's prisoners. This alarming stat includes Russia and China and represents a scholarly consensus. Today we are the most incarcerated society in human history, with a greater per capita prison population than that of the USSR at the height of Stalin's Gulag era. Why weren't any of the presidential candidates talking about this?

Already listless with boredom, with a whole day of sensory deprivation ahead of me, I typically returned to my bunk after workouts to crack open the crossword puzzle book an inmate had given me, only to conk out like a rock. The sleep between 8:30 a.m. and lunchtime, whether fifteen minutes or an hour, was the deepest and most refreshing I got at Canaan. No need for my pup tent.

Time flowed like molasses. Seconds turned to minutes, minutes to hours, hours to days; therein lay the root of my misery and degradation. "Time flies when you're having fun," but what a taskmaster it is when you're not! Like most of you, I was accustomed to spending life neck high in a river of stimuli, addiction enabled by iPhone, computer, and other stimulus addicts, and now suddenly it was cold turkey. With no piano, I planned to meditate my sentence away—*stay* with the boredom, *be* with the boredom, until I transformed myself into a great being. As one such great being Nelson Mandela had quipped, "In my country, we go to prison first, then become president." Problem was, throughout the entire camp, there wasn't a single comfortable place in which to sit, close one's eyes, open one's palms to the universe, and breathe. At home, I meditated in the privacy of my bedroom with flickering candles; my level of mastery didn't remotely encompass being a spectacle among convicts or shutting out endless distractions. The only places where one could be alone were the shower and toilet stalls, more conducive to singing the "Canaan National Anthem" than achieving nirvana. I tried meditating at night in the confines of my pup tent, but with prisoners constantly passing by to fulfill the panoply of bodily functions, it was like meditating in the middle of Grand Central Station. Not a smidgeon of peace or solitude anywhere.

How I had woefully underestimated the gloom! My idealism of making prison an enriching experience was so overwhelmed by boredom that my inner workings turned darkly philosophical and in hindsight overly dramatic. What the fuck was *I* doing here! Me! I had lived a good life, was a good person with a record of good deeds, and this was humiliating! Would I emerge from prison embittered, hard-hearted, unrecognizable to family and friends? The end of January seemed a year away.

Despite most inmates' noble efforts to be good citizens and make the most of a shit situation, despite that we were in a camp and not a hard-core prison, we were all being degraded every second by the agonizing water-torture drip of time, lives trashed to varying degrees by public humiliation, federal seizures of property, isolation from loved ones and the outside world. Forced to shut off large portions of ourselves and never get too personal with anyone, we may have been civil on the outside but tragic on the inside. "Zoo specimens," in the words of Angela Davis, not someone I normally quote.

Wondering what their backstory was, I observed the rather sizable underclass of dead-eyed prisoners who walked around like zombies and slept most of the day, who had no friends and looked like they were at death's door. I began to wallow in all the dystopian pain around me. I took little solace in the fact that I was serving a month, while my fellow inmates had been incarcerated for years and still had years to go! I mean, it wasn't as if I were Hurricane Carter. Who was I to whine when chubby, long-haired George was serving twenty years for selling weed? Undercover feds had been his largest customer, building him up until it was newsworthy to bust him. Your tax dollars at work. His newborn son at the time of arrest was now ten; his five-year-old son now fifteen. When his father died, he wasn't allowed to attend the funeral. Meanwhile, weed has become legal in many states, and the House passed a resolution to legalize it nationally. It wouldn't become the law of the land until the Republican Senate ratified it and the president signed it. Fat chance, but twenty years for a nonviolent offense that is verging on no longer being illegal? George wouldn't harm a fly. Once released, he would likely go back to selling weed. It was all he knew; it had once made him a millionaire. Fine with me. Compared to what the drug companies are getting away with, making billions killing our kids with opioids (including three sons in their twenties of friends of mine), George's was a noble profession.

―

January 4, 2020. Fifth day at Canaan and my wedding anniversary. "Abbott, report to the CO offices!" Not for a conjugal visit but official business and orientation. I was glad to have something new and different to do. I was also eager to learn my actual release date, so I could begin a true countdown.

First was the prison shrink, who seemed to need me more than I needed him. Then I moved to the next-door cubicle of Officer Dunstone, head of administrative matters, who proved to be the most likeable CO in the joint, simply because he wasn't verbally abusive or on any power trip. That said, I was aghast to learn that he wasn't granting me any time reductions on my sentence. When I cited my wife's and Felicity's lenient treatment at Dublin, he didn't see the relevance. He had no records of Marcia Abbott or Felicity Huffman, only the court decision on me, which he considered his marching orders. My multiple court appearances in Boston not only didn't count, but the mere suggestion that they should made him laugh incredulously. Nor did he agree to release me on the Friday before the final weekend. Nor would the day of my release count as a day served. I was to serve "twenty-nine days *and* a wake up." My only hope was a Hail Mary charm offensive. I had connected like Doug Flutie before in business, fundraising, and life, so why not give the pigskin a fling?

"Wait till Anderson Cooper and *60 Minutes* hear about this!" I tried to say it with a straight face; my awkward chutzpah got a laugh out of him. Hungry to talk to someone besides a prisoner and kill time any way I could, I did my best to chat him up and make him like me enough to consider throwing me a bone. He actually seemed curious about this rarefied guy with the rarefied crime and asked a lot of questions. While I told him about the FBI raid, sick daughter, hyenas with cameras, coercive plea—employing humor and evoking empathy whenever possible—he took it all in like the genuine human being he wasn't supposed to be.

"Frankly, I don't know why the hell you're here."

"Thank you—that means a lot." Here I was, five days into it, and already grateful for crumbs. "There are a few other guys, in my opinion, who shouldn't be here. Everyone cherry-picks their facts—'cept me, of course—but seems to me that George and Anthony got the shaft."

"I would agree with you on those guys," Dunstone conceded. "Twenty years for selling weed is ... extreme. And Anthony—they wanted to make an example of him because of his chief of police position. There are more cases like theirs, where the punishment doesn't fit the crime." Dunstone looked at me with a twinkle. "But I'm not the federal judge. It'll be over before you know it. It's the shortest sentence I've ever seen here."

"But my wife ..."

"Your best bet is to call your buddy Trump for a pardon."

"'Tis harder to nail the phone voice recognition," I quipped, in biblical *eye of the needle* cadence, "than to get Trump to grant me a pardon in the middle of impeachment proceedings." On that semijocular note, I left with a spring in my step, simply for having had a normal conversation with a nonconvict. Dunstone's smooth-as-Vaseline manner had made my administrative ass-fucking painless as I headed to orientation.

My orientation in the visitor's room with tall, lanky Officer MacDonald, a self-proclaimed comedian, included three other newly arrived inmates: John, a defense attorney from Long Island in his early sixties; Austin, a slightly unhinged thirty-five-year-old white-collar offender whose lack of boundaries and instant immersion in black market activity made him a consensus SHU candidate; and former US Congressman Chaka Fattah of Philadelphia, who was serving a ten-year sentence for bribery-related charges. Newcomers all, we were Broadway neighbors.

My orientation had been delayed by the New Year's Eve break, so I already knew most of the ropes. All MacDonald's orientation taught me was that he loved to call inmates by their incorrect names and hated New York City.

"So, Abrams," MacDonald addressed me, peering at his clipboard, "I see you're from New York. I assume you don't like dogs." The "Jew York" implication was clear, as if he were conjuring up Auschwitz and rabid German shepherds while Hebrew-izing my surname.

"Actually, I love dogs. Our family has three ... or did until we had to euthanize our dachshund on Christmas Eve."

"Dachshund! That's not a *real* dog."

Asshole! Our family wept at her passing. You'd think he'd approve of the German breed. "It's a big dog in a small dog's body."

"I see we have a wise guy on our hands. Well, Abrams, you look in good shape for seventy."

"Thanks, but I'm not seventy quite yet. I'm still the age teenage boys joke about."

"Trust me, *here* you're seventy. And because you're seventy, and because your sentence is basically the blink of an eye, I'm not assigning you any work detail."

Not such an asshole after all! When I returned to the library, I was almost trampled by inmates filing out through the doorway on their way back to the dorm. They were in a collective funk, especially the ones under fifty. One prisoner "Up Top" at the max pen had stabbed another in the eye with a homemade shiv. The Beast was on total lockdown, meaning that all its prisoners were confined to their cells until further notice. Meaning that some campers had to go up there to make their meals—three meals a day for 1,400 inmates—and do their laundry, by all accounts eight hours a day of nonstop, backbreaking work. A list of the campers assigned to various work details was about to be posted in the dorm, and everyone was heading there like cattle to find out their fate.

"Relax," Terry told me, as I turned to head back there myself. "I'm sure MacDonald exempted you from work detail, right?"

"That's what he told me. Is he true to his word?"

"Not always, but trust me, he's not going to send you Up Top, not at your age and length of sentence. Your finances will take a hit though. No twelve cents an hour for you."

"Twelve cents an hour?"

"That's the entry level prison wage. If you work your way up the corporate ladder, like me, you can earn as much as twenty-eight cents an hour. That's where the *big* money is."

I had to see for myself. I tiptoed through the seagulls, whose eerily restless Hitchcockian vibe caused me to guard my eyeballs. Once in the dorm, I made a beeline for the bulletin board where inmates were congregating. Craning my neck through the crowd to get a glimpse at the newly posted list, I saw that MacDonald had honored his word. Neither Abbott nor Abrams was anywhere to be found. Other less lucky inmates were bitterly resigned, pissed off, or macho about it. They'd been through this drill before and knew the toil that awaited them Up Top. Feeling the guilt of a perfectly healthy greatest generation male whose flat feet disqualified him from fighting Hitler, I also felt a surge of gratitude for my geriatric privilege. Not being assigned a work detail and having had reasonably affable encounters with the guards, who clearly considered my sentence farcical, had shaken me a bit out of my funk. Suddenly I was determined to shed my cockroach identity and make the most out of the twenty-six days (and a wake up) remaining on my sentence.

—

"The journey of a thousand miles," said Chairman Mao, "begins with a single step." My first step on the long march to sanity was doing my own laundry for the first time since college. (If you haven't gathered by now that I'm privileged, then you've just been skimming this book. But don't feel bad; my white skin has gotten thick by now.) The simple after-dinner task of toting laundry bag and detergent to the laundry room, waiting my turn to shove dirty clothes into the one functional washer for 130 inmates, then wet clothes into the one functional dryer, mopping the floor of perpetual leaks, and finally folding and organizing my precious stuff, made me feel much better about … *moi*.

So did the other early-evening ritual: the long, hot shower. The water pressure was worthy of a five-star hotel, though you first had to rinse out the stall thoroughly with scalding water and block from your mind the ubiquitous grime throughout the shower section. The water was hard and full of minerals, resulting in dry skin, but the shower water pressure was Canaan's sole luxury. Simple things like clean laundry in the locker, feeling snug in newly washed sweats and thermals, felt like major achievements. It put me in the mood for nightly chess matches with some truly good players.

The drab gaming tables were on the opposite side of the dorm from my bunk—"Upper Broadway." My first chess opponent, a super-intense Chinese psychiatrist at the tail end of his sentence for Medicare fraud, beat me to a pulp in the beginning. It took me a few nights of spirited rivalry to solve and dominate him, just before he was released and went home to Rochester, New York, where a halfway house awaited him. I enjoyed getting the last laugh (at least where chess was concerned; I mean, he was *leaving*, but leaving a loser, which I knew irked him). I missed the rivalry, but even more the idiot-savant way he referred to prosecutors in his Chinese accent as "persecutors."

My next opponent, a shadowy heroin dealer/addict with scoliosis, who called himself "the only Jew from Maine," had never once lost to the Chinese shrink and played at a much higher level. His aggressive first two or three moves put me on my heels, hemmed me in, destroyed me. Worse was the arrogance in his beady eyes. In between massacres, he took illicit smoking breaks outside at the back of the building, where I also suspect he smuggled in pills, both of which could land him in the SHU. During those breaks, I experimented with the chess pieces and devised ways to neutralize his pesky openings. Soon I was capturing his queen, game after game. After I beat him eight out of nine games, the only Jew from Maine switched to playing poker and dice.

Chess involved no betting, but at night, much of the dorm turned into a casino. Inmates brought armfuls of mackerel packets—the Bitcoin of Canaan—to poker and dice games, but I stayed clear of gambling. Most took place in the back of the building; same with the black market transactions, so I refused to venture anywhere near there. Busybody and fellow Broadway newcomer Austin told me the rumor that last year a hooker had been smuggled into the camp for the price of one hundred mackerel. "What did she do with the mackerel once she did the inmate?" I asked him. Austin had no answer; much like the press, he was into sensationalism, not accuracy. I wondered where in the open dormitory a hooker could have possibly plied her trade, before deducing by process of elimination the shower stalls. A stand-up girl or figment of Austin's imagination?

I was constantly being hustled by inmates offering services for packets of mackerel. Unable to afford certain commissary items, they needed to supplement their meager income from prison jobs. A Latino offered to do my laundry. A persistent Jordanian who worked kitchen crew (whom everyone called "Habibi," Arabic for "darling") offered to make me "shish kebabs, burgers, fish, anything you want" with smuggled ingredients. Trying to drum up business, he presented me with a delicious chicken quesadilla gratis while I played chess. Certain inmates offered to cut my hair at the barber shop. A muscle-bound Caucasian offered personal trainer sessions. An Egyptian doctor offered to teach me Arabic. Apart from a long overdue haircut from a cocaine offender, which proved the worst tonsorial butchering of my life, I followed Anthony's advice to never trust an inmate and kept a wide berth.

Retiring for the night on my rock-hard bunk, with well-earned chess victories dancing like sugarplums in my head, a locker full of clean laundry, a hot shower, and a body slowly getting into shape, filled me with glowing accomplishment and led to somewhat better sleep. But then I awoke the next morning as Gregor the cockroach to begin the metamorphosis anew.

Since I couldn't meditate my sentence away, perhaps I could read it away. The first of the seven books I ultimately read, which Terry nabbed for me from the library because it was so popular, was *After Life: My Journey from Incarceration to Freedom* by Alice Marie Johnson. This remarkable black woman had served twenty-two years in federal prison for a low-level drug offense committed back when she was a pregnant teenager and financially destitute. All Alice did to earn a life sentence was make a few "Blue Star likes Endicott Steel" calls for the drug cartel.

Drug sentences are largely determined by the type and quantity of drugs involved, though Alice never saw or used any drugs herself. US laws don't make any such distinctions. Drug perpetrators are punished the same regardless of their personal role in the offense, though usually the mules like Alice at the bottom of the distribution totem pole fare worse than kingpins. It's all about connections. Kingpins know other big-time criminals to rat out to reduce their sentences. That's how the game is played. It's exactly how Varsity Blues was played. "Be a snitch. Give us bodies to entrap," says the USA police state to incentivize criminals. Thanks to the tireless efforts of Kim Kardashian, who got wind of the case, Alice was eventually pardoned by President Trump, after being turned down several times for whatever reason by President Obama. I found Alice's autobiographical account riveting; as her loveliness shone through the pages, I became emotionally involved in her travails. My opinion of Kim Kardashian as a lacquered floozy gave way to respect.

Even President Trump did his part to enliven prison life. His offing of Iranian General Qassan Soleimani galvanized much of the prison and made me forget, at least for a moment, where I was. The pugnacious Canaan Trumpers (either too old or shielded by dubious doctor notes for work detail) were on fire with glee over the assassination and itching for more. Fox News served up the juiciest red meat we ever got at Canaan (Wednesday was hamburger day, the burgers the size of Holy Communion wafers). While one Fox commentator after another lauded Trump for his courage, I thought more about Iranian reprisals and took comfort that we were in a safe place. For thirty minutes, I was glad to be in Canaan, until the news got stale. While we watched a huge crowd protesting in Teheran, holding anti-American placards and crying "Death to America," a Philadelphia firebrand named Mike proclaimed like Patrick Henry, "Why don't we just bomb the shit out of 'em, right now! How easy that would be! I'm mean, they're all right there in one place. One bomb and badda-bing, they're gone!"

Was he joking? I wasn't sure; he sounded earnest.

By then, the main issue had shifted to the impeachment hearings. On the night of the Democratic presidential debate, some of the Trumpers had obtained special CO dispensation to watch Fox News at night, normally a no-no. The Trumpers requested this Fox News access (in the visitors' room near the CO offices and thus out of the way) not to see the debate but to watch the rally that Trump had scheduled for the exact same time. With the COs solidly pro-Trump and the camp free of disciplinary issues, permission was a virtual rubber stamp. I had seen enough cluster-fuck-narcissist debates to loathe their uselessness, regardless of political party, so I joined the racially mixed Trumpers in the visitors' room mainly for the banter. Much to the group's irritation, Fox News didn't air the rally. Instead of listening to Tucker Carlson, they switched to the Democratic debate in order to heckle the candidates. The nastiest barbs were reserved for Pocahontas, whose scolding demeanor was not well received. By acclimation—86702-054 abstaining—it was decided that if Pocahontas ran sans loincloth in our open dorm at midnight, past 130 horny inmates who hadn't touched a female in years, she wouldn't get any takers. For the first and only time in my life, my heart went out to Elizabeth Warren.

The next morning as I entered the library, Mike, fresh from watching Trump's favorite morning show, *Fox and Friends*, was in a froth over Judge Andrew Napolitano. "He's advocating Trump's impeachment, for Chrissake! Fox should fire his ass! He's a fucking Democrat."

"He's not a Democrat."

"What the fuck do *you* know?"

Entertainment-starved inmates looked up from their computers, no doubt hoping for an old-fashioned fistfight to pierce their boredom. "The judge is a good friend of mine. That's how the fuck I know. We went to college together. I've known him for over fifty years."

On that note, I headed down the hall to the gym, hoping my name-dropping and showing Mike up wouldn't have repercussions. An erudite friend whom I hadn't seen in years—so impressed with my daughter that he dubbed her "the next evolution of mankind"—suddenly popped into my mind. Son of Catherina Graham (owner of the *Washington Post* during Watergate), he used to teach English at Bard College, as well as to inmates at the Eastern New York Correctional Facility as part of the Bard Prison Initiative. Several years ago, the prison debate team challenged the Harvard College Debate Union to a debate. The inmates even agreed to defend a point of view with which they fiercely disagreed, a common practice in debate competition: "Resolved: Public schools in the United States should have the ability to deny enrollment to undocumented students." As a Princeton man (albeit defrocked), I'm delighted to report that the prison debate team cleaned Harvard's clock. Given the street smarts of prisoners, the result didn't surprise me, though the Canaan population needed work. I couldn't imagine Mike, Terry, and his cohorts advocating the position: "Resolved: President Donald J. Trump should be impeached." Mike wasn't stupid, just stuck in dogma—a prison in its own right. After a few days of listening to Mike and others spew strident right-wing inanities and only get angrier, it dawned on me that educational enlightenment might be a prisoner's path out of hell. I would soon learn that rehabilitation had long ago been forsaken by our system in favor of steeper punishments, that society didn't care a lick about its prisoners, perhaps because so many of them were black and brown. Apart from some parlor room discussions with other "socially liberal" white people over what for us was a strictly theoretical topic, I confess that I hadn't really cared all that deeply about prisoners either until being one myself.

CHAPTER 18

A PHD IN THIRTY DAYS

"In America," said Anthony, during one of our talks in his room (he was the only inmate with a room because he took care of a rescue dog), "prisoners are human debris. The feds trash our lives without giving a shit. They seize property—the forfeiture laws in this country are barbaric—then let us rot. There's not a single adult in the United States whom the feds can't arrest and convict if they want. They throw anyone they so choose into prison and treat us like animals. I mean, look how they treated poor Al."

Al, a sixty-something inmate confined to a wheelchair, had "true gentleman" written all over him. Back in early autumn, well before my arrival, Al had slipped and fallen on the slick tiles of the shower room floor, something I'm surprised didn't happen more often. A few times in my sandals, I almost bit the dust myself on that treacherous ice rink. Despite Al's inability to walk, the prison didn't pay for an x-ray for almost *two months*! Barred from using his own health insurance, he was at the warden's mercy. The eventual x-ray revealed a broken femur and pelvis, but by then, Al was also coughing up blood, which the prison medics attributed to the incompatibility of the pain medications, steroids, and ibuprofen he was taking. Our rapport was so instant that I would wheel him around the dorm when he needed to get somewhere. I don't recall what his crime was, only that he'd been sentenced by a ninety-seven-year-old judge! After yet *another two months* of dithering, Canaan was *finally* sending him to Scranton tomorrow to diagnose his additional symptoms.

He told me this as I wheeled him to his bunk after dinner. I never saw him again. From veteran inmates, I learned that the Scranton tests revealed he had advanced bone cancer, something they should have learned promptly after his shower room fall over four months ago. Who knows what could have been done at that point? The prison's "solution" to Al's bone cancer was to ship him off to another penal facility to wash their hands of him and the medical expenses he represented. Rumor had it that Al had strong political connections in Pennsylvania and that a lawsuit was inevitable, but I have no idea whether Al is even alive at this point. Whatever his crime, could it have been worse than Canaan's neglect?

Then there was Clarence, an eighty-two-year-old black man with several missing teeth, imprisoned for failing to declare a couple of winning $1,000 lottery tickets on his income tax. A two-month sentence (twice mine) for depriving the state of roughly $600? Would a white guy have been imprisoned for this? During Clarence's stay, Canaan refused to fill his prescription for prostate cancer pills due to their steep price tag. I was told that Clarence entered Canaan with a PSA of zero and left two months later (in my first week) with a PSA of nearly 4.0, a spike that any prostate aficionado will tell you is dire. Clarence's life didn't matter, possibly because he was black—certainly because he was a prisoner.

Stories abounded about Canaan's medical indifference—they were part of camp folklore—but I can speak from firsthand experience. Halfway through my sentence, my urine turned dark from blood, despite obsessive water drinking. No matter how much water I guzzled, my urine got darker, and I feared my self-fulfilling prophesy of kidney stones. One evening, it turned so dark that I resolved to visit the medical station the next morning, before sunrise to coincide with pill line. Meanwhile, on my way to the chess table, my right sandal slipped on some water outside someone's bunk area. My leg came out from under me and slid violently forward, causing my right knee with the torn ACL to buckle and come out of its socket. In a nanosecond, I did a split and slammed down hard on the concrete floor squarely on my hip.

Quickly I snapped my knee back into its socket; after a few seconds, the blinding pain abated. My hip had also taken a beating. I was able to get up, shake it off, and even win at chess, but the next morning was a different story. I couldn't bend enough to touch my right foot and needed to enlist a passing convict to help slip on my sneaker. My extremely tender right hip was the size of a watermelon. I managed to walk without much pain, but the slightest pressure even from sitting was excruciating. On my way to the med station, I passed the library and stopped in long enough to show Terry my cartoonishly swollen hip. "Jesus," he said, laughing, "you look like Kim Kardashian."

"Don't disparage my new hero."

Once at the med station, I had to wait for the plethora of prisoners to get their prescriptions, one by one. As soon as they cleared out, the medic tried to close the door in my face. "You're out of uniform, and this is pill line."

"I can't put on my uniform. I have an emergency."

"Don't you understand English? This is *pill line*. For medical care, you'll need to fill out a form and make an appointment."

"I think I may have broken my hip."

"You're walking perfectly fine." He scanned me up and down with disgust. "If your hip was broken, you couldn't walk. If you're faking to miss work detail, I'll make sure you're thrown into the SHU for a good long time."

"I don't *have* work detail. Can't you see the bulge in my sweatpants, or do I need to pull them down? All I want is an x-ray."

Reluctantly, he allowed me to enter his sanctum but began busily gathering his papers as if to leave—a man in a hurry.

"I had a horrible fall last evening. This morning, I woke up with this giant contusion, or hematoma, or whatever you call it. Can't even put on my shoe. I'm seventy. I need an x-ray!"

With a put-upon sigh, the medic took down my name and inmate number and entered them into his computer, which surely told him that I would be released in two weeks, give or take. Medically and financially, Canaan wanted no part of me. They'd already received $45,000 in federal money for my touch-down and wanted to keep as much of it as possible. "Can't schedule an x-ray until next week."

"But it's Thursday!"

"So, take ibuprofen and lie down."

"Ibuprofen? I also have blood in my urine and a history of kidney stones."

This new wrinkle pushed the surly functionary over the edge. Clearly, closing up shop by 6:30 a.m. took precedence over my hip or urinary tract. I wondered whether he had ever taken the Hippocratic oath or even knew what it was. "Jesus Christ, Abbott, it's not as if you're having a stroke or heart attack!"

"At my age, shouldn't this be looked into?" How I was itching to throw Al in his face!

"We'll call you next Tuesday and schedule an x-ray. Now, get the hell out of here ... before I file a report on you!"

I never heard from Canaan's medical people again. A few nights later, around 4:00 a.m., I awoke with a bathroom urge, as is the norm for men my age with enlarged prostates. My urine was darker than apple juice. Standing all by myself in the middle of the brightly lit bathroom, it felt eerie. For the first time since I had arrived, I was totally alone. My 129 roommates were sleeping, snoring, talking in their sleep, breathing heavily, passing gas. Using my index finger as a wand, I pretended to conduct it all like an orchestra: the Canaan Philharmonic.

Due to strict no-nudity rules and lack of privacy, there had been no opportunity until now to examine my bruise. I glanced in all directions to make absolutely sure no one was lurking, then quickly pulled down my sweats and thermals to see what my hip looked like in the mirror above the sink. I had never beheld a bruise so massive; it was shocking. My entire lower back was a sheet of jet-black, as was my right leg going down to my knee. The whole shebang was shaped like Africa, the Dark Continent. My conically swollen hip was a dead ringer for Mount Kilimanjaro.

—

"No one truly knows a nation," wrote Nelson Mandela, "until one has been inside its jails. A nation should not be judged by how it treats its highest citizens, but its lowest ones."

I realize I was in a camp, not Up Top, which warehouses some of the most dangerous dudes America has to offer. Not once in my month at Canaan did I feel in physical danger or come into contact with anyone I deemed scary; not once did I detect a racial or sexual overtone. The worst it got was one night when, retrieving a water bottle from my locker with kidney stones on my mind, I carelessly shut the metal door too loudly. A powerfully built doctor, serving a multiyear sentence for Medicare fraud, rushed around from the bunk on the other side and shouted at me so everyone could hear: "You woke me up! You are the most inconsiderate asshole I've ever met in my life!" I stood there mortified as he kept yelling. From that point on, we ignored each other—until the silent feud ended a week later as he passed by my Broadway bunk. I stopped him long enough to demonstrate my skill in opening and closing my locker with the silence of a safecracker. Disarmed, he laughed; we both apologized and bumped fists.

When one thinks prison, one thinks of hard-core places like the Beast. Granted, it's easier to develop a liberal attitude toward criminal justice and prison reform when your only exposure is with nonviolent offenders. Still, it's a mistake to downplay the camp ordeal, even for a month. (Veteran inmates told me that the first month is the most brutal; despite my short sentence, they treated me as one of them.) This is still prison. You're still confined; cut off from loved ones and friends; starved of stimuli and purpose; unable to affect anything in the outside world, which purrs along just fine without you. You never know what certain inmates really think of you or what they're truly capable of. I mean, they're criminals. Other than Slatkin, I'd never been around criminals. Just because we were all in for nonviolent offenses didn't mean there weren't some psychos among us capable of flipping out. You're stigmatized for life; medically neglected; warehoused like livestock; fed disgusting food; and subjected to dehumanizing bunk counts several times a day. Not to mention the crushing boredom.

You go into prison with scars of hurt and humiliation, so how can you not come out with even deeper scars? Some prison alumni prefer to walk away, never speak of it again, and move on. I understand, but slumping off into the sunset like a whipped dog isn't in my DNA. Deny prison all you want, proclaim that it doesn't define you, but you can never completely forget it or wish the trauma out of existence. With social media, it is forever with you, part of your body of work—Choate '68, Princeton '72, Canaan '20. The first sentence in your obituary, unless you later in life happen to cure cancer. You cannot vote; cannot travel to certain countries. When the name "Greg Abbott" comes up in social conversation, or with prospective business partners or lenders, so will "college admissions scandal," "felon" (my new F-word), and "prison," as opposed to "Princeton," "Ithaca Industries," "EarthLink," "family man," "New York Marathoner," "scratch golfer." While Governor Greg Abbott of Texas is the first thing to pop up in Google searches, add "Varsity Blues" to the search bar and see who rules the roost and how horribly I am portrayed. (The Texas governor's office felt compelled to release a statement declaring that he was *not* the Varsity Blues Greg Abbott.) Maybe Old MacDonald was trying to tell me something; maybe

I should change my name to Abrams—EIEIO. He had exempted me from work detail, so getting my arms around my salient reality; putting what happened to me and my family into a larger context by learning, reading, reflecting; making sense of this ordeal and hopefully turning it into something positive by becoming stronger, wiser, and well-informed, became my prison job.

—

Prisoners of Politics: Breaking the Cycle of Mass Incarceration by Rachel Elise Barkow was almost more than I could handle, a breathless cornucopia of information. Its author—director of Criminal Law at NYU; member of the United States Sentencing Commission—is one of the country's foremost thinkers on criminal justice. Like a sugarcane farmer with a machete, I slashed my way through this dense treatise and took copious notes until my fingers ached. Had Varsity Blues not bitten me in the ass, it never would have occurred to me to delve into the subject, let alone crack open this jam-packed scholarly work.

Prisoners of Politics was where I first read that the United States has 5 percent of the world's population and 25 percent of the world's prisoners, that we're not just the most incarcerated nation on earth but in recorded human history. Violent crime was not responsible for quintupling the prison population since 1980; in fact, violent crime had actually *decreased* during the same period that life sentences increased by over 80 percent. This spike in the prison population was due to public policy changes precipitated by politicians demagoguing crime to an uninformed, knee-jerk public. It began with the expansion of the criminal codes in the 1970s, continued through the Reagan era with mandatory sentencing guidelines, and marched unimpeded through the Clinton administration to the present with politically motivated "tough-on-crime" laws. In 1980, America had roughly one thousand federal prosecutors; today, we have more than eight thousand. The "baseless rhetoric and empty symbolism of crime populism," with its misleading sound bites (e.g., Willie Horton) had led to "outmoded and empirically groundless ways of thinking" that were responsible for the spike in sentence lengths. (Speaking of Willie Horton, Barkow documented that Dukakis's furlough program had had a 99 percent success rate; this from a woman who had clerked for Justice Scalia. One couldn't discern any political bias in her book, only that criminal justice and prison reform should be bipartisan causes.) Bombarded by sensationalist news and soulless politicians, the voters lost their appetite for rehabilitation. Retribution was simpler; it washed our hands of the problem. We had become tough on crime instead of smart on crime, and the result was the highest recidivism rate—67.5 percent—in the civilized world.

Our criminal justice system had become bloated, expensive, and cruel while failing to keep us safe. The War on Drugs incarcerated legions of people, mostly of color, while failing to stem drug use. Even as violent crime *decreased*, our prisons grew more crowded with nonviolent offenders. Seven states, relying on data rather than demagoguery, decided to put *fewer* people in prison and experienced a *decrease* in crime, but otherwise we continue heading in the wrong direction. In Louisiana, three hundred people are serving life sentences for nonviolent offenses. Oklahoma prisons operate at 123 percent capacity yet are staffed at only 60 percent; it is the most incarcerated state in the nation and is often called "the prison capital of the world." There are more African American males behind bars in the USA than the *total prison populations* of India, Argentina, Canada, Lebanon, Japan, Germany, Finland, Israel, and England combined.

Sentencing guidelines are equally appalling. The average nonviolent drug trafficking sentence is six years. Double that for a first-time rape offense. One man got a fifty-year minimum sentence for carrying a concealed gun to two $350 marijuana deals—double the sentence of a kingpin who caused a death, an aircraft hijacker, a terrorist who detonated a bomb, and a spy gathering top secret information. One man with three petty theft sentences totaling $230 received a mandatory life sentence. A person who stole nine videotapes from K-Mart for a total of $150 was sentenced to fifty years to life! A woman who forged a $200 check got a twenty-year sentence, whereas Sammy "the Bull" Gravano, who murdered nineteen people, received just a five-year sentence in return for ratting out John Gotti. A man who stole thirty dollars' worth of candy bars was sentenced to twenty-five years to life because he refused to accept the plea.

Trial sentences average five times greater than those from a plea, which is why some lawyers advise their clients to take the plea even if they believe their clients to be innocent. For these reasons, 97 percent of all cases never go to trial. Of those that do, prosecutors, with unlimited resources and a judicial system tilted resoundingly in their favor, win 95 percent of the time.

They frame charges in the highest degree of seriousness. For example, "conspiracy to commit mail fraud," "conspiracy to commit honest services fraud," "racketeering," and "money laundering" to make Varsity Blues defendants seem as sinister as terrorists. They employ sound bites—"criminal," "felon," "trafficker," and the most reviled, "sex offender"—to make relatively harmless people seem like the worst of the worst, thereby failing to define them by their true effect on public safety. A sex offender can be someone who visits prostitutes, urinates in public, flashes, streaks, or moons. A trafficker can be an innocent victim of circumstance like Alice Marie Johnson. Labels like these are regularly misused to demonize defendants, jack up sentences, and bolster legal careers. When the press reported that Lori Loughlin could get up to forty-five years, people applauded, and bloggers went agog with glee. The press knew full well that Lori would never get sentenced to anything near that but said it anyway to stoke vituperative hatred and sell papers.

The more I read about real-world sentencing policy and spoke to inmates who had taken the plea and were sentenced to roughly the same amount of time as their plea stipulated, the more I appreciated the slap on the wrist Judge Talwani had given me. I was serving just 8 percent of the year and a day to which I'd pled guilty. Still too much, in my varnished opinion, but I couldn't find a single case that remotely approached my ratio of leniency. I read *Prisoners of Politics* in a wholly different way from how I normally read other books. I felt connected to its narrative because it was *my* narrative. I was in the correctional system and would be for another year after my release, in the form of probation and community service. How fortunate I was to get a twenty-nine-day (and a wake up) glimpse into hell, enough to expand my awareness and grow as a person but not so long as to be broken as a person.

—

I didn't meet a single white-collar offender at Canaan who didn't get tongue-tied when trying to explain his reason for being there. The drug offenders were candid about their indiscretions—selling, using, making calls, driving the getaway car, whatever—but the white-collar guys had complex stories not always easy to tell. At best, one would admit to sloppy accounting that was immediately rectified but still led to the jailhouse; a tax oversight that was immediately corrected but still led to the jailhouse; a father who took the rap for his son. Like me, most of the white-collar inmates I met had never traveled in criminal circles and had lived productive lives up until their conviction.

I gave up trying to analyze individual cases or find innocent victims for any literary agenda. I would never get objectivity, particularly from those who were appealing their cases. Instinct told me that some were less culpable than others, but ultimately, all I could do was relate to them as fellow flawed human beings and fellow prisoners. Society had branded all of us criminals, but without romanticizing my prison experience and being as clear-eyed as possible, I can affirm that I saw far more goodness in my fellow campers than bad. Actually, I didn't see much bad at all. Though we all were there for reasons (some more justifiable than others), the fellow inmates I got to know, though a bit rough around the edges, were *at least* as kind and courteous as your average Aspenite or Upper East Sider, only more genuine about it.

John, the defense attorney who'd been at my orientation, had defended a murder case in Long Island. As he tells it, the one witness who could exonerate his client, who knew who had actually committed the murder, was in jail. This witness was reluctant to testify for fear of being branded a snitch, the worst thing you can be labeled in prison, so John paid him a visit. For promising, in exchange for honest testimony, that he would spread the word throughout prison that the witness wasn't a snitch, John was sentenced to three years for bribing a witness. Meanwhile, prosecutors use a panoply of rewards and threats to influence witnesses, even threaten to indict family members as blackmail and routinely get away with it. I don't know if there was more to John's story that he wasn't telling me, but it sounded like a flesh-and-blood example of the dirty-dealing imbalance in our justice system that I was beginning to read about.

I don't know if Chan, a successful reseller of health and wellness supplements, was guilty for intentionally peddling vitamin pills containing ephedrine, knowing that they could be converted into meth (*if* you amassed thousands of pills). Was it that, or the jury seeing a photo of his Lamborghini, that did him in? It was curious that he went to prison while the manufacturer of the offending vitamin pills got off scot-free. Even more curious that his biggest local competitor who sold the same pills, a former FBI agent, was not indicted.

I don't know if Anthony (the first black treasurer of a good-sized

Virginia city, who won in all demographics, even white districts, after a brief stint as cornerback for the Atlanta Falcons) was guilty of taking bribes or a true corruption fighter framed by local white interests who considered him an "uppity" obstacle. All I know is how I experienced him, as a physically imposing but soft-spoken gentleman who read tomes on Leonardo di Vinci and was courteous to a fault. He was also writing his own book declaring his innocence, titled *Hung by Lies*.

Hoping not to stoke any race-class sensibilities by pointing out a very common mistake, I informed him that the proper English is *Hanged by Lies*.

"My high school English teacher, who's supported me through all my troubles, told me the same thing." Anthony smiled, exuding humility. "But I'm from the South, and I think my vernacular will fly better there." We agreed with a good laugh that he was there because he was black and I was there because I was white.

Even Mike and I broke the ice. While resuming our Napolitano conversation in the dorm, I discovered that he was an excellent specialty impersonator of the Three Stooges. Our animosities melted as we regressed into childhood, dusting off impersonations of Moe and Curly. Such common ground elevated our political discussions. Mike became less strident, ironically less of a stooge.

I couldn't Google anyone from prison, so I didn't know exactly what former Congressman Chaka Fattah (D, PA) had done to merit his ten-year sentence. All I knew was he impressed me with his upbeat attitude and dedication to the cause of brain science. By his own account, which is all I had to go on, Chaka had been Congress's go-to guy on anything related to brain science. He was now working on multiple book proposals, one proclaiming his innocence and two scientific works on his pet subject. He gave me copies of outlines and asked for comments. He was appealing his case and never allowed anything to dampen his optimism. I doubt he ever went through a cockroach phase. On mornings when he saw me sitting on my bunk in a funk, he stopped by to pick up my spirits. His efforts annoyed me—I resented being outed as a cockroach—but he clearly wasn't doing it for my vote. Like most politicians, he was more interested in telling me about himself than in learning about me, but still he cultivated my friendship. Because the Varsity Blues media had dubbed me a beverage bigwig, perhaps he assumed I could do him some good down the road after he won his appeal.

GREG ABBOTT

While watching TV on the impeachment proceedings, I asked the congressman his opinion; he got up and walked out of the TV room. Apparently, politics was a sore subject with him. He wanted to be known strictly for making a positive contribution to brain science. The only moment when his brilliance and unflappable demeanor abandoned him was when he tried to explain why he was in prison. After opaque hemming and hawing, he delegated the task by recommending I read *Licensed to Lie: Exposing Corruption in the Department of Justice* by Sidney Powell (yes, *that* Sidney Powell, but hold your horses), telling me to pay particular attention to the section on Senator Ted Stevens.

I'd heard other inmates extoll that book, but strangely, it wasn't in the library, so I emailed my wife and asked her to order it from Amazon. Because powdery drugs are oft smuggled inside book pages, Amazon was one of the few sources from which Canaan would accept book shipments to inmates. The only other prison mail I received were *New York Times* crossword puzzle printouts from the minion of George Stephanopoulos, who was still intent on me being the first Varsity Blues parent to spill his guts. For the drug-related reasons stated above, Canaan authorities gave me photocopies. I completed all the puzzles, even the Saturday ones (with time on my hands, the answers eventually came to me), and plowed through several more books before *Licensed to Lie* finally arrived.

—

Licensed to Lie reads like a gripping legal thriller, but, unfortunately, it all actually happened. Sidney Powell's jaw-dropping narrative, which encompasses Enron, Arthur Anderson, and Senator Ted Stevens, documents with superlative passion and prose how notions of professional integrity were cast aside in favor of prosecutorial ambition. It exposes a major human rights problem in the US, one that politicians rarely talk about. The first two tragic pages—which describe the suicide of a young DOJ Criminal Division prosecutor who was under investigation for misconduct in the Ted Stevens case—hooked me.

In *Brady v. Maryland* (1963), the US Supreme Court laid out legal parameters of prosecutorial conduct. The government is no ordinary litigant. A prosecutor's *first constitutional duty* lies in convicting *only* those defendants who are proven guilty beyond a reasonable doubt. The overriding goal is *not* to win at all costs but to ensure that justice is served by turning over all exculpatory evidence and being fully transparent. (Are you listening, Eric Rosen?)

The Enron debacle of 2002 represented the perfect storm for prosecutorial big game hunters to collect enough human pelts to fill the Explorer's Club. The Enron Task Force, directed by political partisan Andrew Weissman, unleashed its Waco mentality on America. They oversaw the prosecution of more than thirty individuals, many of whom they knew were innocent, and brought down one of the world's largest, most respected accounting firms. These deeds could never have been accomplished without a litany of ethical breaches: withholding exculpatory evidence in violation of *Brady*; mishandling and destroying evidence that could absolve defendants; pressuring defense witnesses not to testify by threatening prosecution; fabricating specious charges; relying on fraudulent forensic experts and deceitful witnesses; charging a suspect with more offenses than warranted; and making statements to the media designed to arouse public indignation. Otherwise, they were paragons of virtue.

Sidney Powell, a defense lawyer from Houston (the HQ of Enron), was brought in to represent Merrill Lynch executive Jim Brown. Merrill Lynch, very much a peripheral player with Enron, was involved in no wrongdoing, but the DOJ swept it into its web simply because it was a white-shoe Wall Street firm that they wanted to besmirch as a den of mobsters, and in the process besmirch all Wall Street as mobsters.

When Jim Brown didn't provide the grand jury testimony Weisman wanted, the prosecutor indicted him for perjury and helping Enron defraud its shareholders. He criminalized a legitimate business transaction between Merrill Lynch and Enron, concocting changes that had no legal precedent. With Enron dominating the headlines and antibusiness hysteria sweeping the nation, the media stoked flames, and judges buckled to prosecutorial will. Anything Enron related was fair game; anyone in its orbit was presumed guilty of *something*. Jim Brown, a decent family man who didn't profit a dime from Merrill's anemic relationship with Enron, who wasn't even on the conference call that Weissman cited to incriminate him, became a tragic casualty. While prosecutors withheld evidence that eventually would exonerate him, Brown was convicted and sent to Fort Dix, a tough place where he was forced to spend more than three years.

I had learned about Fort Dix from a couple of inmates who'd spent time there; the nicest thing they called it was a "hellhole." Brown's association with Enron made him a target in prison. I'm not going to recite here the travails he and his wife suffered, or the lies and judicial obtuseness that kept him behind bars and thwarted appeal after appeal. Blithely, the government squandered of millions of taxpayer dollars to send Brown and two of his Merrill Lynch colleagues to prison for conduct that wasn't criminal.

Then there was the 2002 demise of venerable accounting firm Arthur Anderson, Enron's auditor. Only a dozen or so of its 85,000 employees worldwide were involved with Enron; the rest never saw Enron's books. Not content with going after a few culpable individuals, the Enron Task Force shot for the moon and indicted the entire firm on a bogus institutional obstruction of justice charge. Withholding exculpatory evidence and manipulating the judge into giving improper jury instructions, the task force brought down the entire firm and was extolled by the media as heroes. All 85,000 Arthur Anderson employees lost their jobs. Families and loved ones suffered devastating hardships. If there was a problem with Arthur Anderson's culture, why not bring in a first-rate CEO to bang heads and change it? Because it wasn't sexy. Like Sir Edmund Hillary climbing Mount Everest, the Enron Task Force took Arthur Anderson down "because it's there"—and, of course, because they wanted to be at the top of the mountain.

Finally, in this trilogy of government misconduct, the same Enron Task Force crowd embroiled Senator Ted Stevens (R, AK) in a federal corruption trial as he ran for reelection. A World War II veteran who'd served forty years in the Senate with distinction, he was buried in an avalanche of false testimony for accepting favors and found guilty. Eight days later, he was narrowly defeated at the polls. He was the most senior US senator to ever lose a reelection bid, and his loss shifted the balance of power in the Senate from Republican to Democrat. After the verdict, smug prosecutors gloated to reporters on the courthouse steps.

It might have ended there had not an honest FBI agent broken ranks with his colleagues and the DOJ and disclosed the government's willful *Brady* violations and lies to the court. The presiding judge took the matter seriously and ordered an investigation of the lawyers who conducted the case. Legions of ethical breaches were uncovered. The Stevens indictment was dismissed and the conviction vacated prior to sentencing. Senator Stevens was lucky in a sense; *Brady* violations are rarely discovered because prosecutors control the evidence and are rarely questioned. Were it not for the whistleblower, he would have gone to prison and died in shame. Still,

USA VS ABBOTT

his vindication came too late to spare him and his family unwarranted pain and humiliation, to say nothing of the loss of a Senate seat and the shift of senatorial power from one party to another.

There was no mention of Congressman Chaka Fattah in the book. Clearly, the implication he wanted to impart was that he too had been framed by a politicized judicial system that targets anyone it wants. If the Democratic congressman from Philly wants to reach across the aisle and equate himself with a Republican senator from Alaska, sounds like healthy bipartisanship to me.

Yes, it bummed me out months after my release when Sidney Powell got sucked into Trump's election fraud issue, marginalized herself as a wackadoodle, and had her Twitter account cancelled. Doesn't mean her book doesn't have merit. *Licensed to Lie* not only received glowing accolades from all political circles but is echoed thematically by Rachel Barkow, one of our foremost scholars on criminal justice. Lest you assume Powell's book to be a partisan hatchet job, consider this: Long after the Enron Task Force "superstars" were decorated with the Attorney General's Award for Exceptional Service, then springboarded to big promotions at big firms, or plum positions at the FBI, DOJ, or White House, the convictions they had viciously engineered were overturned—though too late to prevent extensive collateral damage. The verdicts against Jim Brown and his Merrill Lynch colleagues were vacated, and three innocent men were at long last released from prison. The Arthur Anderson verdict was overturned in 2005 by the US Supreme Court by a 9–0 margin. Then there's the Senator Stevens travesty. Justice delayed was certainly denied in all these instances.

Neither Powell, Barkow, nor Alice Marie Johnson wrote their books to report one-off episodes. Government abuse is systemic. It occurred repeatedly with Andrew Weissman and his cronies, with Mike Nifong of Duke Lacrosse infamy, and even in Varsity Blues. Even the *New York Times* recognizes this corrupt imbalance. While on a cross-country flight to pick up my wife from Dublin in early December, 2019, I read the *Times Sunday Magazine* cover story about jailhouse informant Paul Skalnik, a grifter who specialized in obtaining murder confessions from fellow inmates. Skalnik's fabricated testimony sent more than thirty men to death row. Prosecutors who knew his testimony was fake continued to vouch for him as a credible (even admirable) witness. Repeatedly they maintained that Skalnik's testimony came with no strings attached, yet each time, Skalnik was released from prison, only to be arrested again, where he once again bore false witness in order to obtain his release. The cycle was plain as day, yet each time, the law looked the other way.

John Rigas, son of Greek immigrants, started a diner in Coudersport, Pennsylvania, then a movie theatre down the street, eventually parlaying several small successes into the founding of Adelphia, the fourth largest cable company in America. According to my trusted friend who litigated many of the government-induced bankruptcy cases involving the Rigas family, Rigas was unjustly destroyed by overzealous prosecutors. Describing Rigas as among the most honorable men he'd ever met, he told me many touching stories of how this beloved patriarch (with no formal education) helped people in need and contributed mightily to his community, supporting an entire town. Was he unjustly crucified with a fifteen-year sentence for sloppy bookkeeping while his hired professionals went free, or did he and his sons loot the company? I only know what my lawyer friend told me, that after almost a decade of litigation, John Rigas still couldn't fathom why they were sending him and his sons to prison.

According to Powell and Barkow, government misconduct is the cornerstone of our judicial system. Prosecutors who withhold evidence and violate *Brady* almost always get away with it due to judges' presumption of trust, lack of healthy skepticism, or just plain laziness. When prosecutors control the crime scene and evidence and defense attorneys are neutered on an uneven playing field, our government is, in effect, *licensed to lie* and our republic threatened. Judges: Wake up and smell the corruption! The thuggish plea deals that thwart due process! Hold prosecutors' feet to the fire re ethics and *Brady* and be ready to discipline anyone who subverts justice. Don't trust them with the evidence and don't allow them to explain the law to you; do your homework. If ignorance of the law is no defense for *me*, shouldn't that principle apply tenfold to you? Weren't our Constitution's checks and balances architected around the principle of *dis*trusting government power?

"Our system of justice," writes Powell, "is crying for a culture change ... What happened to the defendants in this book can happen to anyone." Not that such treachery hasn't been going on throughout history. As Cardinal Richelieu wrote in the sixteenth century, "Give me six lines written by the most honest man in the world, and I will find enough in them to hang him." Or, more recently, to quote a New York state judge, "I can indict a ham sandwich."

The night I finished *Licensed to Lie*, this ham sandwich went to bed seething. I couldn't sleep, knowing that Andrew Weissman was teaching law at NYU, corrupting young minds. The Enron Task Force "conspirators" (a word that fits them far more aptly than my wife or me) abused power to bully innocents. They withheld exculpatory evidence and committed legions of ethical atrocities, destroying thousands of lives and careers in order to advance their own; smearing a true public servant with false charges in order to tamper with a senatorial election and therefore our democracy. They dishonored their profession and the country's justice system they had taken an oath to serve. Yes, yes, and yes again, extending a helping hand to my child at a moment of great stress was wrong, unnecessary, and just plain dumb. But prison worthy? Just who are the *real* criminal elites anyway? Why did I have to resign in disgrace from the company I founded, into which I had poured my heart and soul for a humanitarian cause, while these curs are allowed to practice a profession for which they are proven ethically unworthy?

CHAPTER 19

TWELVE CENTS AN HOUR

Final week, home stretch. I had read more books in three weeks at Canaan than four years at Princeton; made a number of friends from backgrounds vastly different from mine; done my own laundry (stop rolling your eyes); and to some degree, thanks in part to the plethora of NFL playoff games on weekends, had been able to manage the boredom. The junk-food ads—Burger King, McDonald's, Pizza Hut, dripping with meat and cheese—titillated like pornography. Even my workouts continued. Mount Kilimanjaro didn't come in contact with the narrow, stationary bike seat, so miraculously, I could sit and pedal without pain. My urine remained disturbingly dark, and a visit to the urologist was top priority upon my return home, but I felt no kidney stone onset.

One night, with my vanquished Maine chess rival now playing cards and dice for mackerel, I decided to watch some TV before bedtime. Just as I sat down, *American Greed* was beginning an episode on the Varsity Blues scandal. Every inmate in the white TV room, about a dozen guys of all races, creeds, and nonviolent crimes, knew it was about me. A picture of me in a gray suit in front of the Boston courthouse flashed on the screen. Seeing me in suit and tie caused my mates to laugh like it was all a big joke. "Hey, Abbott, you clean up well!" To my relief, that was the last time "Abbott" appeared or was mentioned on the show.

When the narrator brought up the phony athletic recruitment schemes or targeting specific schools, I made sure the room knew I wasn't involved in either. The first segment focused on Singer, how he went from failed college basketball coach to corrupt college admissions coach. After a commercial break, the focus shifted to the two movie stars and their contrasting ways of dealing with the case, and to Devon Sloane simply because the water polo fiasco was too brazen to ignore. In a kind of full circle irony, I remembered that one of the very first *American Greed* episodes ever, back when the series first began, was on the Reed Slatkin Ponzi scheme. When they'd asked me to appear, I couldn't have said no any faster.

This Varsity Blues episode couldn't have been cheesier or more canned in terms of its clichéd banter about the rich and famous; the narrator sounded no less huckster-ish than Rick Singer himself. But when he began mentioning the amounts parents had paid to Singer's "fake charity" to get their kids into college—300k, 400k, 600k—a hush fell over the room.

"I didn't pay nearly that much," I blurted, to silence, and after that, I clammed up until the program ended and people filed out of the TV room for the 9:00 p.m. bunk count. Nothing unkind was said, and I received no looks, but it was obvious that they assumed, correctly, that I had shelled out six figures to help my kid in the college admissions process, a concept they understandably couldn't fathom.

I would be released in a week, so *American Greed* was easy enough to slough off. Just a couple of days after the first lockdown at the Beast had been lifted, a *national* lockdown was imposed on *all* maximum-security federal prisons due to MS-13 gang violence. Once again, the Beast prisoners were confined to their cells until further notice, and the younger campers were summoned Up Top to prepare (and clean up) three meals a day and do laundry for 1,400 inmates. As the national lockdown dragged on, fresh lists were posted on a daily basis. Although I continued to be exempted, I began to give serious thought at the start of my final week to volunteer for a day or two for some task that didn't jeopardize my bruised hip. It was more about obtaining experience—if anything, a selfish impulse; a visit to the zoo, if you will. Several of my over-sixty compadres had obtained doctor-ordered exemptions, which by law couldn't be circumvented. Though older than most of them, I hadn't tried to pull anything like that. Surely I was in good enough condition to handle a grueling day or two Up Top. I was torn between biting the bullet and embracing what would likely be an unpleasant but illuminating experience that I could talk about forever, or just coasting to the finish line.

Turns out, the bullet bit me. As I headed to our 3:00 p.m. dinner, two separate inmates with whom I had never spoken, but who apparently knew my name, approached to say, "You're on the list, Abbott." I got the impression that they took pleasure in informing me. Apparently among certain members of the camp population, sending my privileged ass Up Top for work duty was an issue of some satisfaction. People were milling around the bulletin board, so I went over to check out the newly posted list. Indeed, "Abbott" was part of the four-man laundry crew to report for duty at dawn tomorrow and serve for the rest of the week. The whole *week*? MacDonald had broken his promise, no doubt because he'd run out of able bodies, but at least he got my name right.

—

In prison greens and cramped boots, I climbed into the idling van at 5:45 a.m. and waited for the rest of my laundry crew. It was still dark. The crackling car radio caressed my ears, as did the welcome news that Derek Jeter had been elected to the Baseball Hall of Fame. Though I'm a Dodger fan, there is but one Derek Jeter. One spiteful sportswriter had kept Jeter from joining teammate Mariano Rivera as the only other unanimous selection in history.

"What an asshole!" I told the inmate driver, relishing the illusory feeling of being in the real world. "How do you *not* vote for Jeter?"

"Probably a Democrat," came his rustic non sequitur.

"Probably from Boston," I said, refining his answer a tad.

Our laundry crew was comprised of Donny, a career drug offender from (you guessed it) Maine; a jovial African American named George, whom I hadn't met until now; and Austin, who kept us waiting because he first had to get coffee from the dining hall and then his daily prescription at pill line. Though a white-collar offender, Austin took medication to combat his heroin addiction. Donny looked to be in his midforties; add up the ages of George and Austin, and you roughly get my age. The van transported us to the same entrance at the Beast where I had self-surrendered three weeks ago. That seemed like an eternity ago.

I forget the name of the CO into whose custody we were placed, probably because his attitude traumatized me. Let's just call him Officer Ernst. A powerfully built dude whose vibe suggested that he'd been beaten by his father in preparation for his current vocation, Ernst was triggered by the sight of Austin holding his coffee cup, like Sinatra holding a cocktail.

"Cawwwwffee! Lah di dah! Is that why you cockroaches are late?"

Mum's the word; one doesn't rat out a fellow cockroach.

"You!" Ernst said, pointing at me. He led me inside the CO bathroom and said, "Strip." I undressed down to my thermals, which thankfully was enough for him. "Where are you from?"

"New York City."

"What did you do, embezzle money?"

"No, I don't do such things. I was involved in the college admissions case."

"Ahhhhhhh," he trumpeted, "so *you're* the one!"

"No, I was a parent, not—"

"Get dressed," Ernst barked and then left.

I hustled to get dressed. When I returned to the hallway, Ernst was in the other bathroom with Austin. After the guard came out, Austin took a seeming eternity to return, much to Ernst's impatience. We heard the toilet flush. As soon as Austin emerged seconds later, Ernst flew into his face.

"Who the ever-lovin' *fuck* do you think you are!" he shouted, nose to nose with Austin, red-faced, veins pulsing in neck. "Using the CO facilities! You're a *fucking prisoner*! You are *never* to use our facilities even if it means *crapping in your pants*! *Do you understand*? If you didn't have so much laundry to do, I'd throw your filthy ass in the SHU!"

After the same strip-in-bathroom routine with Donny (a laundry veteran) and George, Ernst led us outside, where a short walkway led to another section of the Beast. The early-morning January air was so biting that I started to trot.

"*Stop*," Ernst ordered, "or they'll shoot you."

I froze in place. "They'd actually *shoot* me for jogging from one building to another?"

"Darn tootin'!" Ernst didn't seem to be kidding. The thirty-foot-high concrete walls and even higher guard towers on either side of us, lined with rows of swirling barbed wire and sheets of electrical panels, took my breath away. They also gave me a twinge of satisfaction that Reed Slatkin, who had destroyed so many lives, spent fourteen years in a place like this, before dying within a year after his release. Did the Varsity Blues haters harbor the same vitriol toward me? Like there's some moral equivalency? Once inside, we came to a checkpoint, where we recited our names and inmate numbers. Moments later, a heavy metal door slammed shut behind us, creating an ominous clang that echoed throughout the long, stark, cavernous hallway ahead. We were in the belly of the Beast. As we trudged toward the laundry section, Ernst never missed an opportunity to bellow to every passing colleague, while pointing at me, "Hey, this guy can get your kid into college!" Over and over and over.

In the dim, dingy laundry area, our work space for the next eight hours, we were greeted by several bulging hampers, each filled seven feet high with prisoner laundry. An aura of disease seemed to envelop these putrid mountains. Donny, the only experienced hand among us who knew the laundry drill, served as de facto foreman. Otherwise, we would have been rudderless.

"Christ," he muttered in a thick New England accent, recoiling in disgust, "this is all from the SHU!" He knew this because the jumpsuits, T-shirts, socks, and underwear were all orange, a color that the SHU people shared with my Princeton Tigers.

"It's been backed up for days," barked Ernst, "so get to work, you maggots!" He directed our attention to a small table containing a box of latex gloves. "Wear those. No proctology exams!" He then retired to his small office adjacent to the laundry area, where he did God knows what for the next eight hours.

We wheeled the hampers one by one to the row of front-loaded industrial washing machines. By the armful and holding our breath, we grabbed the asphyxiating garments and bedding and began stuffing everything into the washers. The machines were deep, requiring that we shove the rancid rags to the very back of the cylinder for maximum output. Somehow, Austin had convinced Ernst that the floor outside his office needed mopping, a task he managed to drag out for nearly an hour. A sleazy move that didn't exactly endear him to his crew.

Fending off the odor, which was practically visible, it was hard to imagine the SHU folks as having any redeeming human qualities. Even by prison standards, they were the worst of the worst, some of the vilest inmates in America who, for reasons of violence or gross misconduct, had been thrown into the 260 dark, vermin-infested SHUs that the Beast had to offer, which currently, we were told, had 100 percent occupancy. We handled their foul, grimy underwear, socks, T-shirts, jumpsuits, sweats, towels, and washcloths. Clothing worn, and worn hard, each with its own unique history (like a bottle of wine?). Some of the laundry grime was jet-black like tar, some a sickly green; some bona fide vomit and excrement. I even came across a woman's nylon panty (pink floral print). George—not my laundry mate but the camper doing twenty years for selling weed—had told me of a talented Beast prisoner under psychological observation who had in rapid-fire urinated, defecated, masturbated, and vomited in an office before the guards came to apprehend him. Since George's prison job was in the medical office, it fell upon him to clean up, which caused him to vomit as well. Amazing none of us vomited.

With all our might—except Austin, who dogged it as best he could (the little shit)—we tugged at the twisting sheets and blankets in futile attempts to dislodge them. When stymied, we bent down into the dank hamper to gather more clothing in order to free up the bedding. I was overworking muscles I hadn't used in ages, sneaking a breath whenever I could and wishing for a hazmat suit, not just gloves. Briefly my mind wandered into a dreamlike state, thinking about life after prison and resolving to do things outside my comfort zone—a rare mental diversion, given how prison does a magnificent job of keeping you in the moment and killing dreams. While the loaded washers chugged, we filled the remaining machines. After each wash cycle, we removed all the heavy, wet material from the machine and dumped it into a "clean" hamper, which we in turn wheeled to the dryers ten feet across the aisle, where we gathered up armfuls all over again.

All four of us could have fit into one of the dryers—they were that huge—but we had to load them to the hilt with wet clothes. I almost disappeared pushing the heavy laundry to the back of a dryer. After a few nonstop hours, the armfuls got heavier and my muscles began to flag. Only once the clothes were washed and dried was I able to breathe normally. It took us over *five uninterrupted hours* to transform the disgusting deathtrap we had inherited into something less repulsive. Once the hampers were full of fluffy, dry laundry, we wheeled everything over to the sorting tables and took our twenty-minute lunch break. Mystery meat and cookies. As I eyed the mountains of clean wash that we still had to sort and fold, my body suddenly felt it. I was weary to the point of teetering, aching, and wilting from head to toe. Lower back precarious, hands lame from all the lifting and tugging at the ornery bedding. I had left it all out on the field. Mount Kilimanjaro, as swollen as ever, didn't even factor into my bodily inventory. I couldn't hide the fact that I felt like a reeling prize fighter in the fifteenth round.

"Hey, Abbaaatt!" said Austin, a la Lou Costello. "How you holding up, old man?"

"Pretty well for someone twice your age who's done twice your work."

I wondered how I could weather another day of this, let alone the week MacDonald had stipulated.

"You're doing great," Donny chimed in. "You're a fuckin' workhawse. It's ridiculous they sent you up here. Are you really seventy? Ya don't look it."

I paraphrased something from Mark Twain: "When people start telling you how good you look, it's a sure sign you're growing old. MacDonald promised me no work duty."

"And he fucked you anyway," said the ever-amiable George, laughing.

"I'm gonna suggest to MacDonald that this be your last day," said Donny.

"Thanks, I appreciate it, Donny, but really, I'm fine." I was lying of course, too proud to accept his offer. Special treatment was why I was there.

"No, seriously, this is hahd fuckin' work. You're really puttin' out too. But this ain't no place for a handsome seventy-year-old."

"Ain't no place for anyone, but I really can use the twelve cents an hour to pay my fines and legal fees." I recalled reading in Rachel Barkow's book about corporate America laying off employees along with their benefits and hiring prison slave labor in their stead. Boeing, Sodexo, Microsoft, Honda, and AT&T were among the culprits, using prison labor for certain tasks like stocking shelves, telemarketing, and, yes, laundry. A hospital in Oregon had moved from using a unionized laundry service to a prison service. Varsity Bleach, anyone?

We began our afternoon of folding, placing the orange socks into one pile, orange T-shirts into another, orange jumpsuits into another, and so on with the boxers, towels, washcloths, blankets, sheets, sweats. (The pink floral woman's panty was pocketed by Austin as a souvenir.) Donny, who knew what Ernst wanted and how he wanted it, placed the piles neatly inside the hampers. For my quasi-arthritic hands and achy-breaky arms and back, folding wasn't as effortless a task as one might assume, especially the bulky blankets and jumpsuits. Many of the jumpsuits had slits sliced in the crotch and nipple areas, presumably to enable inmates so inclined to cop a feel.

Around the folding table, we plowed on diligently, laughing and joking like brothers from distinctly different mothers, singing "Ol' Man River" in mock Negro voices—until Ernst flew out of his office to demand that we assemble two dozen individual packages for incoming prisoners. Each package was to include jumpsuit, T-shirt, socks, boxer short, towel, washcloth, sheet, and blanket to be folded into a nice, neat roll. "ASAFP, you filthy animals," he demanded, with an urgency that sounded like his ass was on the line—like we were being asked to prepare something special for visiting VIPs (Canaan's version of the Petrossian caviar-blini-crème fraîche gift basket?).

While we scrambled, Ernst peered at the filled bins with a critical eye. Not even he could find a flaw over which to grumble. At the beginning of the workday, when first laying eyes on the mountains of nauseating laundry, I never dreamed we could have accomplished so much in a day. I was quite proud of our crew. Being servants to the SHU people for a day had a certain nobility, but fatigue caused me to dread the encores ahead. It was almost 5:00 p.m. when a CO other than Ernst came to tell us it was "quittin' time." We had worked closer to ten hours than eight, which meant roughly $1.20 in my pocket.

Off snapped the latex gloves. As our weary, sweaty crew waited by the barred door, eager as hell to leave, the CO summoned "Abbott" to Ernst's office. What now?

"What the hell were you thinking?" said Ernst, as soon as I appeared in his doorway. "Paying all that money just to get your kid into some fancy Ivy League college? Besides it being wrong—*which it is*—I don't get why the Ivy League is such a big deal."

"I actually agree with you."

"Then why did you do it?" Ernst glanced at the other CO, as if to enlist his agreement. "Why force your kid into a pressure cooker when he or she doesn't have the smarts?"

Such diplomacy caused me to close my eyes and take a long, slow breath. When I finally spoke, it was in a measured tone designed to appeal to the highest in him, whatever that was. "First of all, my daughter graduated with a 4.3 GPA and—"

"I thought 4.0 was the highest you can get." Gotcha!

"She took some AP ... advanced placement courses. She also soloed at *the* Metropolitan Opera, so trust me, she has the smarts *and* the chops. Our story is different from what you've read in the papers or seen on TV. Everyone's story is different, but as far as I know, no one had quite the mitigating factors that we did, which perhaps is why my sentence is so low. I'm happy to sit down and tell you about it." Why I offered to cast pearls to Ernst, I don't know. I'm a sucker for a challenge, but in this case, after ten hours on my feet, I think I just wanted to sit.

Ernst gestured toward a chair, into which I collapsed. I gave him the CliffsNotes version, centering around our daughter's Lyme disease. I explained how Singer sucked us in at a vulnerable moment, opining that a con man works twenty-four seven and can get you every time if you're not vigilant. Ernst was most attentive as I cited false news coverage, hate mail, hyenas with cameras, and numerous character letters. Figuring that Ernst was a Fox News watcher, at least when he wasn't watching *The Swamp People* or *Sponge Bob*, I name-dropped Judge Napolitano and his eloquent character letter, which caused his bushy gray eyebrows to rise a tad. I closed by saying that my daughter had applied to seventeen colleges, not just the Ivies, and that the goal should be to find a school that's a perfect fit for your child, not a parent's narcissism.

"Well, thanks for the explanation. I think your fellow money launderers … [cough] … I mean launderers … are anxious to get out of here."

"Very funny." I rose from my chair and headed for the door.

"See you in a sec, Bernie Madoff."

I wheeled around and momentarily forgot my place. "Don't *ever* call me that! I was hurt by someone just as evil. I know what it's like to be devastated. Don't *ever* call me that!"

This may have been the first time a prisoner had ever spoken to Ernst that way. Thank God the SHUs had 100 percent occupancy, though Ernst was unruffled. "Bernie was here, you know. Just passing through for a few days."

I rejoined my fellow (cough) launderers as Ernst followed and unlocked the door. While we retraced our steps back to the lobby, it became apparent that my efforts to talk to him as if he were a cognitive human being had been a busted 'Enry 'Iggins experiment. "This guy's Bernie Madoff's brother," he chirped to each passing colleague, pointing at me. "He can get your kid into college." The perfect denouement to an unforgettable experience.

As soon as I got back to Broadway, I placed toiletries, towel, and clean clothes on the seat of my plastic chair and carried everything to the shower. I couldn't rip off my grimy clothes and take a hot shower fast enough. Sore muscles relishing the hot water massage, I doubted my seventy-year-old body could handle another day, let alone the rest of the week, of such toil. I was equally sure Donny had forgotten his pledge made hours ago at lunch to ask MacDonald to spare me. Once all the crud was washed off my body and I was swathed in clean sweats and thermals, I felt like a new man. Rather than go to the mess hall to eat whatever vile fare they had saved for us, I heated up some ramen noodles from the hot water spigot in the laundry room, opened a packet of tuna, and mixed everything into my Tupperware bowl. I tore open a sleeve of the prison version of Ritz crackers. While I pigged out on chemicals, Terry, clutching a roll of toilet paper on his way to the bathroom, was suddenly standing over me.

"How was it today?"

"My soul is purified," I tossed off, though I kind of meant it. "Don't know how my old bones will manage tomorrow."

"Didn't you hear the news? They just lifted the lockdown. You're done, you lucky bastard!" Notwithstanding the many months of incarceration still ahead of him, Terry was genuinely happy for me. As my body expelled an orgasmic sigh of relief, Terry gave my shoulder a pat and continued on his mission.

A steady stream of inmates—who passed by my bunk every day but with whom I'd never spoken—were suddenly making respectful overtures. "Hey, Mr. Abbott!" "How ya doin', Mr. Abbott?" None stopped to chat or uttered a word about my day Up Top, but it was evident that my status had been elevated by virtue of having gone through Canaan's rite of passage. Stooping to do the laundry of the most depraved criminals in captivity was the highlight of my prison experience, a lesson in humility that I hope to impart to my children. Not that there's the remotest equivalency between Alexander Solzhenitsyn and myself, but his words resonate: "Bless you prison, bless you for being in my life. For there ... I came to realize that the object of life is not prosperity as we are made to believe, but the maturity of the human soul." That said, I was grateful as hell that my laundry services were no longer needed.

—

The next day, the sun finally came out. Though laden in my heavy green jacket, I shot hoops, dribbling around patches of snow. My muscles were so sore and clenched that I possessed no touch whatsoever. Only with a ridiculous heave could I reach the rim from three-point land, but I was in a playful mood and didn't care—except when inmates stopped to watch. Wanting them to know that this silver fox, former gym rat still had game, that I wasn't the pampered softie portrayed by the fake news, I put on my game face and focused on nailing ten-foot jumpers. I vowed to get my ACL fixed when I got out so I could reestablish lateral movement and play for real again.

With a handful of days left, I eased up on my black market food boycott and made peace with "Habibi," the fat Jordanian who had given me the sullen treatment ever since he'd handed me a complimentary chicken quesadilla and I hadn't followed up with an order. Coasting in my final week, I spent less time in the mess hall as Habibi delivered to my bunk a deliciously grilled fresh fish filet with tartar sauce, cheeseburgers, and kebabs on successive nights. Whatever I wanted, he seemed able to provide, so long as I didn't ask the fatal question: "How?" The one time I made that mistake incensed him, until meal time rolled around and he once again sought my patronage.

Just as Habibi delivered my evening meal, an audible hush punctuated by frantic whispers fell over the dorm. The warden was paying us a visit, his first since my arrival. Quickly, I hid illicit entrée in locker, pretending to read as Little Big Man strode down the aisle, all five feet, four inches of him—a muscular munchkin who would've made a lovely Pennsylvania lawn ornament, or perhaps one of the statuettes gracing the entrance at the 21 Club. Rumor had it that he despised the camp for being too lax, even though we were the cavalry who came to the rescue whenever his Beast was in lockdown, which during my stay was roughly 90 percent of the time.

A directive had come down to reduce the camp capacity from 160 to 130; with Broadway the prime target of this urban renewal, my bunk was to be eliminated. Dunstone, overwhelmed with administrative headaches stemming from this, told me to fend for myself—so I was forced to "give my regards to Broadway," as the song goes, and spend the last three nights as Terry's upper bunk mate. Terry warned me that, early in his stay, he had once fallen from his top bunk. There was no barrier to prevent a fall, and the consequences could be dire at my age and for Mount Kilimanjaro, still as tender as gout. Between that and the bright lights glaring just a few feet directly above me, sleeping was problematic. But I didn't much care. I had gone from counting days to counting hours.

—

One of my favorite inmates was Rev, a three-hundred-plus-pound black preacher from New Jersey who exuded intelligence and spiritual strength.

A graduate of the University of Virginia and Harvard Divinity School, Rev was in prison over irregularities regarding a $150,000 donation to his church from what turned out to be a shady organization. He insisted he got hoodwinked and didn't profit a dime personally. Who knows? Who cares? I liked him. A vehement Trumper, he never blamed race for his problems, but nor was he strident like Mike and always made reasoned, intelligent arguments. That said, during the NFL playoffs, he rooted against the 49ers simply because San Francisco was the home of Nancy Pelosi. At least I could tease him about it; he remained good-natured and seemed to appreciate the interplay. As one who seldom holds a person's politics against him, I believed Rev had a lot to contribute to the world.

That certainly was evident in prison. On my final Saturday, Rev held a fellowship in the visitors' room. Twenty-two inmates attended, a diverse group that included John the defense lawyer, Congressman Fattah, Terry, Mike—people of all races and political persuasions seeking spiritual comfort. As we filed in and took our chairs in a circle, a white guy named Matt played the guitar, and a black guy named Jay the bongos, filling the air with a sublime serenity that I hadn't felt for a long time. It soothed me down to my bone marrow.

Accompanied by Matt and Jay (both in their thirties), we sang ecumenical spiritual songs from the homemade books that Terry had manually laced together in the library. The Rev then encouraged us to share our feelings, the most poignant moment coming when Jay, the black, bald, bearded bongo player, told us that his 120-month sentence had just been reduced by a judge to thirty-four. He had already served twenty-eight, so by his standards, he would be out in no time. A truck driver who had responded to an ad to help his business, Jay became an unwitting mule in a drug conspiracy. From where I sat, there was not a criminal bone in his body. With misty eyes, I peeked around the room while Jay shared his news; tears were streaming down prisoners' cheeks. It was heartening to witness how good news from one inmate brought out colorblind love in all the others; instead of fostering jealousy, it bolstered hopes, spirits, our common humanity. Our musicians, Matt and Jay, were among the gentlest souls at Canaan, or anywhere for that matter. I only hope that society will see them that way and not objectify them as criminals, which I suspect would be a greater crime against humanity than the ones they committed.

Rev read us passages from Ephesians, in which apostle Paul wrote from prison about humility, patience, and unity through love and peace. Rev's message, one that resonated with us all, was for all of us to feel worthy no matter where we were. To my surprise, he even said a prayer for me, asking God to "look over and protect Greg" after his next Tuesday departure.

—

The last two and a half days didn't really feel like prison. I hung up my prison greens and boots for the last time and wore sweats and sneakers even to the mess hall, in front of the COs and the tough-as-nails director, Ms. Williams, a hard-assed black woman trying to make it in an all-male industry who demanded that things be buttoned up. Not even she said a word about my attire. Had I been a long-term inmate, it would have caused a major disciplinary issue. I wasn't flaunting anything, just lazy, or as we used to call it at Choate and Princeton, suffering from senioritis.

"Hey, Greg," bellowed Terry over a lunch of *poulet a la chien*, "ever since you got here, the food's really sucked. Can't wait to see you leave."

"That makes two of us. My new bunk mate is a real asshole by the way."

"You should hear what he says about you."

A ping-pong table materialized in the gym, disappearing just as quickly with the warden's visit. During that brief Club Fed moment, I tested my seventy-year-old reflexes with a host of younger inmates. Back in the dorm, I eavesdropped with some amusement as George the pot dealer reamed Austin over his lack of boundaries, how he might end up with the snot knocked out of him or mired in the SHU. I got acquainted with Tim, who had eleven children with his wife and had adopted five more (yes, you read that right). A one-time assistant to Governor Cuomo, he was working for the federal government when he discovered that his wife and bearer of his eleven children was diddling his boss. Beyond upset, Tim called in sick for almost a year, collecting pay. When the feds finally caught him, they sent him to prison for three years. Your tax dollars at work: first they fuck your wife, then you. Tim was a gentle soul, incapable of hurting anyone, and, when you think about, learning about his wife's infidelity with his boss probably did incapacitate him.

I played chess with Chaka Fattah, who blitzkrieged me three straight times. Never in my life had I been so badly thrashed. I told him he should have been a four-star general rather than a crooked congressman. The following evening, my last—after we exchanged contact into, after he reminisced about his appearances on Fox News and the *Colbert Report*, after we talked our common bucket list fantasy of playing golf at Augusta National—I suggested another game of chess to cap off the evening (and prison term). I wanted one last crack at him. This time, I played much more carefully, assuming I would lose but wanting to restore some semblance of dignity. By some miracle, our seesaw game turned my way and I checkmated him. I was relieved that he didn't insist on a rematch. Beating the congressman at chess was the next-to-last thing I did before going to bed. The last thing I did was wish him Godspeed on his appeal, still not knowing exactly what he had done but thinking that taking ten years out of a man's life is barbaric and insane.

—

January 28, 2020. The only morning I ever showered at Canaan. I put on clean sweats and sneakers that were my own and T-shirt and socks that belonged to the Bureau of Prisons. Other than that, my notes, and *Licensed to Lie*, I left everything else in my locker for Habibi as payment for his black market meals. When the loudspeaker summoned "Abbott" to the van at 7:30 a.m. to take me Up Top for discharge, Terry and I exchanged goodbyes and vowed to stay in touch. Leaving my community gave me a tinge of sentiment. Though skeptical whether friendships forged in prison can thrive on the outside, I think about my former prison mates every day, wondering how they are dealing with COVID, whether any have been released. The place should be turned into a museum to show future generations just how barbaric a society we used to be.

I had no idea whether the welcoming committee Up Top had saved or burned my street clothes. Not a single veteran inmate believed they would be saved; the very notion made them spew laughter. There were three of us leaving the same day. Joining me was a young kid named Kyle (one of my ping-pong opponents), who was stoked about opening up a food truck as soon as he got home, and a callow Uber driver from the Bronx named Salvador, who'd allowed himself to be enlisted as the driver of the getaway car in a busted drug deal.

In the lobby of the Beast, we were asked to sit and wait. After twenty minutes, my pal Ernst appeared holding a small cardboard box, which he handed to me. "Your clothes, Bernie. Go change in the bathroom. And *don't* use the facilities." With fervor of a tot on Christmas morn, I scurried to the bathroom to open my present. Santa had come through; perhaps I wasn't such a naughty boy after all. I fondled my jeans, T-shirt, socks, and parka in disbelief; how luxurious they felt! Once I emerged in my own clothes (a euphoria I cannot begin to describe), Ernst led me around to a plexiglass window, under which a clerk slipped me some papers to sign and a debit card that had $345 on it, representing the money left over from my original commissary deposit, plus the $1.20 I had earned doing SHU laundry. Ernst then handed me the plastic I was itching for, my driver's license ID. Apart from the fact that I was still in the building and had 250 hours of community service ahead of me, I was a free man!

"If I don't declare the buck twenty on my income tax, will I be back here?"

"Still playing around the edges, Madoff?"

I let a giddy chuckle escape; I actually wanted to bear-hug my tormentor. "Well," I said, grinning, my ride awaiting in the prison parking lot, "take care of yourself ... you filthy animal."

"Don't come back. I don't want to see your maggoty face ever again."

Code for telling me to stay out of trouble. When it comes to a hard-assed CO talking to a prisoner, this final exchange is as touching as it gets.

CHAPTER 20

TRUE PERFECTION

November 1963. Ithaca, New York. Boynton Junior High (the acne capital of the world), eighth grade. The year before I went off to Choate, I started a political movement called Abbottism. It was at the apex of the Cold War, shortly after the Cuban Missile Crisis, when Communism was on the march and struck fear in everyone. Abbottism had no ideological basis; it was a very tenuous cult of personality, something I founded while our class was reading George Orwell's *Animal Farm*. Most of the boys in my homeroom class (but none of the girls, who were far too sensible) became instant Abbottists and followed me blindly. When I walked in the hallway, they formed a circle around me, fists raised, laughing like sots and chanting, "Abbottism, Abbottism, long live our leader! Long live the people!" Being a junior high warlord was a heady feeling, but though I didn't know what *tenuous* meant, I knew in my bones and braces that soon my followers would lose interest and Abbottism would vanish into the ash heap of history. I had no army, no KGB, no compelling philosophy to keep them in line.

As it was, Abbottism didn't end via revolt but tragedy. Scarcely a few days into the movement (amazing it lasted that long), we were sitting in homeroom when the school principal somberly announced via intercom, "The president of the United States has been shot." Perhaps because the principal had offered no other details, I assumed it was a minor flesh wound and that JFK would be AOK. Moments later, the principal's voice returned with words that will forever haunt my memory: "The president of the United States is dead."

GREG ABBOTT

Just like that, our notion of America as an idyllic Camelot of unlimited possibilities came crashing down, bedeviling a stunned nation with doubt. Not that this is an original thought, and forgive me for buying into the JFK myth, but one can only speculate what trajectory our country and its consciousness might have taken had that event not occurred.

"War will exist," said a prescient JFK, "until that distant day when the conscientious objector enjoys the same reputation and prestige that the warrior does today."

Imagine any other president saying that, let alone in the early 1960s? (While you're at it, imagine today's press ignoring a president's sexual affairs with a mega movie star and a Mafia gun moll, or the fact that he was kicked out of Princeton for cheating and demoted to Harvard, but I cunningly digress.) Our dashing, charismatic leader, who offered so much hope and optimism in tense, uncertain times, whom my parents didn't vote for but nonetheless respected as their president, was gunned down by ... well, you tell me.

As if it were yesterday, I remember my father, an ardent Goldwater supporter (was there any other kind?), weeping during the funeral while the military band played "Hail to the Chief" and John-John saluted the flag draped over the horse-drawn casket. Watching Dad weep at such a moment made an indelible impression on me and taught me so much about our country. We were all Americans first and foremost, a distinction that withered any party allegiances. Naivety and privilege have a certain inherent wisdom when it comes to knowing how things *should* be. Yes, the civil rights movement was in its infancy; yes, our society had numerous blind spots and millions of disenfranchised citizens. Still, for a nation with roots in witch burning and slavery, we have come a long way, because being on the cutting edge of history has always been integral to our national character. We hardly invented slavery yet lost more lives fighting against it in our Civil War than in all our other wars combined. We rebuilt our vanquished enemies after World War II. People from all over the world still want to come here. If that doesn't make America exceptional, then I give up. We can be messy and are far from perfect, but as that great American Voltaire reminds us, in six words that decimate the far left, "Perfect is the enemy of good."

USA VS ABBOTT

Twelve years ago, two years after my mother's passing, my brother called me from Boston at 7:00 a.m. I had just roused my daughter (pre-Lyme) and was waiting to take her to school.

"Are you sitting down?" Brother warned, his ominous tone causing my stomach to churn. As I plopped into a chair, he almost giddily blurted the news: "Mom's Jewish."

He went on to explain in painstaking detail the mountain of research he had amassed to prove this fact beyond a particle of doubt. Somehow, my brother always had a suspicion, despite that we'd grown up in a mildly anti-Semitic household—standard stuff in the 1950s and '60s, where as long as one didn't "hate the Jews more than absolutely necessary," one was within acceptable bounds of behavior. We'd been raised as Episcopalians, who demonstrated our mainstream commitment by golfing on Sundays (and thus inevitably cursing the Lord). Our *Leave It to Beaver* mom radiated WASP as well as anyone. She freaked out when I dated Jewish girls. Much later in life, she belonged to the Everglades Club in Palm Beach, which didn't even allow Jews as lunch or golf guests, to the point of unceremoniously escorting them off the premises in the middle of their salads or putts. She also belonged to the LA Country Club, which didn't allow Jews as members but, in laid-back California fashion, tolerated them as guests. I wonder how Mom felt when she was dining at those exclusionary clubs. Proud as hell, I imagine (with mixed emotions); the culmination of a multigenerational, distinctly American journey.

From all historical documentation my brother assembled—town records, birth certificates, shipping manifests—my maternal grandfather had fled the pogroms in Lithuania in 1906 and immigrated to the United States on the vessel *Kaiser Wilhelm*. Our ancestors hailed from the same Lithuanian village as the parents of Moe, Curly, and Shemp, something I shared with Mike in prison when we were doing our Three Stooges impersonations, which seemed to confer on me enough provenance to overcome our political divide. Great peacemakers, those Stooges. Our great-great-grandfather had been a rabbi!

My brother drove down from Boston to Sayre and with our long-lost cousin visited the Jewish cemetery where our grandparents were buried, the Star of David and the Freemason symbol emblazoning the door of the mausoleum. Our maternal grandmother, though buried there, was German Lutheran, which means my brother and I are one-quarter Jewish—enough, I'm told, to be booted from the Everglades Club but welcomed at Auschwitz. When I said earlier that no one kept a secret better than my mother, I wasn't just whistling "Dixie" or "Hava Nagila." She had a conniption when, after she generously offered to type my senior thesis, I affectionately dubbed her "my Episcopalian Jewish mother." Too close to the bone.

I wished I could have discussed this with her, told her it was all OK. Questions abounded as to why she had so masterfully concealed her Jewish identity, but I was left having to fill in the blanks myself. A legacy of persecution, fear, and trauma? The desire to start life afresh and redefine oneself in America? I'm sure those reasons and others lay behind this massive, lifelong coverup, just as I'm sure that I could never have kept such a secret for so long. My mother's internal discipline put mine, and that of everyone else I've ever known, to shame. Looking back, I could always trust her to keep a secret. Had she been black, of course, such a charade, and perhaps everything else in this book, except my arrest and prison term, would have been impossible, but that is a wholly different discussion.

My credential as a *goyem* who'd made it in the schmatte business was shattered. My self-image of Anglo with just enough dash of ethnicity to be exotic also bit the dust. Anglo-schmanglo—I was pure mutt. Some of my (fellow) Jewish friends were critical that my mother would hide her Jewish identity, labeling her rather insultingly a "self-hating Jew," but who are they or anyone to judge? Who knows what ancient folklore and exigent pressures her family endured and passed down to her? The American dream is essentially transcendent, and when my mother's family came to our shores, being a mainstream American meant being Protestant. Maybe they weren't very religious Jews any more than we were religious Episcopalians. Maybe, for them, religion was less of a belief system than a brand. After all, in Lithuania, hadn't they been branded ... like cattle? Maybe it was paramount for my mother's family to assimilate and become Americans all in, rather than hyphenated Americans. Isn't starting fresh and creating a new and better life what America is all about?

My mother's Jewish background may explain her drive to give her sons the best education possible and expose us to alien bastions like Choate. That same loving impulse might also partially explain my poor judgment a generation later in succumbing to Rick Singer. In any case, my brother's mind-blowing surprise gave me that big, elusive belly laugh that I hadn't experienced since the night Slatkin was sentenced to fourteen years and my fellow victims giddily celebrated the triumph of justice. Somehow, I felt liberated from invisible shackles I never knew I had.

My genetic dog's breakfast of Syrian-Jewish-German contains all sorts of traditional stigmas. The explosiveness inherent in that combination is a comedian's dream, but I consider myself as American as anyone (apart from my Choate schoolmate Russell Red Elk, yet another different discussion). For centuries and continuing to present time, people from all over the world have clamored to become Americans. Being an American is, or should be, an elite honor because it is the very antithesis of elitism—an homage to *everyone's* humanity *and* autonomy. One can't move to France and become a Frenchman, to Germany and become German, to China and become Chinese—nor would anyone in his or her right mind want to when one can be an American, *at least in theory*. As Americans, we are *all* privileged. (Never lose sight of that!) When functioning as intended, America is a boundless, inclusive, free, empowering, open country that exhibits its flaws for all the world to see. Therein lies our greatness—and why we are constantly criticized for falling short of our ideals. We are an idea, a unifying set of principles rooted in natural law that almost force us to become less hypocritical with each generation. It is our God-given freedoms, not government, that account for the fact that we are the most innovative, wealth-creating society on the planet. It is our unwavering Constitution, not our fickle government, that is our true protector. We do not exist to serve the state; the state exists to serve us. At least that was the idea. (If I ever revive Abbottism and dust off my customized MAGA hat, it will be along those lines; though maybe, instead of a MAGA hat, a less egocentric MOFA hat: "Make Orwell Fiction Again.")

Alas, I only wish that my paternal Syrian ancestors had Anglicized their surname with something farther down in the alphabet. When I first registered as a freshman at Princeton, the student volunteer behind the table declared, "Congratulations, Abbott, you're first in your class ... until grades come out." A no-brainer assumption, but I never aspired to be first in my class. Nor did I aspire to have a high-profile criminal case be called *The United States of America vs. Abbott et al*. Would have preferred to be among the *et al.*, or better yet, not *at all*. I'm sure my paternal ancestors never considered such a possibility when opting to be at the top of the alphabetical heap.

I want the American dream for everyone, yet I grieve. Well before the pandemic, George Floyd's murder, and January 6, our pursuit of happiness had become warped, if not a prison in its own right. Our society is overheated, overmedicated, overweight; our freedoms and way of life in peril from multiple divisive directions. Watching MSNBC and Fox News is like beholding parallel universes, living in the twilight zone. Technology, despite its benefits, has dehumanized human interactions and punched holes in human hearts. Big Tech, co-opted by government, wields totalitarian power over our lives in ways the world has never seen: obliterating all notions of personal privacy, enabling politically motivated censorship, stoking divisions, weakening our republic. Pardon the not-so-micro aggression I'm about to commit, but our elite universities have become useful idiots for Marxism, sworn enemies of free speech in favor of oppressive political correctness and reverse racism. Culture-cancelling propaganda centers who preach diversity but demand iron-fisted conformity—to such a degree that it boggles the mind how parents clamor to get their kids into them, and throws into question the spine, wisdom, and moral compass of the ideologues "educating" our offspring. Why is it virtuous for US universities to outsource admissions in the name of diversity but an un-American travesty when US firms outsource manufacturing? Why do colleges always get a pass? Perhaps, when all is said and done, by shining a light on the *whole process* and not just the offending parents, Varsity Blues will have been for the best.

To say nothing of our degenerate political climate—hopelessly partisan, craven to its core. Instead of uniting and uplifting us as Americans, or underscoring the *real* truth that most Americans love one another (Mandela: "Love comes more naturally to the human heart than its opposite"; MLK: "Love is the only force capable of transforming an enemy into a friend"), our parasitic "lea-ders" rub salt in common human problems—depression, anxiety, alienation, race, poverty, stress, addiction—with shame-and-blame identity politics that split us into warring factions. These useless windbags erect their fiefdoms by focusing on our differences, not in what we have in common. Their raison d'être is the perpetuation of social ills, crippling the populace while convincing us we need them. They can't make us safer or more prosperous; can't stem our soaring debt; can't secure our borders or our environment; can't instill confidence in our democratic institutions; but they sure can demonize, prosecute, and incarcerate the citizens who pay their salaries. Anonymous put it most succinctly: "Amateurs built the ark, experts the *Titanic*."

Which brings me to our criminal justice system, our modern-day form of witch burning and slavery. "Nothing can be more abhorrent to democracy," wrote Winston Churchill, "than to imprison a person or keep him in prison because he is unpopular. This is really the test of civilization."

Incarcerating a handful of "rich and famous" people who committed nonviolent, victimless crimes doesn't begin to even the playing field or reform inequities in our justice and educational systems. Did anyone sleep any easier during my incarceration? It may make some noble and/or self-righteous and/or envious people feel good, just as mass and prolonged incarceration of people of color for petty drug offenses may make some loathsome, unevolved racists feel all warm and fuzzy. Perhaps it was needed for symbolic reasons, to prove that privileged people can be punished in America. But isn't it a disingenuous example when you consider all the far more serious, politically protected exceptions running around: subprime bankers who got bailouts; paid "protestors" (and their puppet masters) who burn cities and destroy public monuments and places of business without consequence; steroid-bloated mega-millionaire athletes who sully the record books of their sports and the idealism of our youth; opioid peddlers who hook and kill our youth while raking in billions; prosecutorial terrorists and feds who emulate the Gestapo; tech magnates with CIA clearance (and emotional baggage galore) who censor speech to sway elections and stifle public discourse in their quest for world domination; "public servants" who participate in insider trading, destroy evidentiary hard drives and cell phones, who lie, steal, collude, administer justice on a partisan basis, and flirt with treason for a living? I'll leave it to you to compare the magnitude of their misdeeds to that of mine, to decide who is more deserving of public indignation and the slammer.

Facing the comprehensive problem—whether in college admissions or criminal justice—takes clarity and courage, not thuggery and tabloid journalism. I challenge anyone to make a cogent case that my arrest did anything to improve our system, or to name any other country that would have sent me to prison for what I did. Again, because it is at once stunning and compelling, having 5 percent of the world's population and 25 percent of the world's prisoners is a blight on modern America. Doesn't mean we're the most brutal nation on earth, but given our professed values, it's shameful. It doesn't mean, as my friend in law enforcement absurdly suggested, that our justice system is simply "more efficient" than that of other countries. It means systemic *in*-justice: squandering taxpayer money; endless prison terms for nonviolent crimes; criminalizing virtually any human frailty for political gain. The triumph of punishment over redemption; ignorance over reason; politics over law. In one way or another, these issues touch *all* American citizens and therefore have the potential to unite us—to make us realize, in the words of Rosa Parks, that "there is just one race, the human race." *All* people make mistakes. *All* of us are sinners. *All* of us have technically violated the law at some point in our lives and may be deemed "criminals" whenever the government so decides. Criminals of the world, unite!

"Personality is a mysterious thing," wrote Oscar Wilde, once a prisoner himself simply for being homosexual. "A man cannot always be estimated by what he does. He may keep the law, and yet be worthless. He may break the law, and yet be fine. He may be bad, without ever doing anything bad. He may commit a sin against society, and yet realize through that sin his true perfection."

I pretty much went straight from prison to home confinement, not because of any judicial order but because of the Wuhan lab virus (sorry, not into euphemisms). Microscopic bugs have been the bane of my existence. Let's be careful how we "pull together" during this pandemic, that in the quest of securing our safety we don't instead fall prey to yet another government power grab spurred on by the drive-by media mob. "The welfare of humanity," wrote Camus, "is always the alibi of tyrants." Like him or not, the Gipper's warning is spot-on: "Freedom is always one generation away from extinction." Balancing unity with autonomy is the essence of America the beautiful, and we must always continue to see our citizenhood through that paradoxical lens and never be docile.

Meanwhile, the Varsity Blues prosecutors have been credibly accused of committing *Brady* violations. Documents indicate that the feds "may have" (in the protective couching of my lawyer) pressured Rick Singer to lie, "may have" scripted him to propagate the myth that the defendants knew the Key Worldwide Foundation was a sham charity, when in fact he told me (with considerable pride) that it was a bona fide charity helping underserved schools and children. I had no reason to believe otherwise when donating to a 501c3 entity—good enough for the IRS, so why not me? Yes, our behavior was out of bounds, but why taint us further simply to send us away for longer? Defendants fighting the case on the basis that Singer's testimony was corrupted have jumped all over this, and I wish them Godspeed, not because they're angels but because they're human and the forces against them are far more dangerous than they will ever be.

USA VS ABBOTT

Those going to trial filed a motion to have the case thrown out (as it likely would have been in the Warren Court era of my youth), but Judge Gorton denied it. Those who pled guilty late in the game also drew Gorton and had the book thrown at them, with sentences ranging from six to nine months. Based on his harsh rulings and comments, and stubborn refusal in the face of COVID-19 to stipulate home confinement instead of prison, Judge Gorton appears to harbor a rigid orthodoxy against Varsity Blues defendants, staunchly believes in draconian punishments, and will likely stick it hard to those who exert their Sixth Amendment rights. For America's sake, I hope I'm wrong. It will be interesting, to say the least, how much time (if any) mastermind Rick Singer will get after all his patriotic cooperation for ratting out fifty-two individuals. Currently he is running around Newport Beach, a free man.

But now I stop. This book is about me, yes. It is about my life, the Varsity Blues saga, and our criminal justice and prison systems. Yet at the core, it is a love letter to my daughter. The one true victim of our actions, who knew nothing of them and otherwise would no doubt have stopped us. A lovely soul with a solid head on her shoulders (*Ghost of Versailles* aside), wise and kind beyond her years, who throughout her life has done everything right apart from contracting a serious autoimmune disability. Thus saddled, she conducted herself with valor, neither complaining nor indulging in self-pity but forging on with academics, opera, and service. An angel with amazing voice, generous spirit—"the next evolution of mankind"—who since birth never gave her parents a single reason not to believe in her or be anything but incredibly proud of her. Whether we committed a crime or simply cut an ethical corner, it was simultaneously wrong and rooted in pure love. By committing our parental "sin against society," in the words of Oscar Wilde, did we possibly "realize [our] true perfection" through this imperfect expression of love? Naturally, I'd love to couch it that way.

To our daughter's many friends who never stopped recognizing her inherent goodness and stuck by her, you forever have my respect and gratitude. To her former school friends once blessed by her true blue loyalty, who have taken to gossip behind her back, who exploit the scandal to falsely impugn her abilities and character; and to their parents who may influence them, whose insecurity may impel them to take pleasure in our family misfortunes and pass down a smug, cowardly legacy to their kids, I say: welcome to prison, whose metes and bounds are measured by judgment and meanness, attachment and envy, selfishness and greed, status seeking and conformity, pettiness and fear.

Take it from me, there is something liberating about being publicly humiliated. One can just as easily be imprisoned lying in a plush Fifth Avenue king-size bed as a metal prison bunk. Prison for most people is a state of mind—so free yourself! Prison is hating people richer than you or poorer than you; lighter than you or darker than you; righter than you or lefter than you; cooler than you or nerdier than you. Prison is holding grudges; needing to be right; embracing dogma, self-righteousness, and sanctimony; safeguarding one's ego and reputation at crippling spiritual cost. Prison is getting so invested in outcomes—Harvard, Princeton, Yale, Duke, USC—that you forfeit all mystery and joie de vivre. Everyone has his or her own journey, so to judge someone "loser" or "winner" based on such shallow criteria is to become one's own jailer.

With all her tribulations, none of which she had a hand in creating, my daughter is way ahead of the game in terms of obtaining a true education. She has accrued depth and resilience light-years beyond most of her peers. She already has a history of extending her heart to social outcasts and the physically handicapped. She readily realizes one of life's most important truths: it isn't happy people who are grateful, but grateful people who are happy. She is to be admired, respected, and envied, though she would never want anyone to envy her because that is the antithesis of who she is. How utterly useless is a politicized education, rooted in vengeful dogma and brainwashing? What happened to the notion of inner exploration, thinking for oneself, of the glorious, unfettered First Amendment without which true education is not possible? And what happened to laughter—the ultimate truth? Let's "decriminalize laughter" like Elon Musk says and not take ourselves and our labels so goddamn seriously. "A day without laughter," said Charlie Chaplin, "is a day wasted." Let's come to grips with the one unavoidable hallmark of living in a free society: you *will* be offended now and then. You can't have it both ways. Challenging one another, mixing it up and occasionally getting your ass kicked in an argument, happens to be the way we learn and grow, work out our differences, become better, kinder, more tolerant people, and unite as a vibrant society. Fie on the thin-skinned pussification of America! If you want a "safe space," go to a prison camp. You get three meals a day, clothing, shelter, TV, medical care—all for free! Everyone's equal; life's pressures are lifted. People stay in their lane and out of trouble. The only thing missing is sparkling-eyed freedom. And boy, am I glad I'm out!

You can tell a lot about a person by his or her favorite poem. This Philistine's was always "Casey at the Bat"—that is, until I read my daughter's shortly after my release:

> If you can keep your head when all about you
> Are losing theirs and blaming it on you;
> If you can trust yourself when all men doubt you,
> But make allowance for their doubting too;
> If you can wait and not be tired of waiting,
> Or being lied about, don't deal in lies,
> Or being hated don't give way to hating,
> And yet don't look too good, nor talk too wise;
>
> If you can dream—and not make dreams your master,
> If you can think—and not make thoughts your aim,
> If you can meet with Triumph and Disaster
> And treat those two impostors just the same;
> If you can bear to hear the truth you've spoken
> Twisted by knaves to make a trap for fools,
> Or watch the thing you gave your life to, broken,
> And stoop and build 'em up with worn-out tools;
>
> If you can make one heap of all your winnings
> And risk it on one turn of pitch-and-toss,
> And lose, and start again at your beginnings,
> And never breathe a word about your loss;
> If you can force your heart and nerve and sinew
> To serve your turn long after they are gone,
> And so hold on when there is nothing in you
> Except the Will which says to them: "Hold on!"
>
> If you can talk with crowds and keep your virtue,
> Or walk with Kings—nor lose the common touch,
> If neither foes nor loving friends can hurt you,
> If all men count with you, but none too much;

GREG ABBOTT

If you can fill the unforgiving minute
With sixty seconds' worth of distance run,
Yours is the Earth and everything that's it in,
And—which is more—you'll be a Man, my son!

Take gender out of the last line and "If," by Rudyard Kipling (a canceled colonialist), embodies the person my daughter is in the process of becoming. Fresh from completing year one at an elite international university sans Lyme, she won the award as its best first-year biology student. Stick that in your woke crack pipe!

President Kennedy once addressed the French people as follows: "I do not think it altogether inappropriate to introduce myself to this audience. I am the man who accompanied Jacqueline Kennedy to Paris, and I have enjoyed it."

I am the man who bows to the goodness of my daughter, to the uniqueness of all my children, and for that I consider myself the most privileged man on earth.

Printed in the USA
CPSIA information can be obtained
at www.ICGtesting.com
CBHW022039210924
14741CB00054B/151

9 781663 237521